eat
great

lose
weight

eat great lose weight

Tried-and-true recipes and tips from real weight-loss winners

Jane Kirby, R.D., and David Joachim

RODALE

Notice

This book is intended as a reference volume only, not as a medical manual. It is not intended as a substitute for any treatment that may have been prescribed by your doctor. If you suspect that you have a medical problem, we urge you to seek competent medical help. Keep in mind that nutritional needs vary from person to person, depending upon age, sex, health status, and total diet. The foods discussed and recipes given here are designed to help you make informed decisions about your diet and health.

Cover and Interior Designer: Carol Angstadt
Cover Photographer: Mitch Mandel/Rodale Images, Will Yurman/Liaison Agency
Interior photography credits for this book are on page 331.

Front Cover Recipes: Slow-Cooked Pork Stew (page 153), Chicken Fajitas (page 143), Peanut Butter Cake with Chocolate Frosting (page 279), and Chicken Fettuccine (page 183)

Library of Congress Cataloging-in-Publication Data
Kirby, Jane, 1953–
    Eat great lose weight : tried-and-true recipes and tips from real weight-loss winners /
Jane Kirby and David Joachim.
        p.   cm.
    Includes index.
    ISBN 1–57954–076–7 hardcover
    1. Reducing diets—Recipes.   I. Joachim, David.   II. Title.
    RM222.2.K5443   2000
    613.2'5—dc21   99–055663

Distributed to the book trade by St. Martin's Press

2   4   6   8   10   9   7   5   3   1   hardcover

Visit us on the Web at www.rodalecookbooks.com, or call us toll-free at (800) 848-4735.

RODALE
WE **INSPIRE** AND **ENABLE** PEOPLE TO IMPROVE
THEIR LIVES AND THE WORLD AROUND THEM

Acknowledgments

Books don't just happen. They develop from a tiny germ of an idea and take shape as they grow and mature. That kind of alchemy is hardly the result of a single person. Rather, it's an evolution that stems from the input of many contributors. It is here that we want to acknowledge these people. Our sincere thanks to:

The staff at Rodale Books, particularly Anne Egan, the project's director, without whom the germ would not have sprouted.

Kristen O'Brien, who effortlessly contacted, cajoled, and coordinated the contributions of our esteemed experts.

Nancy Zelko, who meticulously researched every fact and statistic quoted in this book.

Wendy Hess, R.D., for her impeccable nutrition analysis.

Mitch Mandel, for his beautiful photographs.

Carol Angstadt, for her inventive and inviting design.

All the health experts and spas that shared their weight-loss advice and recipes: Dean Or-nish, M.D.; Deepak Chopra, M.D.; Deirdra Price, Ph.D.; Howard Rankin, Ph.D., of the Carolina Wellness Retreat; Don Mauer; Kathie Graham, R.D., of the Spa at Doral; Sarah, the Duchess of York, and Weight Watchers International, Inc.; Joan Lunden; Marsha Hudnall, R.D., of the Green Mountain Program at Fox Run in Vermont; Richard Simmons; Jeanne Jones for Canyon Ranch Health Resorts; Michel Stroot of the Golden Door; and Bill Wavrin of Rancho la Puerta.

The generous supporters of *Prevention*'s Recipe Sweepstakes: Mary Rodgers from Cuisinart; Julia Stambules from All-Clad; Jack Saunders at LamsonSharp; and Beverly Kastell at Hamilton Beach.

The loyal readers of *Prevention* magazine who so enthusiastically shared their weight-loss success stories, tips, and recipes with us.

And to everyone who has ever struggled to reach a healthier weight. It is your tenacity and success that encourages us all.

—Jane Kirby, R.D., and David Joachim

In all Rodale Press cookbooks, our mission is to provide delicious and nutritious recipes. Our recipes also meet the standards of the Rodale Test Kitchen for dependability, ease, practicality, and, most of all, great taste. To give us your comments, call (800) 848-4735.

Contents

Weight Loss That Works • ix

Wisdom from the Winners • 1

What Works in the Kitchen • 31

Bring on the Breakfasts and Brunches • 53

Lickety-Split Lunches • 79

Snacks, Nibbles, and Mini-Meals • 103

Snappy Weeknight Suppers • 125

Delightful Weekend Dinners • 181

Simply Sides • 227

Slimming Salads and Dressings • 247

Sweet Treats • 277

Two Weeks to a Slimmer You • 316

Credits • *331*

Index • *333*

Conversion Chart • *358*

Weight Loss That Works

The people who share their advice in this book lost a combined total of more than 120,000 pounds. And they've kept it off for an average of 6 years. Some folks have kept it off for 10 years or more. That's true weight-loss success.

To find these weight-loss winners, we set up a Web site in conjunction with *Prevention* magazine. We also got in touch with the National Weight Control Registry, a unique database of people who have lost at least 30 pounds and kept it off for at least a year. Then we went straight to the phone lines and talked with these folks.

Our goal in writing this book was to bring these weight-loss winners directly to you—to bring you their stories, their strategies, and their wonderful recipes.

For expert advice, we also talked with the nation's top weight-loss professionals, including Kelly Brownell, Ph.D.; Dean Ornish, M.D.; and Deepak Chopra, M.D. We even tapped into the perspective of weight-loss spas and celebrities like Sarah, the Duchess of York.

This book contains the combined wisdom of trained professionals and everyday folks who found out what really works. We organized everything into an easy-to-follow plan. Charts and tables simplify the process of figuring out whether you need to lose weight, how much to lose, how to do it safely, what's good to eat, and how much to exercise. We know there isn't a one-size-fits-all method for everybody, so we made the book as flexible as possible. You can customize the plan to meet your individual needs and match your own lifestyle.

Proven weight-control strategies are the core of this book. But if you ask us, the recipes are the best part. This is the food that successful dieters eat to lose weight and maintain their slimness. Straight from their kitchens to yours! (With a slight detour in the Rodale Test Kitchen.) We were amazed at how good these recipes were. They range from simple breakfasts and salads to more indulgent main dishes. Yes, indulgent. Don't be alarmed by some of the higher-fat meals. We included "Splurge Meal" menu suggestions with these recipes for those times when you want to indulge. And when you don't want to overdo it, look to the "Slimming Meal" menus.

Either way, you'll never feel deprived. This is easy-to-make, great-tasting food from everyday folks. How do Double Chocolate Chip Fudge Brownies grab ya? How about Blueberry-Pecan Pancakes? Hot Black Bean Dip? Grilled Pork Chops? Roast Sirloin Steak? Every recipe gets our hearty seal of approval, especially the Peanut Butter Cake with Chocolate Frosting. Yum!

What's the point of rattling off these recipe names? The point is *Eat Great*. That's what this book is about, first and foremost. Whether you want to lose 10 pounds or 100 pounds, you can't do it if you have to eat food that you don't like. This book shows you how to eat well and enjoy the experience of eating while losing or maintaining weight.

Wisdom from the Winners

You've heard the heartbreaking statistics: "Ninety-five percent of people who lose weight will gain it back." It's enough to make you exchange your scale for a frequent buyer's card at the plus-size store.

Don't believe it. Plenty of people lose weight and keep it off. And you can, too. That's worth repeating.

Plenty of people lose weight and keep it off. And you can, too.

But what about that 95 percent failure rate? That's a widely quoted statistic that comes from a study of only 100 people at a nutrition clinic at New York Hospital in the 1950s. It does not represent the real world of today, where lots of people lose weight and keep it off on their own. Our evidence: Thousands of weight-loss winners are coming out and speaking up. The innovative National Weight Control Registry at the University of Pittsburgh School of Medicine has identified the largest group of weight-loss winners ever recorded, and they have lots of

good advice to share. We also interviewed dozens of successful dieters. They're people just like you. Some lost weight on their own. Some joined weight-loss programs. Some had to lose weight for health reasons. Others wanted to make a better impression at their high school reunions. And a few had simply had enough of being overweight.

Break the Rules

The patterns of success that we saw in our interviews were the same as those at the National Weight Control Registry. And they weren't what you might expect. The registry has tracked more than 2,000 people who have lost at least 30 pounds and kept it off for at least 1 year. Amazingly, the average loss for those in the registry is about 65 pounds, and they have maintained it for more than 6 years. What these people told us flies in the face of conventional weight-loss wisdom. Consider these myth-busting truths.

It Worked for Me!

Connie Bissonnette

VITAL STATS

Weight lost: 43 pounds

Time kept it off: 7 years

Weight-loss strategies: Strength training, low-fat diet

Weight-maintenance strategies: Exercise, healthy eating

Connie went from old and achy to 43 pounds trimmer and feeling younger with weight training. Now, she teaches others to do the same.

"My knees hurt and I was always tired. I found myself napping whenever I could. At 53, it didn't occur to me that my sluggishness could be caused by anything else than simply getting old.

"I was a full-time university lab instructor and was about 30 pounds overweight. My blood pressure began to creep up. My son Jeff, who was working on his master's degree in human performance, told me that I'd feel better if I exercised. But excuses came easy. 'Are you kidding? With my knees? Where am I supposed to find the time? I'm not spending all that money on shoes and going to a gym. I barely have enough energy to get through the day.'

"Jeff persisted and planned a simple 10-minute workout for me. Just 3 days a week of seated leg lifts, wall pushups, and lifts with milk jugs halfway filled with water. It was so easy that I had no trouble sticking to it. After a few months, my knees were feeling better, so Jeff toughened up my program and challenged me to a single diet change: Stop using butter on my morning toast.

"After about 6 months, my jeans were looser. But what impressed me most was how good I started to feel. I had more energy and my knees didn't bother me anymore. I began to do more exercises and started walking for about 30 minutes two or three times a week. Soon, I could run with our dogs and heft a 40-pound bag of dog food without trouble.

"I was hooked. I wanted to learn all I could about exercise and diet. My son even suggested that I become a personal trainer. At first, I thought he was joking. But then, he said, 'You already know this stuff and you're a good teacher.' Because I was ready to retire and wanted to find a part-time job close to home, I considered what he said. Two months later, I became a certified personal trainer. Today, most of the clients I have are 40, 50, and 60. I have a contract that if they are not happy after three to six sessions, they can have a full refund. I haven't refunded a single penny.

"Even at 58, I still add muscle. I enjoy weight lifting, and I want to see how far I can go. In fact, I just competed in my first body-building contest." ∎

It's never too late. Being heavy as a child doesn't sentence you to a life as an overweight adult. At the registry, 46 percent of the participants said that they were overweight as children at age 11 or younger. Twenty-five percent first became heavy between ages 12 and 18. Only 28 percent became overweight as adults. That means most of these weight-loss winners overcame a lifetime of being overweight.

Forget your "ideal" weight. Ideal weight is just that: an ideal. The fact is that most people who consider themselves successful at maintaining a weight loss drop only about half the pounds that they'd hoped to drop. Weight-loss researcher Thomas Wadden, Ph.D., proves the point. He and his colleagues asked 60 overweight women (their average weight was about 218 pounds) to write down three different numbers: their ideal "goal" weight, weight loss that they considered "acceptable," and weight loss that they saw as "disappointing." Most set their ideal weights about 72 pounds less than their current weights (an average ideal of 146 pounds). The average "acceptable" weight loss was about 55 pounds (which would put them at an average of 163 pounds). A loss of only 38 pounds was considered "disappointing" (an average weight of 180).

After 6 months of dieting, exercising, and behavior modification, plus 6 months of maintenance, the average weight loss sustained by these women was only 36 pounds. Two pounds *less* than their "disappointing" weight loss. The good news? All were absolutely thrilled with their new weight. Even though they hadn't reached the loss that they initially called "disappointing," they felt better physically and emotionally than they had ever expected.

A weight loss of only 10 percent of your current weight is enough to bring down high blood pressure, lower cholesterol and triglycerides (substances that can put you at risk for heart disease), and improve your overall medical health. And that translates into feeling better instantly. So reach for a reasonable goal weight, not an ideal. That's exactly what Susan Cursi did. Susan is 5 feet 5 inches tall and now weighs 130 pounds. She lost 50 pounds and has kept it off for 5 years. But she had to get real first. "I realized that I may never be as skinny as I was in high school. But when I lost just 25 to 30 pounds, I felt so much better."

Keep trying. Contrary to rumors, yo-yo dieting (or continually losing weight and gaining it back) does not lower your chances of ever losing weight permanently. The research that started that rumor was done on rats, not humans. Even so, it caused some weight-loss "experts" to think that it might be healthier to stay heavy than to continue trying to lose weight. Nothing could be further from the truth. A national task force was organized to do a comprehensive survey of 43 human studies on the subject (known among doctors as "weight cycling"). Guess what they concluded? Repeat dieting does not increase body fat, make future weight-loss attempts more difficult, or permanently lower metabolic rate (the rate at which your body burns calories).

Proof positive: Nearly all the weight-loss winners (91 percent) in the National Weight Control Registry are veteran dieters. And these folks lost an average of 60 pounds and kept it off for 10 years. The people we interviewed had similar dieting patterns. So what triggered the lasting success? Among other things, they all said that this time, they were

(continued on page 6)

FACTS YOU DON'T WANT TO KNOW

More than half of American adults are overweight, and a third of our children are heavy, too. Why so many? Partly because the "overweight" bar was lowered in June 1998 by the Heart, Lung, and Blood Institute at the National Institutes of Health. The official cutoff for being overweight was lowered from a Body Mass Index (BMI) of 27 to a BMI of 25. (To find out your BMI, see page 8.) The research is clear. When a person's BMI goes over 25, chances of getting heart disease, diabetes, sleep apnea and other breathing problems, and some forms of cancer increase.

Here are some other surprising statistics. These tell the underlying story of why so many Americans are overweight and what it means to their health.

Number of Americans considered overweight in 1970, 1996, and 1999, respectively: 1 in 5, 1 in 3, 1 in 2

Percentage of Americans who regularly eat away from home: 57

Percentage of daily calories eaten outside the home: 25

Calories in 1 pound of fat: 3,500

Calories in one McDonald's Super Value Meal: 1,425

Number of Super Value Meals that equal a pound of fat: 2½

Percentage of Americans who drink soft drinks: 50

Average annual consumption of soft drinks: 54 gallons per person

Percentage of consumers who check fat content on nutrition labels: 62

Percentage of consumers who check calorie content on nutrition labels: 55

Average pounds that women gain between ages 25 and 54: 16

Average pounds that men gain between ages 25 and 54: 10

Number of daily calories that a 54-year-old woman must eat *less* than she did as a 25-year-old in order to avoid gaining weight: 132

Percentage of Americans with hypertension (high blood pressure): 39

Percentage of obese Americans with hypertension: 35

Percentage of healthy-weight Americans with hypertension: 17

Percentage of increased risk of diabetes with 11-pound weight gain: 25

Percentage of new cases of diabetes attributed to 11-pound weight gain: 27

Average dress size of American women: 12

Average dress size of female models: 6

Average height of American women: 5 feet 4 inches

Average height of female models: 5 feet 10 inches

Average weight of American women: 138

Average weight of female models: 120

Average percent body fat of American women: 32

Average percent body fat of female models: 18

Number of American women who have bodies like fashion models: 1 in 40,000

Number of American women on diets to lose weight: 30 million

Number of American men on diets to lose weight: 16 million

Percentage of American adults on diets in 1964 and 1994, respectively: 15 and 38

Size of a bottle of cola in the 1930s: 6 oz

Minimum size of a bottle or can of cola in 1999: 12 oz

Size of a serving of popcorn according to the Food Guide Pyramid: 2 cups

Size of an average small popcorn served at movie theaters: 10 cups

Size of a medium muffin according to the Food Guide Pyramid: $1\frac{1}{2}$ oz

Size muffin that most Americans consider average: $5\frac{1}{2}$ oz

Number of servings of added sugars recommended daily: sparing consumption

Number of servings of added sugars that Americans eat daily: 20 teaspoons

Number of servings of fat recommended daily: sparing consumption

Number of servings of fat that Americans eat daily: $6\frac{1}{2}$ tablespoons

Percentage of Americans who think it's very important to eat plenty of grains, breads, cereal, rice, and pasta: 30

Percentage increase of pretzel, corn chip, popcorn, and cracker consumption between 1970 and 1996: 200

Percentage of Americans who say that they need to lose weight who count fat but not calories: 27

Percentage of Americans who say that they need to lose weight who count calories but not fat: 14

Number of Americans who report that they are in fair or poor health: 1 in 10

Percentage of Americans who lost weight with exercise and continue to keep it off with exercise: 100

Number of American men who never exercise: 3 in 10

Number of American women who never exercise: 1 in 2

Number of dollars spent annually on health care in the United States: $988.5 billion

Number of dollars spent annually on obesity-related health care in the United States: $99.2 billion

Number of dollars that Americans spend annually on weight-loss products and programs: $33 billion

Number of the leading causes of death (heart disease, cancer, stroke, and diabetes) that have a weight component: 3

Percentage of body weight that needs to be reduced to lower health risk: 10

going to make long-term behavior changes. They more closely watched what they ate, and they exercised more.

Adrienne Jacobson dieted for years. She tried everything: weight-loss pills, liquid diet products, even starvation. Finally, she found a registered dietitian who designed an eating plan based on her lifestyle—a diet that she could stick with for the long haul. She met with her dietitian once a week for positive reinforcement and fine tuning. She has maintained a loss of 36 pounds for 3½ years.

Mark Ballard dropped an amazing 125 pounds—but not the first time he tried. "My first weight-loss attempt was a fast that I did in high school. From there, I moved on: Weight Watchers, the Cambridge System, Slim Fast, Nutri/System, Cabbage Soup." Mark eventually found that a sensible low-fat eating plan and exercise worked for him. If you've tried before, it couldn't hurt to try again. This time could be different.

Ignore your family's weight history. Genetics tell you only that you have a tendency to be overweight. Your genes do not predict your ability to lose weight. "I saw pictures of my grandmothers, great-grandmothers, and great-great-grandmothers, and they were all overweight and short like I am. My mother was only about 5 feet tall, and she was also overweight," says Jean Ross. Despite her family's weight history, Jean dropped 35 pounds and went from a size 22 to a size 12. How about the weight-loss winners at the registry? Forty-six percent reported having at least one parent who was overweight.

Trust your instincts. People told us that one of the keys to permanent weight loss was getting triggered by something deep inside, coming to a turning point, an incident or

time in their lives that made them say, "This is it. This time will be different." For Richard Daly, it was his overall health. "I looked down at the floor beside my easy chair and counted eight cola cans that I'd emptied in less than an hour. The next thing I knew, I was in the hospital, diagnosed with diabetes and learning how to give myself insulin to bring down my sky-high blood sugar." Right then, Richard knew that he had to make a change for good.

More than three-fourths (77 percent) of the men and women in the registry said that there was a trigger or a turning point that also got them motivated. Thirty-two percent said that their triggers were either medical conditions (like back pain, breathing trouble, or fatigue) or emotional events such as divorce. "I had asthma, poor circulation, chronic constipation, and heartburn," says Lynne Watson. But poor health wasn't enough. Lynne went on and off diets for years until her powerful emotions finally moved her. "I sat alone on Christmas Day 1985 and realized that I had two choices: end my life or take control of it. I decided to grab control; I didn't want to die." For Lynne, the trigger had to come from deep within. Once she found her motivation, she lost 105 pounds.

Be honest with yourself. Not everyone has to be hit with an earth-shattering event. For more than 11 percent of the people at the registry, the trigger was simply seeing themselves in a mirror or a photograph. That's all it took for Senator Matt Salmon of Arizona. "I was rummaging through some snapshots of my formerly athletic self. I realized that I now look like a walrus. I couldn't believe I'd let myself get so bloated. I was ashamed and embarrassed." Matt started a basic eating and exercise strategy and lost 70 pounds.

Luanne Barrett had a similar experience.

"I looked at a photo. My heart sank. My weight had crept to more than 170 pounds. It was time to do something about my weight—and my lifestyle." Luanne took control and lost 27 pounds.

How Much Should You Weigh?

Most people want to know what the "right" weight is. The honest answer is that there is no ideal weight that applies to each person. Everybody is a little different. But there are ways to tell whether your body shape and weight are putting you at risk and what weight range is considered healthy for you.

Do the math. Two simple formulas will tell you whether your weight is healthy or unhealthy: Body Mass Index (BMI) and waist circumference. As your BMI goes up, so does your risk of high blood pressure and increased blood cholesterol levels. Likewise, the more weight you have around your middle, the greater your chances of developing diseases like adult-onset diabetes, heart disease, and some forms of cancer. See page 8 to check your BMI and see where you stand.

Measure your middle. It's important to check your waist circumference, even if you're not overweight on the BMI chart. A large waist measurement means that you're shaped more like an apple than a pear and could have increased risk for disease, such as diabetes and heart disease. Waist circumference is particularly useful for older people whose weight has shifted with age. Their risk for major diseases goes up, not because of weight gain but simply because their weight has collected around their middles. Older men are often aware of their changing shapes because men's pants are sized by waist

measurement. But women's clothing is not. Women are often less aware of increased waist size as they age.

To check your waist circumference, place a tape measure just above your belly button at your natural waistline. Pull the tape snug but not tight. Jot down your waist size in inches. A circumference of more than 40 inches for a man and 35 inches for a woman means that your health could be at risk. Losing some weight now will make a difference.

Find your healthy weight range. Your best weight is not a particular number on a scale. In fact, pegging one number as your goal always keeps you 1 pound away from failure. Instead, think of your target weight as a range. This strategy gives you leeway for your body's natural monthly and seasonal weight fluctuations. To find yours, see "Find Your Target Weight Range" on page 10.

Follow Your Own Plan

Knowing that weight loss is different for everybody, we designed this book to be flexible. You can personalize your own weight-loss strategy. If you like the psychological approach, see "What's Your Weight-Loss Personality?" on page 12. Knowing your general response to life might help you figure out the weight-loss strategy that suits you best. Or, if you just want some healthier recipes in your diet, scan through the recipes until you find a few that you like. (For tips on making your own recipes more healthy, see What Works in the Kitchen on page 31.) If you want to exercise more, see "Burn, Baby, Burn" on page 27. Or, if structured meal plans are for you, pick a calorie level (see how on page 17), then follow the simple 2-week slimming plan on page 316.

(continued on page 10)

IS YOUR CURRENT WEIGHT HEALTHY?

Body mass index (BMI) is a tool that health professionals use to determine if someone's weight is unhealthfully high or low. Generally, the higher BMIs are associated with unhealthy amounts of body fat—not just total pounds. To determine your BMI, find your height in the column at the left and then move across until you find your weight. Your BMI is the number at the bottom of the column.

Height	Weight (lb)										
4'10"	86	91	96	100	105	110	115	119	124	129	134
4'11"	89	94	99	104	109	114	119	124	128	133	138
5'	92	97	102	107	112	118	123	128	133	138	143
5'1"	96	100	106	111	116	122	127	132	137	143	148
5'2"	99	104	109	115	120	126	131	136	142	147	153
5'3"	102	107	113	118	124	130	135	141	146	152	158
5'4"	105	110	116	122	128	134	140	145	151	157	163
5'5"	109	114	120	126	132	138	144	150	156	162	168
5'6"	112	118	124	130	136	142	148	155	161	167	173
5'7"	116	121	127	134	140	146	153	159	166	172	178
5'8"	120	125	131	138	144	151	158	164	171	177	184
5'9"	123	128	135	142	149	155	162	169	176	182	189
5'10"	126	132	139	146	153	160	167	174	181	188	195
5'11"	130	136	143	150	157	165	172	179	186	193	200
6'	134	140	147	154	162	169	177	184	191	199	206
6'1"	138	144	151	159	166	174	182	189	197	204	212
6'2"	141	148	155	163	171	179	186	194	202	210	218
6'3"	145	152	160	168	176	184	192	200	208	216	224
6'4"	149	156	164	172	180	189	197	205	213	221	230
BMI	18	19	20	21	22	23	24	25	26	27	28

Underweight: Less than 18
Normal: 18–24
Overweight: 25–29

Obese: 30–34
Very obese: 35–39
Extremely obese: 40 and above

29	30	31	32	33	34	35	36	37	38	39	40
138	143	148	153	158	162	167	172	177	181	186	191
143	148	153	158	163	168	173	178	183	188	193	198
148	153	158	163	168	174	179	184	189	194	199	204
153	158	164	169	174	180	185	190	195	201	206	211
158	164	169	175	180	186	191	196	202	207	213	218
163	169	175	180	186	191	197	203	208	214	220	225
169	174	180	186	192	197	204	209	215	221	227	232
174	180	186	192	198	204	210	216	222	228	234	240
179	186	192	198	204	210	216	223	229	235	241	247
185	191	198	204	211	217	223	230	236	242	249	255
190	197	203	210	216	223	230	236	243	249	256	262
196	203	209	216	223	230	236	243	250	257	263	270
202	209	216	222	229	236	243	250	257	264	271	278
208	215	222	229	236	243	250	257	265	272	279	286
213	221	228	235	242	250	258	265	272	279	287	294
219	227	235	242	250	257	265	272	280	288	295	302
225	233	241	249	256	264	272	280	287	295	303	311
232	240	248	256	264	272	279	287	295	303	311	319
238	246	254	263	271	279	287	295	304	312	320	328
29	**30**	**31**	**32**	**33**	**34**	**35**	**36**	**37**	**38**	**39**	**40**

FIND YOUR TARGET WEIGHT RANGE

Your Body Mass Index (see page 8) will tell you if your health is at risk, but use this chart to determine your weight goals. Remember that these numbers represent a range (in most cases, about 15 pounds) that is appropriate for men and women at various heights. They are not absolutes, so use them only as a guide. Find your height in the left column and move across the chart to find your range.

Height	Weight (lb)	
	Men	Women
4'8"	74–90	72–88
4'9"	79–97	77–94
4'10"	85–103	81–99
4'11"	90–110	86–105
5'	95–117	90–110
5'1"	101–123	95–116
5'2"	106–130	99–121
5'3"	112–136	104–127
5'4"	117–143	108–132
5'5"	122–150	113–138
5'6"	128–156	117–143
5'7"	133–163	122–149

Height	Weight (lb)	
	Men	Women
5'8"	139–169	126–154
5'9"	144–176	131–160
5'10"	149–183	135–165
5'11"	155–189	140–171
6'	160–196	144–176
6'1"	166–202	149–182
6'2"	171–209	153–187
6'3"	176–216	158–193
6'4"	182–222	162–198
6'5"	187–229	167–204
6'6"	193–235	171–209

Play the numbers. The most surefire method of losing weight is to take in fewer calories than you use. That's what this book is based on. If you are overweight, you are simply taking in more calories than you need. The solution is to take in fewer calories (by altering your diet gradually) or use up more (by slowly getting more active).

Lose weight gradually. Here's the science behind the principle of calorie balance. One pound of fat is equivalent to 3,500 calories. For every 3,500 calories you cut, your weight will drop 1 pound.

But cut too many calories too quickly, and you may not lose any weight at all. It's too sharp a change for your body. Studies show that on fewer than 800 to 1,000 calories a day (by eating less, exercising strenuously, or a combination of the two), your body will turn down its thermostat to conserve every calorie it gets. Your body goes into survival mode and doesn't know if you're a prisoner of war suffering from starvation or a prisoner of your own head. That's why rapid weight-loss diets don't work.

Barbara Miltenberger knows this principle

firsthand. "As soon as I saw the weight coming off, I thought, 'If it's working at this rate, I'll try eating less so that I'll lose more,'" she admits. "Then I stalled and put on even more weight because I was undereating. And my metabolism slowed down. I'd start losing again when I'd eat a little bit more." In the end, Barbara lost more than 40 pounds the safe, reliable way: slowly.

Drop 1 or 2 pounds a week. Safe, effective weight loss is considered to be 1 to 2 pounds a week. That's not as slow as you might think. In just 2 months, you could be 20 pounds slimmer.

To lose a pound a week, you need to reduce your calories by 500 each day (500 × 7 = 3,500 calories = 1 pound). To lose 2 pounds a week, reduce your calories by 1,000 a day (1,000 × 7 = 7,000 calories = 2 pounds). Reducing calories means eating fewer of them and burning off more.

See how many calories you eat now. Before changing the way you eat, it helps to know how many calories you eat to maintain your current weight. There are a few ways to do this. Some folks keep a food journal and average out the number of calories they eat using a fat-and-calorie-count book (these are available in most bookstores). "It took a few extra minutes a day, but keeping a food journal helped me become aware of how much I was eating," says Alan Mathis, who lost 130 pounds.

A journal will yield a wealth of information about your eating habits. If you're not very aware of your diet, give it a try. Keep a small notebook in your pocket or purse for just 3 days, including at least 1 weekend day. Jot down what you eat, when you eat, how much, and how you felt when you ate. Write down every last bit of food and drink. Then review it to see the average number of calories that you eat in a day. You'll also discover your snacking patterns and the emotions that prompt you to eat.

This method may be too time-consuming for many people. If you are generally aware of what and how much you eat, see "How Many Calories Do You Eat Now?" on page 18 to figure out the average number of calories that you eat to maintain your current weight.

Make a reasonable calorie budget. Once you know how many calories you eat each day to maintain your current weight, it's easy to plan a diet to lose weight. You can cut 150 calories simply by choosing a glass of diet soda instead of a can of cola (most colas have about 150 calories).

Get Balance

After you pick a daily calorie level, you could eat a day's worth of calories in hot-fudge sundaes or in steamed broccoli. It really doesn't matter for weight loss. But if you want to keep the weight off long-term and stay healthy, a balanced diet is the way to go. Here are two ways to get balance.

Eat from the pyramid. The U.S. Department of Agriculture organized the six food groups into a visual guide known as the Food Guide Pyramid. Here are the recommended number of servings in each food group, according to the pyramid.

- 6 to 11 servings of bread, cereal, rice, or pasta

- 3 to 5 servings of vegetables

- 2 to 4 servings of fruit

- 2 to 3 servings of milk, yogurt, or cheese

(continued on page 16)

WHAT'S YOUR WEIGHT-LOSS PERSONALITY?

Knowing your general approach to life can help you choose the weight-loss method that suits you best. Here's a list of questions that will help you pinpoint your weight-loss personality. Every question has four different statements that may or may not apply to you. Rank each statement 1, 2, 3, or 4, where 1 describes you least and 4 describes you best.

Transfer your scores to the Scoring Table on page 14, then add them up. Your highest score will reveal your weight-loss personality. Read the corresponding description to find out the most effective approach for you to lose weight and keep it off.

1 Least like me

2 Hardly like me

3 Somewhat like me

4 Most like me

1. When it comes to new health information, I:
   a. read several different sources to make sure that they are giving the same advice.
   b. like to see statistics and how the information was compiled before believing it.
   c. don't have time to read the news.
   d. like to try new things, especially if it's worked for someone else.

2. When I dress in the morning, I:
   a. wear what makes me feel good that day.
   b. dress after hearing the day's weather forecast.
   c. wear what I planned at the beginning of the week for that day.
   d. wear what fits my mood.

3. I grocery shop:
   a. when we're out of food, and I buy what looks good.
   b. by buying only what's on the list that I compiled from my weekly menu.
   c. by compiling a list of what's on sale.
   d. without a list and buy what seems good for my body.

4. When I pass my favorite fast-food restaurant, I:
   a. stop if it's mealtime, but check nutritional information first.
   b. almost always stop to get my favorite food, even if I'm not hungry.
   c. stop if it's mealtime and get my favorite food.
   d. only stop if I've planned it into my weekly meals.

5. When contemplating my weekend activities, I prefer:
- a. to plan several days in advance.
- b. intellectually stimulating activities.
- c. to keep my options open until Friday.
- d. activities that help my personal growth.

6. The activity I like best is:
- a. choosing newspaper and magazine subscriptions for my family.
- b. organizing kitchen and bathroom cabinets.
- c. finding activities to help everyone in my family grow personally.
- d. decorating the house so it's an enjoyable, fun place to live.

7. In relationships with others, I:
- a. am sometimes late because I get involved in something fun and forget the time.
- b. am known to get impatient when I'm not understood.
- c. am considered idealistic.
- d. often have expectations of how others should behave.

8. Those who know me well say that I am:
- a. reliable and dependable.
- b. empathetic and inspirational.
- c. fun to have around when things become dull.
- d. intelligent and clever.

9. If I'm trying to lose weight, I will:
- a. plan my meals in the morning, following my guidelines.
- b. ignore my food plan if I'm busy or if it doesn't sound good to me.
- c. plan meals weekly and eat what's on my plan even if it doesn't sound good to me that day.
- d. fix something in the healthy category, but not necessarily follow a meal plan.

10. When it comes to filing taxes, I:
- a. don't get to it until the very last minute.
- b. save my receipts throughout the year, then file my taxes by January 15th.
- c. enter my financial information on a computer and then use it to fill out my tax forms.
- d. would rather hire someone to do it.

(continued)

WHAT'S YOUR WEIGHT-LOSS PERSONALITY?—CONTINUED

SCORING TABLE AND PERSONALITIES

Transfer your answers to the table below. (Note that the spaces are not always in a-b-c-d order.) Total your points in each column. Match the symbol underneath the column with the highest score to the personality types. If your two highest totals are nearly equal, read the descriptions for both types to see which fits you best.

1.	a___	b___	c___	d___
2.	c___	b___	d___	a___
3.	b___	c___	a___	d___
4.	d___	a___	b___	c___
5.	a___	b___	c___	d___
6.	b___	a___	d___	c___
7.	d___	b___	a___	c___
8.	a___	d___	c___	b___
9.	c___	a___	b___	d___
10.	b___	c___	a___	d___
Total	___	___	___	___
	O	**A**	**S**	**I**

O = Organized

You thrive on routines and schedules. Your kitchen cabinets are likely to be highly organized and everything has it's place in your home. You're usually prepared for anything. Your weight-loss strategy:

- Calculate your current daily calorie intake on page 18. Subtract 500 or 1,000 from that number so that you can lose 1 to 2 pounds a week. Match your calorie level to the menu plan on page 316 and follow the menus.
- Chart your progress. Use a checklist to record what you eat and how much you exercise every day.
- Plan a week or two of menus at a time.
- Try to be flexible. Structure and organization might feel so comfortable that you get stuck in a pattern that isn't working.

A = Analytical

You're an information gatherer. You enjoy complexity and the challenges of problem solving. Your weight-loss strategy:

- Design your own program.
- Calculate the number of calories you are eating now on page 18. Subtract 500 per day to lose 1 pound per week. Keeping a

food journal and using a calorie-counter book may help you chart the calories that you eat daily.

- Turn to "What to Eat" on page 17 to read about the building blocks of a balanced lower-calorie diet. Use the information to make your daily food choices.
- You may benefit from a one-on-one meeting with a dietitian. Call the American Dietetic Association at (800) 366-1655 to find one in your area. A dietitian can help you analyze how you're eating now and make suggestions for changes.

S = Spontaneous

You live life as it comes, expanding each moment to overflowing. You look for variety and maximum flexibility. You hate schedules and have a crisis approach to life. Your weight-loss strategy:

- Skip rigid food plans. If they don't fit into your lifestyle, you'll just ignore them.
- Stock up on a selection of healthy, low-calorie, and low-fat foods to eat when you're hungry. Keep problem foods out of the house.
- Read through the recipes that begin on page 53 and flag the ones that sound appetizing and are low in calories and fat.
- Eat at least five fruits and five vegetables each day.

- Eat only from salad-size plates. Drink from juice glasses. Stock up on preportioned foods such as low-calorie frozen dinners and individually packaged healthy snacks.

I = Inspirational

You're always interested in improving yourself, mentally and physically. People often confide in you because you're a great listener—and you have a wonderfully kind, effective way of inspiring others. Your weight-loss strategy:

- Join a weight-loss group. You like people, so group settings or the buddy system works extremely well. Read the profiles of weight-loss winners throughout this book. Just look for the logo, "It Worked for Me!"
- Keep tempting foods out of the house, but don't rule out your favorite foods entirely. Deprivation leads you to overeat, so be sure to plan occasional desserts.
- You're likely to enjoy an extra scoop of something you love, so dish up only a single serving. Don't eat out of the bag. Avoid serving meals "family style." Plate food before it gets to the table.

- 2 to 3 servings of meat, poultry, fish, dry beans, eggs, or nuts

- Sparing use of fats like butter and oil

Notice that a range of servings is given in each food group. If you eat the lower number of servings a day, you'll get about 1,600 calories. If you eat the larger number of servings, your calorie total will be about 2,700. Either way, you'll get a good balance of vitamins, minerals, and fiber.

Try the exchange program. A similar food-grouping system was organized by the American Dietetic Association and the American Diabetic Association: the Dietary Exchange System. The advantage of this system is its greater level of detail. Plus, it's easier to keep track of what you eat if you're trying to lose weight. To use the exchange system, choose the calorie level you need to lose 1 to 2 pounds a week. Then see "What to Eat" to determine how many servings of the various food groups you should eat each day. The recipes in this book include dietary exchanges to make meal planning simpler.

Make servings count. Knowing serving sizes is crucial to making any meal plan work. Unfortunately, because more of us are eating in restaurants (and their portions are huge), we've gotten accustomed to eating more than we should. The average take-out muffin is about five times the size it should be. Even healthy foods like potatoes are nearly three times the size that health experts recommend. When in doubt of what makes a serving, minimize, don't supersize. You'll find more specifics on the pages that follow.

Bread. Sometimes called starches, the bread group encompasses all carbohydrate-rich foods like cereals, grains, pastas, breads, crackers, and snacks. Starchy vegetables like corn, green peas, plantains, potatoes, winter squash, and yams are included here. In general, one serving (cooked, where applicable) is:

- ½ cup cereal, grain, pasta, or starchy vegetable

- 1 slice bread

- 1 ounce of most snack foods (see "Counting treats" on page 20 for a detailed list)

Fruit. These can be fresh, frozen, canned, or dried fruit or fruit juice. One fruit serving equals:

- 1 small to medium piece fresh fruit

- ½ cup canned fruit (with a small amount of juice), cut fruit, or fruit juice

- ¼ cup dried fruit

Milk. Fat-free milk and yogurt are included here. To count cheeses, see the meat group. Cream and other dairy fats are counted in the fat group. One serving of milk equals:

- 1 cup (½ pint or 8 fluid ounces) fat-free milk

- 1 cup fat-free or low-fat yogurt

Vegetable. Includes all vegetables, except the starchy vegetables mentioned above. Go for the richest colors you can find. Dark green and dark yellow vegetables are the most nutritious. These include spinach, broccoli, romaine lettuce, carrots, bell peppers, and chile peppers. In general, one vegetable serving is:

- ½ cup cooked vegetables or vegetable juice

- 1 cup raw vegetables

WHAT TO EAT

In the chart below, pick the daily calorie level that is closest to the one you have chosen to reach your weight goals. Then scan the food groups to see how many servings of each food to eat in a day. Of course, these numbers are meant only as a guide. Some days, you may end up eating more or less in any given food category.

Food Group	Daily Calorie Level				
	1,200	1,500	1,800	2,000	2,500
Bread	5	6	8	9	10
Vegetable	2	5	5	4	5
Fruit	3	3	5	5	6
Milk	1½	2	2	2	4
Meat	5	6	6	8	10
Fat	3	4	5	5	6

Meat. When buying meats, choose ones labeled "lean" or "very lean." "Select" and "choice" grades are leaner than "prime." Look for "ground beef" rather than meat labeled "hamburger" because the latter may contain more fat. This group includes meats and other protein-based foods like cheese, eggs, and beans. Note that the serving size for meats and cheese is 1 ounce. Don't worry, you can still eat plenty of meat. We recommend that you get somewhere between 5 and 10 servings (5 to 10 ounces) from the meat group a day. Just remember that there may be several ounces (or several servings) of meat in any one meal you eat. Bacon is counted in the fat group. Generally, one serving of meat equals:

- 1 ounce cooked lean beef, pork, lamb, skinless poultry, fish, or shellfish
- 1 ounce cheese
- ½ cup cooked dried beans, peas, or lentils
- 1 egg

Fat. Most fats have the same number of calories per serving. But some fats are better for you than others. The good monounsaturated and polyunsaturated fats are generally found in plant foods like olive oil and nuts or in some seafood. Generally, one serving of fat equals:

- 1 teaspoon butter, regular margarine, or vegetable oil
- 1 tablespoon regular salad dressing
- ⅛ of one medium avocado
- 8 to 10 olives
- 6 to 10 nuts
- 2 teaspoons peanut butter

(continued on page 20)

HOW MANY CALORIES DO YOU EAT NOW?

Here's a quick way to estimate the number of calories that you currently eat to maintain your weight. First, determine your activity level using the descriptions at right. Then, find your weight along the left-hand column. Follow across the row until you find the column that matches your activity level. The corresponding number is approximately how many calories you now take in each day. Remember, to lose 1 pound a week, drop that number by 500. To lose 2 pounds a week, drop the number by 1,000.

WOMEN

Current Weight	Very Light	Light	Moderate	Heavy
		Activity Level		
120	1,584	1,716	1,848	1,980
125	1,650	1,788	1,925	2,063
130	1,716	1,859	2,002	2,145
135	1,782	1,931	2,079	2,228
140	1,848	2,002	2,156	2,310
145	1,914	2,074	2,233	2,393
150	1,980	2,145	2,310	2,475
155	2,046	2,217	2,387	2,558
160	2,112	2,288	2,464	2,640
165	2,178	2,360	2,541	2,723
170	2,244	2,431	2,618	2,805
175	2,310	2,503	2,695	2,888
180	2,376	2,574	2,772	2,970
185	2,442	2,646	2,849	3,053
190	2,508	2,717	2,926	3,135
195	2,574	2,789	3,003	3,218
200	2,640	2,860	3,080	3,300
205	2,706	2,932	3,157	3,383
210	2,772	3,003	3,234	3,465
215	2,838	3,075	3,311	3,548
220	2,904	3,146	3,388	3,630
225	2,970	3,218	3,465	3,713

Very light: Sitting, standing, playing cards, reading, typing, cooking, sewing, sleeping, lying down
Light: Restaurant work, housecleaning, child care, golfing, walking slowly

Moderate: Heavy housework, biking, skiing, tennis, brisk walking
Heavy: Construction work, climbing, manual labor

MEN

Current Weight	Very Light	Light	Moderate	Heavy
			Activity Level	
190	2,759	2,989	3,219	3,449
195	2,831	3,067	3,303	3,539
200	2,904	3,146	3,388	3,630
205	2,977	3,225	3,473	3,721
210	3,049	3,303	3,557	3,812
215	3,122	3,382	3,642	3,902
220	3,194	3,461	3,727	3,993
225	3,267	3,539	3,812	4,084
230	3,340	3,618	3,896	4,175
235	3,412	3,697	3,981	4,265
240	3,485	3,775	4,066	4,356
245	3,557	3,854	4,150	4,447
250	3,630	3,933	4,235	4,538
255	3,703	4,011	4,320	4,628
260	3,775	4,090	4,404	4,719
265	3,848	4,168	4,489	4,810
270	3,920	4,247	4,574	4,901
275	3,993	4,326	4,659	4,991
280	4,066	4,404	4,743	5,082
285	4,138	4,483	4,828	5,173
290	4,211	4,562	4,913	5,264
295	4,283	4,640	4,997	5,354
300	4,356	4,719	5,082	5,445

- 2 teaspoons tahini paste
- 1 tablespoon sesame seeds
- 1 slice bacon
- 2 tablespoons half-and-half
- 2 tablespoons coconut
- 3 tablespoons reduced-fat sour cream

Counting treats. You've probably gotten used to many of the foods that you consider treats. If a little bit helps you stick to a healthy eating plan, there's no reason to stop eating these foods. Just eat moderate amounts. Here's how to count them using the dietary exchange system. Note that things like sherbet and jelly are included in the bread group. That's because these foods are mostly carbohydrates.

- Angel food cake ($\frac{1}{12}$ of a cake) = 2 bread
- Brownie, unfrosted (2" square) = 1 bread, 1 fat
- Cream-filled cookie (2) = 1 bread, 1 fat
- Doughnut, plain (1) = $1\frac{1}{2}$ bread, 2 fat
- Fruit spread, jam, or jelly (1 tablespoon) = 1 bread
- Fruit juice bars (3-ounce bar) = 1 fruit
- Fruit roll-up ($\frac{3}{4}$-ounce roll) = 1 fruit
- Hot dog (1 ounce) = 1 meat
- Ice cream ($\frac{1}{2}$ cup) = 1 bread, 2 fat
- Pie, fruit, with 2 crusts ($\frac{1}{6}$ of pie) = 3 bread, 2 fat
- Potato chips or tortilla chips (1 ounce) = 1 bread, 2 fat
- Pudding made with 1% milk ($\frac{1}{2}$ cup) = 2 bread
- Sherbet or sorbet ($\frac{1}{2}$ cup) = 2 bread

Eat Smart

Food-grouping systems like the Food Guide Pyramid and the Dietary Exchanges may help you eat a more balanced diet. But they're not the whole picture. We uncovered some other key principles to eating smart and losing weight. Once you have balance in your diet, here's what weight-loss winners recommend to keep the weight off for good.

Eat when you're hungry. The people in the National Weight Control Registry eat an average of five meals a day. The fact is, most folks need to eat every 2 to 4 hours. Otherwise, we override our built-in mechanism that tells us when we're hungry and when we've had enough. We're starved, so then we overeat. Learn to recognize your hunger cues—grumbly tummy, energy crash, irritability—and eat in response to them.

"Naturally slim" people eat only when they're truly hungry, according to Vicki Hansen, author of *The Seven Secrets of Slim People*. These lucky people eat differently than the rest of us. They eat only when they are really hungry. All of us were born with this ability. But we let appetite, cravings, and years of conditioning to clean our plates short-circuit our hunger mechanism. The fact is, denying hunger and skipping meals always backfire. You'll overeat when you do allow yourself food.

Stop when you're full. Your body tells you when it has had enough to eat. But the signs are subtle. You may need to relearn how to recognize these signals. One way is to eat slowly. It takes your body about 20 minutes to feel the food you eat. If you eat too quickly, you'll eat right past the point of being satisfied and eat too much. Another trick is to wear clothing with zippered waist-bands instead of the elastic kind. Elasticized skirts and slacks are very forgiving, but something snug around your waist will signal you to stop eating as it tightens up.

Eat a good breakfast. Breakfast helps you avoid overeating later in the day. Go for foods that have some protein and a little fat in addition to carbohydrates and sugar. They will give you the energy you need to make it through the morning. Good choices include whole-grain cereal with 1% milk, eggs and toast, or a fruity breakfast shake. Beware of sugary breakfast foods like kids' cereals and Danishes. While initially satisfying, these are out of your system in about 30 minutes, leaving you hungry for more.

Count calories, not just fat. Sure, fat has more calories than protein or carbohydrate foods (9 calories per gram versus 4 for protein and carbohydrate foods). But that doesn't mean that eating only low-fat foods will help you lose weight. Research done at the University of Vermont in Burlington showed that there's more to weight loss than counting fat grams. One group of dieters was asked to restrict their fat to 22 to 26 grams per day but not to count calories. Another group was asked to count calories but not fat. After 6 months, the calorie counters lost more than twice as much weight as those who restricted fat. Why? One reason is the incredible number of low-fat products on the market that are not low in calories. By only counting fat grams, you could be taking in more calories than you need.

Don't pass on pasta. Every few years, a new diet hits the locker rooms and bookstores promising the secret formula for easy and permanent weight loss. One formula

that has come in and out of style severely limits or even bans carbohydrate foods. That means bread, pasta, cereal, and starchy vegetables like potatoes and beans.

Revolutionary? Hardly. In the 1960s, the plan was promoted by Dr. Irwin Stillman. It was also called the Drinking Man's Diet. It has resurfaced as The Zone, Protein Power, Carbohydrate Addict's Diet, and a retooling of the old Atkins Diet. The difference today is how the diets are packaged. Nutrition knowledge has come a long way from 1960 to 2000, and the recent crop of books uses lots of scientific-sounding jargon to sell the plans. It's very convincing until you analyze the diets and realize that regardless of the promises and premises, all the plans are basically low in calories. And that is why people lose weight on them. Don't be fooled. Breads, pasta, and grains are the basis of a healthy diet.

Fill up on fiber. Combined with a good supply of water, fiber-rich foods are a dieter's dream. They're filling and come packaged with lots of vitamins, minerals, and other helpful plant nutrients. What are the best sources of fiber? Whole grains like cereals, whole-wheat bread, and brown rice; watery vegetables like salad greens, tomatoes, zucchini, green beans, and broccoli; and fruits like apples and oranges.

Look at portion sizes. We're used to seeing our plates full. But if you're eating from a huge dinner plate, it's probably too much food. Try using smaller plates. Remember, a cup is about the size of your fist. A portion of meat or fish is about the size of a deck of cards. See "Eyes on the Size" on page 162 for other visual cues to healthy portion sizes.

LOW-FAT? LOOK AGAIN

Hundreds of low-fat foods are out there. But low-fat doesn't mean low-calorie. And calories count. Take another look at that nutrition label. The reduced-fat version is often just as high in calories as the regular version. The reason? Sugar is added to make up for the flavor and texture lost by taking out fat. So, if the calories are the same, why not go for the better-tasting original? You may even eat a smaller portion because you'll be satisfied sooner. Here are the numbers. You be the judge.

Food	Serving Size	Calories
Cool Whip	2 Tbsp	25
Cool Whip Lite	2 Tbsp	20
Oreos	3	160
Reduced-Fat Oreos	3	130
Fig Newtons	2	110
Fat-Free Fig Newtons	2	90
Honey Maid Graham Crackers	2 sheets	120
Low-Fat Honey Maid Graham Crackers	2 sheets	110
Wheat Thins	18	137
Reduced-Fat Wheat Thins	18	120
Original Club Crackers	4	70
Reduced-Fat Club Crackers	5	70
Alouette Gourmet Spreadable Cheese	2 Tbsp	60
Alouette Light Spreadable Cheese	2 Tbsp	50
Skippy Peanut Butter	2 Tbsp	190
Skippy Reduced-Fat Peanut Butter	2 Tbsp	190
Cheez-It Party Mix	½ cup	140
Reduced-Fat Cheez-It Party Mix	½ cup	130
Orville Redenbachers's Original Butter Popcorn	1 cup popped	35
Orville Redenbacher's Light Butter Popcorn	1 cup popped	20
Stouffer's French Bread Pizza with Pepperoni	1	390
Healthy Choice French Bread Pizza with Pepperoni	1	340
Franco-American Turkey Gravy	¼ cup	25
Franco-American Fat-Free Turkey Gravy	¼ cup	20
Old El Paso Refried Beans	½ cup	100
Old El Paso Fat-Free Refried Beans	½ cup	100

If you're going out for fast food, choose a kid's meal instead of the "Super Combo." You'll save about 438 calories per meal at most restaurants. Having a salad? Eat as much as you want. But be sparing with what goes on top.

"I usually misjudge portions of salad dressing and mayonnaise," says Theresa Revitt, who lost 80 pounds. "They're really high in fat and calories (100 calories per tablespoon), so I still measure them."

Make Peace with Yourself

Losing weight may be mostly about reducing calories. But it's also about your relationship to food: how you look at the food you eat and at yourself. Many successful dieters told us that they had to make peace with their relationship to food and their bodies before they kept the weight off for longer than a month or two. Here's what they recommend.

Accept your cravings. The faster you give in and have a small portion of the food that you're craving, the better off you'll be. You can pack in plenty of calories trying to eat around the one thing you truly want. So go for it. Have a small serving of the food you crave and get over it.

Or, use the 90-10 principle that Verona Mucci-Hurlburt used to go from a size 18 to a size 8. "If you watch what you eat 90 percent of the time, the other 10 percent is not a problem."

Eat cake! Eat all the foods you love, says weight-loss expert Deidra Price, Ph.D., who wrote *Healing the Hungry Self.* "You won't gain weight when you eat chocolate, cookies, candy, cake, and chips," she says. "As long as you eat them in moderate amounts *after* (not instead of) a meal." What's a moderate amount of these foods? Whatever you can fit in the palm of your hand is a moderate serving for you.

Love who you are. Positive body image is central to lasting weight loss. It's so important that the Green Mountain Program at Fox Run, a weight-loss center in Vermont, specializes in it.

"If people accept their bodies, they will have an easier time losing and maintaining weight," says nutrition director Marsha Hudnall, R.D. "If you have a negative attitude and hate your body, it's more difficult to eat healthy and exercise."

Don't go it alone. More than half (55 percent) of the folks at the registry finally lost weight when they joined some kind of formal program. "Programs provide structure, a supportive group setting, and follow-up," says Kelly D. Brownell, Ph.D., professor of psychology at Yale University.

A group can help you feel safe. "It's like an extended family," says Susan Cursi, who joined a program to help keep her focused. "You can call someone and say, 'I'm having a hard day. I need your help.'"

But many people lose weight without going to formal programs. Some use a less formal support system. Debra Mazda lost 135 pounds after starting her own group. "It was just a bunch of women who got together once a week, and we would compare notes."

Gloria McVeigh lost 35 pounds and her friend lost 50 when they dieted together. "We spoke daily on the phone about our personal lives, swapped recipe ideas, and compared exercise routines. We always motivated each other to keep going."

It Worked for Me!

Alan Mathis

VITAL STATS

Weight lost: 130 pounds

Time kept it off: 5 years

Weight-loss strategies: Learning control, eating low-fat, walking, running, keeping a journal

Weight-maintenance strategies: Stays sensitive to how his body feels, concentrates on feeling healthy rather than on weight

Dropping 130 pounds gave Alan the confidence to put on a bathing suit, go dancing, and do the things he enjoys most.

"It wasn't unusual for me to eat 12 hot dogs while watching a ball game on television. By age 25, I weighed 290 pounds and was diagnosed with Type II (adult-onset) diabetes. By age 31, I was up to 330 pounds and had to take insulin twice a day. I muddled through life, constantly sweating and exhausted. I didn't enjoy a single day of good health. Chest pains, which at first I thought were heartburn, finally got my attention.

"I started making changes. Fat-free yogurt, a bagel, fruit, and black coffee for breakfast. Lunch might be a bagel and tuna with mustard, lettuce, and tomatoes and some fruit or vegetables and a diet soda. No more fast-food burgers and breakfast sausage biscuits. A typical dinner was 2 to 3 ounces of chicken or other lean meat or fish and 12 to 16 ounces of vegetables. I switched to low-fat or nonfat versions of yogurt and cheese.

"Keeping a journal was one of my key tools. I used it to monitor how much I ate. Exercise also became a part of my program. About 2 weeks into my new eating habits, my wife suggested walking instead of driving to the bagel shop for breakfast. It was only a mile, but it took us 40 minutes. After a month, it only took half the time. Soon, the walk seemed too short. So I started walking after work, too: 45 minutes in the park 2 or 3 days a week.

"Within 6 months of beginning my new way of life, I stopped taking insulin. In a year, I'd lost 105 pounds. And I took off another 25 pounds in the next year. I have lost about 20 belt sizes since I started making changes.

"Now, I run four times a week. The distance depends on whether I am training. Last year, I ran three half-marathons. I went to my high-school reunion, and I looked younger than any of my classmates.

"I've learned to listen to the signals that I get from my body. If I'm feeling sluggish, or if I eat too much of the wrong things, my body feels the difference." ■

Move It to Lose It

Weight loss doesn't have to be about what you give up or cut out. The most successful dieters we spoke with were focused on what they *added in*. Some said, "I now put more vegetables on my plate." Some said, "I'm more aware of what I eat." Exercise falls into the same category. It's an add-in, something you can do. Granted, it may be tough at first if you've been inactive for a while. But the payoffs are incredible: more energy, better looks, better physical health, even better mental health.

Yes, better mental health. We're not talking simply about "runner's high" or an "endorphin buzz." Each time you get physically active, you send a message to yourself that you are doing something positive. Some psychologists even prescribe exercise for depressed patients to improve their moods. In some cases, the results are about as effective as prescription antidepressant drug therapy. The bottom line is that when you feel good about yourself, it gets a lot easier to stay with your weight-loss commitment.

Start slowly. There's no need to run out and buy exercise equipment. If you're among the 78 percent of Americans who do no exercise at all, just going for a walk or playing with the kids will get you moving again. Do some kind of activity for just 10 minutes a

MOOD FOODS

It's always best to deal with your emotions before you eat, says Cheryl Hartsough, a nutritionist at the Professional Golfers Association of America National Resort and Spa in Palm Beach Gardens, Florida. But sometimes, you may be anxious or depressed, and nothing but food will do. When that happens, it's good to know that you can avoid foods that will worsen your mood. Better yet, you can eat foods that may improve your mood. Follow this chart that Hartsough developed to satisfy your cravings without busting your weight-loss plan.

If You Feel . . .	Avoid These . . .	And Try These . . .
Anxious	Cake, chocolate, ice cream	Fresh fruit, dried fruit, pasta, whole-grain bread, potatoes, rice
Depressed	Cake, ice cream, pastries	Whole-grain foods like cereal, pasta, rice, beans
Sleepy and lethargic	High-fat foods, sweets, pizza	Low-fat, high-protein foods like fish, chicken, turkey, nonfat or low-fat cheese

day. Then, slowly work up to a total of 30 minutes of moderate-intensity activity. That's the amount recommended by the Centers for Disease Control and Prevention and the American College of Sports Medicine. "Moderate" means things like brisk walking and swimming.

Another way to look at it is to expend a minimum of 1,000 calories a week. Or, for increased weight loss, try expending 1,500 to 2,000 calories a week. That equals 200 to 300 calories a day or 60 minutes of moderate-intensity activity. To step up your weight loss to this level, try walking more, walking faster, and walking longer. See "Burn, Baby, Burn" to check the number of calories you can expect to burn by doing your favorite activities.

Sneak it in. Exercise doesn't have to be done in one lump sum. Finding a continuous 60 minutes is difficult for just about everyone. What counts most is the day's total amount of activity. Three 20-minute periods of exercise burn the same number of calories as one continuous 1-hour workout. Even 10 minutes here and there can add up to sufficient exercise. "I could never find the time for long walks and aerobic exercise classes," says Lorraine Stevens, who eventually reached her goal weight. "But I can always find 10 minutes. I can climb stairs at work for 10 minutes. I can walk around the parking lot for 10 minutes on my lunch hour. I can even jog in place in a hotel room for 10 minutes." Lorraine is 5 feet 8 inches tall and has kept her weight between 145 and 148 for years.

Walk, walk, walk. Don't worry about counting your pulse or getting into your target heart zone as you walk. It's not important. Research shows that for calorie burning, a greater amount of exercise at a lower intensity is better than small amounts of high-intensity exercise. You'll know you're walking at the right pace if you can talk but can't sing.

Muscle up. Studies have demonstrated that when a person diets, the weight that is lost is 75 percent fat and 25 percent muscle. And that's not good. As muscle is lost, so is your ability to burn and use calories efficiently. That's one of the reasons why so many dieters who don't exercise reach a plateau and stop losing weight, even though they are still eating a very calorie-restricted diet. For every pound of muscle that you build, your resting metabolic rate increases by 60 calories a day. Translation: For every pound of muscle you build, you will burn more calories and lose more weight. "It wasn't until I put on more muscle through resistance training that I was able to keep the weight off—almost effortlessly," says Mucci-Hurlburt.

Prioritize. Lack of time is the number one reason most people give for not exercising. Amy Reed, who lost 80 pounds, lets the beds go unmade to make time for exercise. "I have to schedule it in and let go of other things, like a perfectly clean house." Some solutions to the time crunch: Get a significant other to watch the children. Make family time a time to walk together. Get up a half-hour early. Or use your lunch hour to walk.

Get a buddy. Better yet, get several friends and make a commitment to them. Chances are, one of you will want to keep moving, even when the others don't. Chris Koehler lost 37 pounds with the help of his daughter, Katie. "Her enthusiasm was contagious. We'd walk 3 miles a day through the park and into downtown. It only took about 35 minutes. All of a sudden, those walks that

BURN, BABY, BURN

Almost every activity burns calories. Even sitting quietly. Of course, moderate-intensity activities like swimming or aerobic dancing will burn more. The important thing is to choose activities that you enjoy. That's the only way you will stay active. Below are more than 20 activities and the calories that they burn after 20 minutes.

Activity	Calories Burned in 20 Minutes	
	140-lb Person	190-lb Person
Sitting quietly	27	36
Raking	68	92
Cleaning	78	106
Weeding	92	124
Walking (normal pace on asphalt road)	102	138
Golf	108	146
Stacking firewood	112	152
Weight training	120	148
Bicycling (leisurely 9.4 mph)	127	172
Dancing the Twist	131	178
Scrubbing floors	139	188
Tennis	139	188
Aerobic dancing	141	178
Mowing	142	192
Snow skiing (moderate speed)	151	204
Football	168	228
Field hockey	170	230
Basketball	176	238
Boxing (sparring)	176	238
Swimming	183	278
Jumping rope (80 per min)	209	282
Running (9 min/mile)	245	332

had been so easy to forget became an essential part of my day."

Make it fun. Check out the classified section in any newspaper and you'll see lots of ads for ski machines, exercise bikes, and stair climbers. Did the owners of this expensive equipment reach their weight-loss and fitness goals? We doubt it. More likely, they got bored with their machines because they simply are not fun to use.

Anne Geren lost 55 pounds and kept it off for 13 years without any exercise equipment. She tuned in to her love of dancing and discovered Jazzercize. "If somebody told me that I had to go out and run 5 days a week, I'd still weigh 185 pounds." Pick an activity that you love.

Get centered. Very large people who are not used to exercising may feel clumsy at first. It takes a little time for your body to adjust. Comfortable footwear that has a wide sole and good support will help. So will walking on a flat, paved surface rather than a bumpy sidewalk. And if you've never weight trained before, you'll be surprised at how quickly your body responds. Lisa Getz, who had never weight trained before, lost 4 pounds and $2\frac{1}{2}$ inches in just 3 weeks. She was having trouble balancing while doing lunges at first. "Now, I'm much more in control," she says. "It feels like my legs have come out of hibernation and are alive again."

Fear not. Fear stops us from doing all kinds of things. The best antidote for fear is action. You might think that you can't start exercising because you're not in good shape or you weigh too much. "I call that the cleaning-up-for-the-maid syndrome," says Karen Andes, a San Francisco personal trainer. You don't need to join a gym. You don't need a special outfit. For the most part,

we're talking about walking, jogging, or running. You can saunter, meander, or stroll. Take it at your own pace. You don't have to go to a special place, either. Although, you may find it motivating to go to the school track, the mall, the woods, or some other walker-friendly environment. If you don't like walking, you can take the stairs instead of the elevator whenever possible, get off the bus a little earlier and walk the rest of the way, park at the far end of the parking lot, or pace while waiting for the train instead of sitting. Be sure to give yourself credit for every bit of exercise you do—even if some days you don't make your goal. Some activity is always better than none.

Seven Habits of Highly Effective Losers

People who lose weight have the most useful tips because they've done it. Of all the advice shared by the weight-loss winners in this book, here are the techniques mentioned most often.

1. Stop dieting. Get out of deprivation mode and back into enjoying the food you love. All of the successful weight losers at the registry as well as the people we talked to told us that they never felt deprived. Only about 40 percent of them thought that losing weight was hard. And more than a quarter said that it was easy. They said that to lose weight once and for all, they had to be stricter with themselves than they had been in the past, but most didn't call it dieting. The food choices they made (more fruits, vegetables, and grains) and the lifestyle changes they made (regular mealtimes and exercise) didn't feel like being "on a diet."

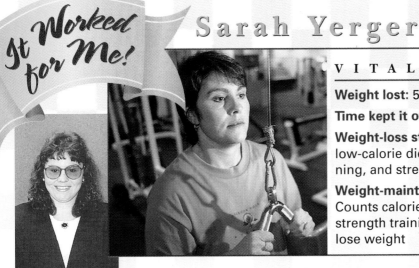

It Worked for Me!

Sarah Yerger

VITAL STATS

Weight lost: 55 pounds

Time kept it off: 5 years

Weight-loss strategies: Low-fat, low-calorie diet; aerobics, running, and strength training

Weight-maintenance strategies: Counts calories, runs and does strength training, helps others lose weight

A comment from a saleswoman got Sarah motivated. She dropped 55 pounds and has kept it off for 5 years. Now she has more energy than ever.

"At 5 feet 4 inches and over 200 pounds, I knew that if I didn't make some changes to my lifestyle, I would die of an early heart attack. Both of my parents died by age 50.

"After examining my mother, the doctor warned us. He told us that she could die of a heart attack within months. She did. And it scared me into action. I joined a health club and began low-impact aerobics classes.

"My new friends at the gym kept me going. But it was a nasty comment from a saleswoman that really pushed me to lose weight. A friend asked me to be in her wedding, and I could barely squeeze into a size 18. The saleswoman insisted that I buy the size 20. Hurt and determined, I ordered a 16. Suddenly, I had a goal and a point to prove.

"To lose the weight, I took stock in how I was eating and made changes. My candy bars, cheese steaks, and beer and chicken wing dinners were replaced by smaller, healthier meals.

Once I began measuring food, like a cup of spaghetti and ½ cup of sauce, I realized that I'd been dishing up three times that amount.

"Breakfast, which I used to skip, became a piece of fruit and dry toast. For protein, I added a cup of low-fat yogurt. Lunch was often water-packed tuna and raw vegetables. For dinner, I ate fish or pasta and salad. I also started drinking lots of water, which helped me feel full and cut my nine-cups-a-day coffee habit down to just two.

"I lost about 2 pounds a week. In just six months, my weight dropped to 150 pounds. The bridesmaid gown didn't need to be altered one stitch. I made my goal. But I didn't stop there. I felt so good, I started running three times a week. Now, I also lift weights for half an hour twice a week.

"I've started helping others to make the commitment to heal. I am very active in volunteer groups in my area. It helps me stay committed to my choice.

"Every time I lace my running shoes or choose a celery stick over a candy bar, I'm reminded that nothing is inevitable. Life is about choices, and I've chosen health." ■

2. Exercise daily. The registry shows that just about everyone did some form of exercise. On average, they burned 2,800 calories a week by walking and weight training. That's a lot! You don't have to commit to that much. But try to stick with daily activity of some kind, even if it's only 10 minutes of brisk walking at first.

3. Drink more water. The brain is about 75 percent water. It's the first organ to be affected by dehydration, clouding your thinking and making you feel fatigued and irritable. Office workers who spend much of their time in air-conditioning (which takes the humidity out of the air—and their bodies, to some extent) lose about 10 cups of water a day. Dehydration-related fatigue is what may be behind most people's hunger cravings. Next time you think you're hungry, have a drink of water instead. "Drinking lots of water keeps me from snacking when I'm not hungry, and it gives me more energy," says Revitt. "It also stopped what I thought were hunger headaches, which were probably due to dehydration."

4. Eat every 2 to 4 hours. If 4 hours go by and you haven't eaten, you're setting yourself up for the starvation-binge scenario—a calorie and fat disaster for anyone. Eating every 2 to 4 hours avoids it. When you eat small meals regularly, you're never too hungry or too full. And you'll more easily find your natural hunger and satiety clues.

5. Limit fat. Current wisdom from the government recommends limiting fat to 30 percent of total calories. That's what you'll see on the nutrition labels of food packages. But the folks at the registry did even better. On average, they limited daily fat to about 24 percent of total calories. Why cut back on fat? Because it's so calorie-dense. Fat has more than twice as many calories per gram as carbohydrates or proteins.

6. Eat more vegetables. Concentrate on what you *can* eat and what you can add to your diet. If you're like most Americans, you should be eating more fruits and vegetables. People who eat lots of fruits and vegetables naturally eat fewer calories and fat than people who don't.

7. Watch portion sizes. You can eat anything you want and still lose weight. No food is too fattening. But size matters. It could spell the difference between a good-for-you meal and a fattening one. If you need to, at least in the early stages of your weight-loss plan, use measuring cups and spoons. Or, see "Eyes on the Size" on page 162. Soon, you'll instinctively know what a teaspoon of mayonnaise looks like on your sandwich or a tablespoon of dressing on a salad, 1 cup of spaghetti on your plate, 3 ounces of chicken, 2 tablespoons of chocolate sauce . . . You get the idea.

What Works in the Kitchen

Healthy cooking starts in your supermarket. Long before you get to the kitchen, your shopping habits determine the foods you'll have on hand to cook with—and to snack on. If you stock bags of potato chips in the pantry, they'll get eaten. If you have pounds and pounds of butter in the freezer, you'll use it. Likewise, if you keep fresh red bell peppers in the crisper, you'll eat those, too. Before you rush off to the recipe chapters, read on about how you can shop faster, cook quicker, reduce the calories in your favorite recipes, and stock the healthiest foods available.

Shop Smart

Food retailing is marketing at its best. Everything in the supermarket is scientifi-cally engineered to entice you to buy more. Every food's location in the market is calculated to keep you in the store longer in the hope that you'll spend more money. Take milk and eggs, for example. These frequently purchased foods are located farthest from the door, which means that you have to pass by many, many temptations to get what you need. In-store bakeries and delis (often located near the entrance) send aromas throughout the store to tickle your nose and coax you to buy.

Even pricing policies are designed to prod you to shell out a few more bucks. Coupons often require that you buy two items to take advantage of their cents-off deals. Simply putting a number on an item's price sign such as "2 for $1.00" rather than selling the item for 50 cents each encourages us to buy more, according to Brian Wansink, director of the Food and Brand Research lab at the University of Illinois at Champaign-Urbana. The perception is that you're getting a greater value, despite the fact that you are spending more money.

Here's what weight-loss veterans recommend to keep your slim-down strategy from getting sabotaged before you even make it back home.

Have a plan. Knowing exactly what you need from the store helps minimize splurge purchases. And don't forget to check your cupboards, freezer, and refrigerator to avoid duplicating purchases. Wansink's research showed that the more of a product we have in the cupboards, the more willing we are to eat it. "I stopped shopping for an army, even for low-fat foods like chicken breasts," says Victoria Bennett, who lost 60 pounds and kept it off for 5 years. "I used to think that everybody had to have two or three chicken breasts. Now, I just make sure that everyone has one."

FOOD LABELS FOR WAIST WATCHERS

We know you can find the calories and fat grams on a food label. They're as easy to find as the nose on the Jolly Green Giant's face. But here are a few numbers that you might not always check and what they mean.

Serving size. That's the first thing to look at (even before fat and calories) because all the information is based on one serving. Compare the food manufacturer's serving size to the size that you'll actually eat. For instance, do you usually eat about 1 cup of ice cream (the size of your fist)? That's twice the standard ½-cup serving, which means doubling all the figures. "Servings per container" can also help. To see how much fat and calories are in an entire container of food, multiply the figures by the "servings per container" number. You'll be amazed at some foods. For ex-ample, the average bag of regular corn chips has more than 2,000 calories and 100 grams of fat.

Calories and fat. Focus on the absolute numbers here—calories and grams of fat per serving—rather than percentages. The Daily Value (DV) percentages are based on 2,000 calories a day, which is probably more than you'll be eating if you're trying to lose weight. For the true numbers on pack-aged mixes, read the "As prepared" column. Many mixes need fats or eggs added in preparation.

Fiber. Choose foods with the most fiber. Research shows that people who eat lots of fiber also eat fewer calories. Fiber-rich foods help you feel full so that you don't overeat. Try to get at least 25 grams of fiber a day.

LOOKEE HERE! "FAT-FREE!"

Health claims on the front of a label can be very misleading. Don't buy it before checking the Nutrition Facts Label for specific nutrition information. Often, fat-free products are loaded with calories. And it's the total number of calories that you really need to watch. Here are some other labeling terms and what they mean by law.

If the Label Says . . .	The Food Has . . .
Fat-free	Less than ½ gram of fat in a serving
Low-fat	3 grams of fat (or less) per serving
Lean	Less than 10 grams of fat per serving, with less than 4 grams of saturated fat and 95 milligrams of cholesterol
Extra-lean	Less than 5 grams of fat per serving, with less than 2 grams of saturated fat and 95 milligrams of cholesterol
Less	25 percent less of a nutrient than the food it is compared with
Reduced	At least 25 percent fewer calories, fat, or sodium than the regular version
Light/lite	⅓ less calories or no more than half of the fat of the higher-calorie, higher-fat version; or no more than half the sodium of the higher-sodium version
Cholesterol-free	Less than 2 milligrams of cholesterol and 2 grams (or less) of saturated fat per serving

Make a list when you're hungry. Try planning meals when you're belly is growling. It will make your menus more interesting.

But don't shop when you're hungry. Have a bagel or some fruit before you go out. You'll have more control. Don't forget to feed the kids, too. Hunger makes controlled shopping difficult for adults and nearly impossible for children. "Grocery shopping after school is always a disaster—unless we have a snack before we head to the store," says Liza Arnow. "My daughters' hunger alarms go off at 3 o'clock in the afternoon. If we have a snack first, then shop, we're all less likely to be drawn to unhealthy foods." A preshopping snack also helps you resist the temptation of high-fat free samples.

Build a pyramid in your cart. For a balanced and varied diet, your filled grocery cart should match the proportions in the Food Guide Pyramid. Bread, cereal, rice, and pasta should occupy the largest space. Fruits and vegetables come next. Then meat and dairy. Fats, oils, and sugary foods should take up very little room.

Grab a basket for fill-in shopping. Don't automatically reach for a huge cart every time you enter a supermarket. It's too easy to fill it up with foods that you don't need, says Dr. Michael Hamilton, an obesity expert at Duke University in Durham, North Carolina. "I sometimes recommend that people shop frequently—every day if possible—instead of loading up the cart and refrigerator once a week."

Wise Buys, Aisle by Aisle

Balance, variety, and moderation. These are the keys to any healthy diet, especially a weight-loss or weight-maintenance eating plan. Sure, cutting calories will drop pounds. But balance and variety with occasional indulgences will help keep you satisfied and keep the weight off long-term. It will also provide the nutrients that you need for more energy.

Load up on cereal, bread, pasta, and rice. These foods are the foundation of a long-term weight-loss strategy. Plus, they keep in your cupboards the longest. Just don't overdo the refined grains like white bread and white rice. Whole grains are higher in fiber than refined grains. That makes them more filling and satisfying, too.

- When buying breads and cereals, look to see that the first ingredient is a whole grain, such as wheat or oats.

- Items from the in-store bakery usually don't have nutrient labeling. Scan the ingredient list and look for items made with whole-wheat flour.

- Pass up those giant muffins, biscuits, and scones. They're loaded with fat. If you can't resist, look for a smaller size.

- Most bakery bagels are the equivalent of three servings of bread. Frozen bagels are usually two servings worth.

- Baked goods should have 3 grams of fat or less per serving.

- Cereal should have 3 grams of fiber or more per serving.

- Seeded crackers have slightly more calories than plain ones, but they have more fiber, too. If you can handle the extra calories, go for the seeded ones.

- Brown rice has almost three times the fiber of white rice. It also has a pleasant, nutty flavor. Quick-cooking brown rice is available in most grocery stores.

THE PRESSURE TO EAT AND EAT

You know how to lose weight. Eat fewer calories and exercise more. Right? So why is it often so hard to stick with your plan? Here are some of the roadblocks that may stand in your way.

Bigger is better. Restaurants, not nutritionists, set portion sizes for America, and your healthy weight is the least of their concerns. They offer huge steaks and all-you-can-eat buffets because consumers perceive them as a higher value. Fast-food places let you "super-size" your meal for pennies. Convenience foods are packaged so that each one seems like a single serving. We've forgotten what a real portion is. Most of us think that a medium bagel is about 4 ounces. But the USDA calls that 2 servings. When Coke was introduced in the 1930s, a bottle was a mere 6 ounces, or about 70 calories. Today, a small soda at many movie theaters and take-out restaurants is 22 ounces, or about 256 calories. A large soda is a whopping 44 ounces, or 515 calories—more than seven times the original.

And it's not just take-out food that's bigger. Home cooks are super-sizing too. The *Joy of Cooking*, in its 1964 edition, instructed its readers to cut a 13" × 9" pan of brownies into 32 bars. The latest edition doubles the size of the brownie. One pan makes only 16 bars.

Food is everywhere. Not long ago, gas stations had no food. If anything, they had a candy machine tucked away in a corner. Today, we buy our gas at mini-marts where fuel is a small part of the merchandising. The gas station has become a convenience store with all kinds of tempting goodies. Also, think of the amount of food available in shopping malls, the ever-present fast-food restaurants on America's main streets (and even in our schools), and the walls of candy that line our movie theaters and drugstores. Food sales have become a huge industry in America.

Advertising works. Plenty of studies demonstrate that the more TV a person watches, the heavier he or she is likely to be. It's true for children as well as adults. Experts point to two possible explanations: First, when you're sitting in the TV room, you're not active and not burning many calories. Second, depending on the time of day, the ads on TV are heavily promoting prepared snack foods and soft drinks. It's a double whammy. Not only are you getting the "buy me" message that stays with you all the way to your next shopping trip but you're also getting prompted to "go get something to eat now." For many people, TV and snacking go hand in hand.

So what's your defense against clever food marketing and the relentless pressure to eat? One simple word: "No." Know when to say no. Just be aware of when you need to eat and when you don't.

- Ramen noodle soups are cooked in oil before packaging. Some have more than 14 grams of fat per cup. If you love them, try preparing the soup using regular spaghetti instead.

Get sweet on produce. For the best buy and best flavor, choose what's fresh and in season. When buying canned and frozen fruits and vegetables, look for those made without sugar and fats. Some waist watchers reduce calories by giving sugar-packed frozen fruits a quick rinse before using. Nutrition experts also say:

- Reach for richly colored fruits and vegetables. They have more nutrients than the pale ones. Dark greens like spinach, watercress, and arugula are healthier than iceberg lettuce. Deep orange or red-fleshed fruits like oranges, melons, and mangoes are richer in vitamins than pears, apples, and bananas.

- Most produce is fat-free and weighs in at less than 40 calories per serving—as long as it's not packed in cream sauce, butter, or added sugar. The exceptions: avocado and coconut. Both are high in fat and calories.

- Shop the salad bar when you need ingredients for a recipe but don't want to purchase too much. Or stop there when you need precut produce for a quick meal.

- If you don't eat salad because you can't bear to make it, give the pre-bagged salad mixes a try. Buy the ones without dressing packets or garnishes. Or toss these to someone in the family who isn't counting calories. Also, see "Dressings to Live By" on page 254 for quick and easy low-calorie salad dressings.

- Although 100 percent fruit and vegetable juices count as a serving of fruits or vegetables, they lack fiber, so they're not as filling or satisfying as a whole fruit or vegetable. Likewise, unfortified fruit drinks are mostly water, sweeteners, and flavorings. Try to keep these to a minimum since they're really just empty calories.

- Dried fruits have most of the water removed from them, which concentrates the flavor and nutrients but also ups the calories. Keep an eye on portion size ($1/4$ cup is one serving).

Dive in for dairy. This is one area of the store where low-fat really is a guarantee of fewer calories.

- Buy 1% milk or fat-free milk. Two percent milk is not low-fat (because it has more than 3 grams of fat per serving).

- Look for low-fat and fat-free yogurt. If you prefer flavored yogurt, vanilla and coffee have the fewest calories.

- Choose cheeses labeled "reduced-fat," "part-skim," "low-fat," or "fat-free." Don't forget strong-flavored cheeses like Parmesan and blue. A little of these goes a long way.

- Buttermilk has no butter and is available fat-free. Some folks find its thicker texture more satisfying than skim milk.

- Butter, margarine, and oils have about 100 calories per tablespoon. Whipped has approximately 70, and light varieties have 50 to 60.

Make meat lean. Meat is definitely on the menu. The leanest cuts of beef are flank, sirloin, and tenderloin. The leanest varieties of pork are fresh, canned, cured, and boiled

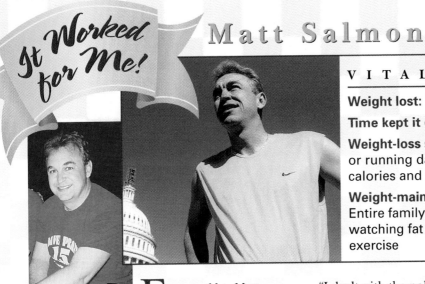

It Worked for Me!

Matt Salmon

VITAL STATS

Weight lost: 70 pounds

Time kept it off: 2 years

Weight-loss strategies: Walking or running daily, cutting calories and fat

Weight-maintenance strategies: Entire family is committed to watching fat intake, daily exercise

Former athlete Matt Salmon's career in politics slowed him down and packed on the pounds. Then he figured out what works.

"I was a long, lean athlete in high school. Later I stayed in shape playing tennis and basketball. But when I was elected to the Arizona State Senate, my exercise routine and healthy eating habits were replaced by political dinners and fundraisers. Each prime rib added another notch to my belt. I kept telling myself, 'I'll exercise after the next election.' But there was always a next election. I just bought bigger suits instead. After 2 years in the U.S. House of Representatives, I added even more weight. I looked like a walrus. I was ashamed and embarrassed. But I also started to have back pain, sinus problems, and chronic heartburn.

"I tried a few of the fad diets that made the rounds on Capitol Hill. Once, I lost 22 pounds. But within a month, my new suit trousers wouldn't fasten across my reinflated belly. I finally had to admit that fad diets don't work and changed my lifestyle.

"I dealt with the political dinners and airplane meals by requesting low-fat or vegetarian meals. And I cut out high-fat desserts. That was hard. But I was no longer willing to trade my health for 10 minutes of pleasure. For snacks, I ate fat-free yogurt, fresh fruits and vegetables. I even kept a bag of raw baby carrots in my briefcase. I began to read food labels. I was amazed at how much fat was crammed into my favorite foods, like bologna.

"I began easy exercise: walking 20 minutes a day, occasionally revving up to a jog for a few minutes. After a month, I was jogging the whole time. Two months later, I had lost 40 pounds, my heartburn and back pain were gone, and I was sleeping better. Eventually, I even decided to train for a marathon! As I trained, the pounds kept coming off. By race day, I had lost a total of 70 pounds, and my waist had gone from 40 inches to 34.

"My whole family now watches the fat grams and eats a more healthy diet. I've become a weight-loss advisor to other members of Congress, too. I tell them, 'Count calories, cut out fat, and meet me at the gym.'" ■

ham, Canadian bacon, pork tenderloin, rib chops, and roast. Lean lamb includes roasts, chops, and legs. Be realistic about portion size when stocking meats. "If you can't pass on some high-fat favorites, stick to the most flavorful ones," says Helen Fitzgerald, who lost 51 pounds. "A single slice of bacon is enough to flavor eggs or a potato."

- Reach for meat labeled "select." It is leaner than meat graded "choice" and much leaner than "prime."

- Look for "ground turkey meat" for the lowest fat. If it's labeled simply "turkey," it may contain the skin, which makes it very high in fat and calories.

- Avoid self-basting turkeys. They have fat injected into the meat. Buy a regular turkey and baste it with your favorite broth instead.

- Buy fresh seafood. Its taste is beyond compare. If you stock frozen seafood, look for varieties without high-calorie breading.

- Light tuna has less fat and fewer calories than solid white pack. Many people actually prefer the flavor of light tuna, too.

- Check lunchmeat labels carefully. Ones made from turkey or chicken don't always have fewer calories and less fat than the beef and pork ones.

Get the Right Tools

You don't need to completely restock your kitchen for low-calorie cooking. In fact, you probably already own most of the really useful fat-fighting and timesaving gadgets.

Sharp knives. One of the greatest deterrents to cooking, low-cal or otherwise, is not being able to quickly and safely cut and chop. The basics: a serrated-edge bread knife (great for tomatoes, too), a paring knife (about 3 inches), and a chef's knife (8 to 10 inches) for chopping.

Food processor. It speeds up chopping, grating, and blending—jobs that otherwise may seem too daunting done by hand. A mini chopper is good for small jobs like mincing parsley or chopping an onion or garlic.

Nonstick skillets. Nonstick coatings have come a long way since the early days of scratch-and-peel Teflon. Today's nonstick pans are chip-resistant and durable. Invest in top quality if you can. Look for pans with a tough, textured coating and a heavy weight so that they're less likely to warp. These also deliver more even, high heat without hot spots. Of course, the best advantage of nonstick pans is that they require less cooking fat. "I've found a way to make home fries without any fat," says Kara Kelly. "I use chicken broth and a nonstick pan instead of lots of butter or bacon fat." An added bonus is that nonstick pans clean up faster.

Microwave oven. If you use it for nothing else than zapping leftovers or "steaming" vegetables and fish without added fats, it's worth it.

Gravy strainer. Even if you don't make gravy, this measuring cup with a pour spout that starts at its base is handy to have around. Instead of skimming away the fat from the top of soups, for example, you pour away the fat-free broth from the bottom and leave the high-calorie fat behind.

Measuring cups and spoons. No, you don't need to portion out every ingredient or serving of food with exact gram accuracy before it passes your lips. But watching por-

MEAT BEATS CHEESE FOR PROTEIN

Many dieters cut out meat because it's high in calories and fat. Instead, they eat cheese and peanut butter for protein. It is a good idea to eat less meat and to make it lean. But replacing meat with dairy and nuts won't save you any calories. In fact, it'll cost you. For instance, to match the protein in 4 ounces of roasted lean pork tenderloin, you'd have to eat nearly 4½ ounces of peanut butter, which piles on an additional 550 calories. For vegetarians who want to lose weight, better protein choices are eggs (especially the whites), low-fat tofu or tempeh, beans, and grains. If you're a meat lover, here are a few protein comparisons that demonstrate why a little meat isn't such a bad idea, even when you're slimming down.

To match the protein in 4 oz of . . .		You'd need this much Cheddar cheese . . .	Or this much peanut butter . . .
Well-done ground beef patty		**4.6 oz**	**4.4 oz**
Protein	32 g	32 g	32 g
Calories	301	521	740
Fat	18 g	41 g	64 g
Broiled beef tenderloin		**4.6 oz**	**4.4 oz**
Protein	32 g	32 g	32 g
Calories	239	521	740
Fat	11 g	41 g	64 g
Roasted lean pork tenderloin		**4.6 oz**	**4.4 oz**
Protein	32 g	32 g	32 g
Calories	186	521	740
Fat	5 g	41 g	64 g
Roasted boneless, skinless chicken breast		**5 oz**	**4.8 oz**
Protein	35 g	35 g	35 g
Calories	187	570	807
Fat	4 g	45 g	64 g
Baked or broiled salmon		**4.4 oz**	**4.3 oz**
Protein	31 g	31 g	31 g
Calories	245	502	723
Fat	12 g	40 g	62 g

tions is the easiest way to cut calories. This is especially true of the little things like salad dressing and oil. The difference between a teaspoonful of olive oil and an offhanded splash is about 100 calories. Just ask Theresa Revitt. "I usually misjudge portions of salad dressing, mayonnaise, and ice cream," she says. "They're really high in fat and calories and cause the most damage if overdone. So I still measure them." Until you're comfortable eyeballing a teaspoon, tablespoon, half-cup, and cup, you might want to pull out the ol' measuring cups and spoons. Or, tie an attractive measuring teaspoon to your olive oil bottle and a tablespoon to your salad dressing. Also, see "Eyes on the Size" on page 162.

Plastic bags. Use them to store cut-up vegetables and fruits so that they're ready to cook or to take along for snacks. Resealable bags also make marinating easier and less messy.

Plastic spray bottles. A refillable spray bottle is less expensive than can after can of chlorofluorocarbon-filled cooking spray. Just fill a bottle with olive or canola oil. Use it to lightly coat skillets and baking pans or to spray a shimmer of oil over foods before roasting. Squeeze bottles (like the ones used for ketchup at diners) can shave calories, too. They allow you to dribble a tiny bit of high-fat sauces or gravies only where you need it.

Popcorn popper. If you like popcorn (it makes a great snack), invest in an air popper or one that can be used in the microwave without added oil. Once popped, coat the popcorn with a light mist of water or oil spray before adding salt or herbs. The seasonings will stick better.

Pantry Pointers

When you're really hungry and trying to lose weight, staring into a pantry full of only fattening foods is a nightmare. Don't be caught off guard. Keep low-calorie, low-fat foods and ingredients on hand. When you have them at the ready, you'll be less tempted to pop a frozen deluxe pizza in the oven. Below are basic ingredients to stock for healthy cooking. For a list of the best snacks to keep around, see "50 Low-Calorie Snacks" on page 121.

Beans. You can buy them dry, cook them, and freeze them. Or stock lots of different kinds in cans. "I like to add beans to whatever other vegetables I have on hand," suggests Lorraine Stevens, who lost 35 pounds.

"I stir-fry them for about 5 minutes, then add a fat-free barbecue sauce." Beans are also great pureed into sandwich spreads and dips, added to soups or pastas, and sprinkled on salads.

Extra-virgin olive oil. Keep a small bottle on hand for uncooked dishes like salad dressings or dips. Its pronounced flavor allows you to use less. Olive oil spoils easily, so keep it in the fridge. It will thicken and turn cloudy, but a few minutes at room temperature will return it to a golden liquid without damage to the quality or flavor. You might want to stock a less expensive olive oil for cooking and sautéing.

Fresh produce. With a microwave oven, cooking fresh vegetables doesn't take any longer than the frozen kind. And they're a lot less caloric than ones packed in sauce or butter. "I've been known to eat a whole bag of vegetables," says Verona Mucci-Hurlburt, who went from a size 18 to 8. "And with only

(continued on page 44)

It Worked for Me!

Teresa Tomeo

VITAL STATS

Weight lost: 60 pounds

Time kept it off: 12 years

Weight-loss strategy: Low-fat, low-calorie diet

Weight-maintenance strategies: Low-fat, low-calorie diet with occasional splurges; walking

The only thing keeping Teresa Tomeo from a career in TV journalism was her weight. Teresa got motivated and dropped 60 pounds.

"'You're a good reporter, but if you want to make it on TV, you have to lose weight.'

"Believe it or not, a friend and mentor spoke those words. And, believe it or not, I needed to hear them. I was 25 and a successful newswoman for a Detroit radio station, but I was ready to try on-camera work. My friend, an NBC producer, summed up my situation with a journalist's stone-cold objectivity: I was too fat.

"The words stung, but he wasn't telling me anything that the scale hadn't already. At 5 feet 6 inches, I weighed 190 pounds and wore a size 18. In the image-conscious world of TV, my look would never fly. So I took action. I went to a medically supervised clinic called the Quick Weight Loss Center in Warren, Michigan. I wanted real-world foods, healthy recipes, and sensible amounts. The clinic supplied me with a calorie chart and balanced eating plan. I recorded my calories and weighed in once a week.

"For 6 months, I ate fish and chicken and lots of fruits and vegetables. At work, I ignored the doughnuts, bagels, and cheese trays sent by fans and advertisers. And I drank water like a camel—a half-gallon a day—since the nutritionists at the clinic harped on how water makes you feel full.

"At first, the weight came off quickly—4 pounds the first week, 3 the next. In 3 months, I'd lost 30 pounds! Then the weight came off more slowly, usually 1 to 2 pounds a week. But with each pound I lost, I had more energy and confidence. After 7 months, I'd lost 60 pounds and felt great. What's more, I looked great, and in the summer of 1988, I landed a job for a local TV station.

"Now, at 40, I adhere to the same eating principles as I did back then, but with an occasional treat. I'm more disciplined if I can indulge in my mother's lasagna every once in a while. And I still have my on-camera figure; I weigh about 135 pounds and wear a size 8.

"The one thing I still struggle with is exercise. I wish that when I was relearning how to eat, I'd also learned how to exercise regularly. If I had, I could be less rigid about my diet." ■

CALORIE-SAVING SWAPS IN THE KITCHEN

Sometimes a simple switch is all it takes to make a low-calorie meal. For instance, Canadian bacon has 120 fewer calories than regular bacon. Experiment with the calorie shavers below. You may not like a sweet potato more than a white potato, but most people do prefer the taste of light tuna over higher-calorie white tuna. Unless indicated, the foods and their alternatives have the same serving size.

Instead of Using . . .	Try . . .	And Save This Many Calories . . .
Soups and stews		
Bacon (1 oz)	Canadian bacon	120
Chicken broth (14-oz can)	Skimmed chicken broth	27
Green peas (½ cup)	Broccoli	55
Pork chops (4 oz)	Pork tenderloin	48
White potato	Sweet potato	100
Entrées		
Broiled burger, medium doneness (3 oz)	Well-done broiled burger	20
Salmon (4 oz)	Cod	126
T-bone steak (4 oz)	London broil	116
Tuna in oil (3½-oz can)	Tuna in water	80
Turkey breast cutlets	Skinless chicken breasts	36 per 4 oz
White tuna in water (6-oz can)	Light tuna in water	30

Instead of Using . . .	Try . . .	And Save This Many Calories . . .
Baking		
Butter (1 cup)	Drained applesauce (¾ cup) plus butter (¼ cup)	530
Chocolate (1 oz)	Cocoa (3 Tbsp)	100
Cookie crumb crust made with eggs (12")	Crust made with egg whites	360
Cream (½ cup)	Fat-free evaporated milk	145
Cream cheese (1 oz)	Neufchâtel cheese	25
Whole egg	2 whites	45
Whole milk (1 cup)	Fat-free milk	48
Whole-milk yogurt (1 cup)	Fat-free yogurt	24
Salad dressings		
Oil (½ cup) and vinegar (½ cup)	Oil (⅓ cup), vinegar (⅓ cup), and strong tea (⅓ cup)	20
Sour cream (¾ cup)	Cottage cheese (½ cup) plus buttermilk (¼ cup)	266
In casseroles		
Cheddar cheese (1 oz)	Reduced-fat mozzarella	42
Flour tortilla	Corn tortilla	50
Ground beef (1 lb)	⅔ cup soaked bulgur plus ½ lb ground beef	210
Ground beef (1 lb)	Chopped mushrooms (4 cups)	810
Ground beef (4 oz)	Ground turkey breast	100
Whole milk (1 cup)	1% cottage cheese or ricotta cheese whirled in a blender	268

a quarter-cup of homemade sauce, it's only about 3 grams of fat."

But, don't you hate it when your fresh vegetables spoil before you can get to them? Here's what stays freshest longest: green beans, broccoli, cabbages, carrots, potatoes, peppers, bananas, apples, and citrus. Keep a supply of canned and frozen corn and peas on hand, too, since the season for fresh is so short. Most people prefer canned corn because it is sweeter and more tender than frozen. As for peas, the frozen kind are far tastier than canned.

As a general rule, wash produce only just before you use it. And store it in the right place for maximum flavor and freshness. At right are the foods that keep best *out* of the fridge and why.

TWO FAT FAUX PAS

Some low-fat cooking techniques were not meant to be. Here are two methods that many people use in the hopes of cutting calories. Avoid them. They don't save calories, and they may cost you flavor.

Skinny chickens. You don't have to cook chicken without the skin to save calories. Very little of the fat from the skin gets into the meat—just enough to keep it moist. Leave the skin on during cooking so that the bird doesn't dry out. You will save about 30 calories per chicken breast, though, if you don't eat the skin *after* it's cooked.

Extra-lean burgers. The leanest ground beef in the meat case is not always the tastiest (or least expensive) choice for burgers. The calorie and fat difference between a grilled or broiled burger made with regular ground round and one made with extra-lean hamburger is slim. Here's why: During cooking, the leanest beef loses water and only a little fat. That makes extra-lean burgers extra-dry, too. The fattier beef loses mostly fat, but remains moist. This principle applies only to burgers that are grilled or broiled on a rack so that the fat drips away. If you're pan-frying the burgers (or using the ground beef for something like meat loaf), stick with the leanest beef you can find. Here are the numbers for quarter-pound burgers, grilled or broiled.

Ground beef	Raw		Well-Done	
	Calories	Fat (g)	Calories	Fat (g)
Extra-lean (17% fat)	264	19	186	11
Lean (21% fat)	298	23	196	12
Regular (27% fat)	350	30	198	13

- Tomatoes: taste better at room temperature
- Winter squash: shells protect them without refrigeration
- Potatoes: get too green if kept too cold
- Onions: moisture collects under their skins and spoils them
- Basil: cold blackens tender leaves
- Unripe fruits: refrigeration stops the ripening processes

Keep all your other produce in the crisper drawer in unsealed plastic bags to allow air to circulate.

Herbs and spices. Flavor is the name of the game when you're cooking low-calorie. Herbs and spices are an easy way to boost any food's flavor. To get the most taste, add fresh herbs just at the end of cooking. Dried herbs, on the other hand, should go in toward the beginning to coax out their "sleeping" aromas while the food cooks. (Crushing dried herbs helps release their flavors, too.) Generally, you can substitute a third of any dried herb for fresh.

A good stock. Use it in salad dressings to replace some of the oil, to cook vegetables for more flavor (instead of using water), to start a homemade soup, or to replace butter or oil for sautéing. The taste of homemade stocks beats that of store brands by a mile. If you can, store homemade stocks frozen in ice-cube trays to punch out 2 tablespoons whenever needed. Another alternative is to use stock bases, which are available through gourmet stores. They're pricey but delicious.

Vinegars. Sherry, rice, raspberry, wine, and balsamic vinegars are all more flavorful and mild than pungent and acidic white vinegar or cider vinegar. Use them for dressings and marinades, to sauté chicken breasts, or to splash over broiled fish.

Aged cheese. The stronger the flavor, the less you'll need. Intensely flavored cheeses like extra-sharp aged Cheddar, Asiago, imported Parmesan, and smoked cheeses like Gouda can really add a shot of flavor to soups, salads, pastas, and casseroles. Place the cheese where you can see it (on top of a dish) so that it's the first thing you'll taste.

Whole grains. Here they are again—we can't recommend them enough. Whole grains don't have fewer calories than refined ones, but they do have extra fiber, which helps fill you up and keep you satisfied. Store them in the fridge, since whole grains go rancid more quickly. Oatmeal is a good breakfast staple for sprinkling over cereal or tossing into baked goods. Whole-wheat pastry flour can replace all-purpose flour in just about any baking recipe. Some other whole grains to try: Quinoa (KEEN-wa), an ancient grain, is one of the best grain sources of protein. It cooks up like rice (even faster) and can be used in casseroles, salads, or desserts. Brown rice takes a little longer to cook than white (35 versus 20 minutes), but it has three times the fiber. Bulgur (cracked wheat) can be used to make salads and to toss into chili. Experiment with different cooking liquids. The Herbed Rice recipe on page 236 is a great place to start. "For variety, I cook rice and other grains in tomato juice, apple juice, or beef or chicken stock," says Helen Fitzgerald. "Rice done in pineapple juice is especially good for Chinese dishes."

CALORIE-SAVING SWAPS AWAY FROM HOME

Eating out is fast, easy, and fun. But the temptation to eat (and eat) is everywhere. Here are some healthy options to consider whenever you face a meal, market, or any food choice. Keep these in mind as you plan your menus and write your shopping list. Unless indicated, the foods and their alternatives have the same serving size.

Instead of Choosing . . .	Try . . .	And Save This Many Calories . . .
Vegetables		
French fries (½ cup)	Coleslaw	76
Macaroni salad (½ cup)	Cob of corn, no butter	163
Mashed potatoes (1 cup)	Medium baked potato	89
Potato salad (½ cup)	French bread/roll	122
Meat, poultry, and fish		
Beef chimichanga	Beef burrito	212
Chicken breast with skin	Chicken breast, no skin	102
Chicken nuggets (6)	Grilled chicken fillet	142
Chicken parmigiana	Chicken piccata	40
Fettuccine Alfredo	Fettuccine marinara	300
Ham and cheese sandwich with mayonnaise	Ham sandwich with mustard	269
Italian sausage link	All-beef hot dog	37
Sausage and pepperoni pizza slice	Vegetable pizza slice	120
Slice of turkey breast (1 oz)	Slice of salami	36

Instead of Choosing . . .	Try . . .	And Save This Many Calories . . .
Snacks and treats		
Apple pie slice	Scalloped apples (1/2 cup)	300
Cherry pie slice	Fruit salad (1/2 cup)	424
Granola cereal (1 cup)	Grain cereal with dried fruit	317
Jumbo soft drink (64 oz)	Kid's soft drink (8 oz)	75
Creamsicle	Ice cream bar with fruit swirl	25
Dove bar	Popsicle	250
Fried tortillas chips (1 oz)	Baked tortilla chips	20
Guacamole (1 Tbsp)	Salsa	58
Ice cream (1/2 cup)	Italian ice	140
Ice cream sandwich	Fudgsicle	55
Onion dip (1 Tbsp)	Salsa	22
Peanuts (1 oz)	Popcorn (2 cups popped)	175
Premium ice cream (1/2 cup)	Regular ice cream	100
Potato chips (2 oz)	Baby carrots (2 oz)	280
Soft-serve ice cream (1 cup)	Soft-serve frozen yogurt	65
White cake slice with frosting	Angel food cake slice, no frosting	138
Beverages		
Fast-food milkshake (1 cup)	Low-fat milk	140
Half-and-half (2 Tbsp) in coffee	Fat-free milk	30
Sweetened iced tea (1 cup)	Unsweetened iced tea	60
Wine (2 glasses)	Wine (1 glass)	120

De-Calorize Your Favorite Recipes

Any dish tastes great with lots of butter, cheese, and other fats thrown in. But you don't have to give up taste and flavor for weight-savvy cooking. The people we talked with found lots of ways to cut calories in their favorite recipes without severely sacrificing flavor. Of course, your tastebuds need a little time to adjust, so make changes gradually.

Toss that yolk. Whenever a recipe calls for two eggs, throw out one yolk, and you'll save about 45 calories and 5 grams of fat. This trick works with baking, casseroles, scrambled eggs, egg salad, you name it!

Swap fruit for most of the fat in baked goods. You can't take out all the oil or butter in baked goods and still have something worth eating. But you can reduce the fat to about one-fourth of the original amount. Replace the rest with prune pie filling (sold as lekvar), apple butter, apple sauce, mashed bananas, or pureed canned pears. Reconstituted and pureed dried fruits like apricots and apples also work. The trick is to pair the fruit with the other flavors in the quick bread, muffins, or cake. For instance, prunes and chocolate work well. If you can't stand prunes, applesauce works with chocolate, too. Applesauce is also a

THREE CHEERS FOR CHEESE

Low-fat cheeses have come a long way since they were first introduced. Granted, they're not the same as full-fat versions, but today's low-fat varieties taste a lot better. And folks have figured out how to make them melt better, too. Here are a few tips to help get that gooey, melted, stretchy texture that makes cheese so fun.

Shred it cold. Low-fat cheese shreds easiest when it's well-chilled.

Shred it finely. Big chunks don't melt well. The key is shredding it as finely as possible, then distributing it evenly throughout the food you're using it with.

Add moisture. Low-fat cheese is low in moisture (because fat is moist and there's less of it). For the best results, use it with foods high in moisture, such as soups, sauces, lasagna, and casseroles. Low-moisture foods such as pizza don't work as well.

Turn down the heat. High heat tends to make low-fat cheese dry and gluey. Think "low-fat, low heat." When adding cheese to a soup or sauce, reduce the heat, then gradually stir in the cheese until it melts.

Cover it. To create a creamier texture, cover foods to keep in moisture. When microwaving with low-fat cheese, use a low setting, cover the food, rotate often, and stir frequently.

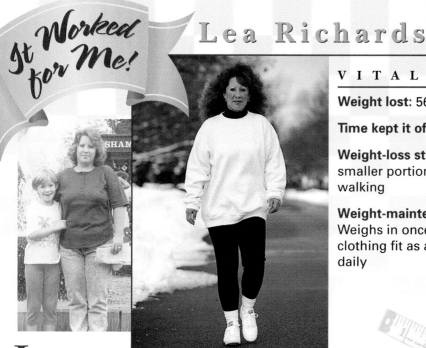

It Worked for Me!

Lea Richards

VITAL STATS

Weight lost: 56 pounds

Time kept it off: 7 years

Weight-loss strategies: Eating smaller portions, low-fat diet, walking

Weight-maintenance strategies: Weighs in once a year, uses clothing fit as a gauge, walks daily

Lea walked every day to reduce the stress in her life. After 5 years, she was calmer and a lot leaner.

"One particularly stressful night, I just had to get out of the house. So I went for a walk. I was gone only 10 to 15 minutes, but that little bit of exercise helped me vent my emotions and calm me down. It didn't take long before that little evening walk became a habit. I walked every day, through snow banks if I had to. My walk was my time, my chance to shed the day's stresses.

"Soon, I started walking farther, increasing my mileage by about a half-mile every 6 months. Over the course of 3 years, I worked up to four 15-minute miles a night. Destressing wasn't the only benefit. In a few months, I had also dropped a dress size!

"As I became a more dedicated walker, I also became a more conscientious eater. I started paying attention to portion sizes by measuring my servings. What an eye-opener. I'd been eating two, three, even four times the recommended amounts of foods like pasta and meats. I also cut back on rich ingredients like cream, butter, and cheese. I still allow myself treats, but always in moderation.

"Now, I use my clothing as a gauge of how well I'm keeping my weight in check. I don't concentrate on the scale. Instead, I just weigh in once a year. And I walk every day. At this point, my exercise and eating habits have become second nature. Now, I'm addicted to walking. And it sure beats living in a too-large body clothed in stress." ■

better choice when you want the finished product to remain light in color. For the best results, drain applesauce in a colander for 10 minutes to remove excess liquid. If you're using bananas, keep in mind that they will darken when baked.

Cake flour is best. Fat carries flavor, but it also tenderizes baked goods. When you have less fat, you need more tenderizing. Enter cake flour. All-purpose flour is a good choice for full-fat baking, but the low-fat baker's choice is pastry or cake flour. It has less structural strength and needs less tenderizing than all-purpose. The less fat, the more important this substitute will be.

Switch from chocolate to cocoa powder. In baking, 3 tablespoons of cocoa has the same chocolaty flavor as 1 ounce of solid chocolate, but 100 fewer calories. This is an easy switch for chocolate cakes, cookies, brownies, and sauces. Depending upon the liquid in the recipe, you might want to add a little extra moisture in the form of low-fat milk or other dairy products.

Bake a crispy pie crust. Traditional graham cracker and chocolate cookie crusts are held together with lots of melted butter. But egg whites have the same binding properties as butter. You can substitute one lightly beaten egg white for every $\frac{1}{4}$ cup of butter in prebaked crusts. This fat saver is not recommended for unbaked crusts because salmonella-contaminated eggs are a fact of life.

Use strong tea in salad dressings. Simply cutting the oil in a vinaigrette results in a very acidic dressing (because there's less oil and more vinegar). Adding strong black tea (the common kind) mellows the vinegar's acid without diluting the dressing the way, say, plain water would.

Stretch your beef budget with bulgur. Meatballs and meat loaf come out fluffier and leaner when you substitute bulgur for part of the ground beef. For every pound of beef, mix in $\frac{1}{2}$ cup of soaked and drained bulgur (start with $\frac{1}{3}$ cup dry). Bulgur is a form of cracked wheat available in the grain aisle of most supermarkets.

Beware the oil sponges. Grill, broil, or bake eggplant, but avoid sautéing or frying it in oil. Eggplants are sponges that absorb just about any amount of oil they get. In dishes that call for cooked eggplant, cut it in half or slice it, coat with a little nonstick spray, salt, and pepper, and bake at 375°F, or until tender. You'll never miss the fat.

Sweat instead of sautéing. To really cut back on fat, when recipes call for onions and garlic to be cooked in oil, use a nonstick pan and two tablespoons of broth or water in place of the oil. Use low heat and cover the pan to coax out the vegetable's natural juices.

Make and use yogurt cheese. Drained yogurt (or yogurt cheese) makes a good substitute for sour cream and heavy cream. If you drain it well, it can even stand in for cream cheese. Spoon a 16-ounce container of low-fat plain yogurt into a colander lined with cheesecloth or a coffee filter. Allow the yogurt to drain in the refrigerator over a bowl for 8 to 24 hours, depending on how firm you want the "cheese" to be. For a delicious dessert topping, drain low-fat vanilla yogurt for 4 to 8 hours, or just until thickened. One caveat: Don't use yogurts containing aspartame or gelatin; they don't separate properly.

Roast garlic. When it's roasted, garlic transforms into a rich, buttery, nonbiting, nonodorous spread. It makes a great substitute for some of the mayonnaise in potato, pasta, and chicken salads. It's also good spread on bread in place of butter. Cut the top off a head of garlic to expose the cloves, sprinkle with a couple teaspoons of water, seal in foil, and bake at 400°F for 45 minutes. Unwrap the garlic, cool until easy to handle, then squeeze the creamy roasted garlic from its skin.

Brown butter. Browning boosts flavor so that you don't need to use as much. Heat butter in a skillet until it becomes fragrant and begins to turn nutty brown (but not burnt). This is a great trick when making dishes such as mashed potatoes. Try drizzling it over corn on the cob, too.

Toast nuts. Like butter, a little browning pumps up the flavor of nuts so that you can use less without missing a flavorful morsel. Simply toast them in a dry skillet over medium heat for a few minutes, shaking the pan often, or until the nuts are fragrant. Then, place them where you'll really taste them—on top of muffins or a casserole (not buried inside) or sprinkled over a salad.

Marinate, marinate. Lean meats, poultry, and seafood are less tender than fatty ones. Marinating does double duty by tenderizing and adding flavor. Experiment with different marinades made from soy sauce, broths, citrus juices, vinegars, and your favorite herbs and spices.

Get fired up. Grilling intensifies flavors like no other cooking method can. The high heat of the grill concentrates a food's tastes. Grilling over charcoal also imparts a smoky aroma. Instead of sautéing vegetables, chicken, meats, or fish, try marinating and grilling them instead. The flavor boost is remarkable.

Fry in the oven. "I bake instead of frying," says Jean Ross, who lost 35 pounds. Baking at high heat creates results similar to deep-frying, but without nearly as much fat. This method works especially well for oven-fried potatoes (instead of french fries), homemade tortilla chips (or corn tortillas cut into wedges), and breaded chicken, meats, and seafood. The basic method: Preheat the oven to 450°F. Place the food on a nonstick baking sheet and coat the food with nonstick spray. Bake until crisp, turning occasionally.

Bring on the Breakfasts and Brunches

Easy Huevos Rancheros 54

Meatless Mexican Chorizo 56

Roasted Home Fries 57

Fat-Free Skillet Home Fries 57

Easy Ham and Cheese "Soufflé" 58

Breakfast in a Cup 60

Savory Hash-Browned Potatoes 62

Good Morning Muffins 64

Quick Breakfast Crisp 65

Blueberry-Pecan Pancakes 66

Jumbo Cinnamon-Raisin Muffins 68

Lemon Scones 70

Hot Banana-Wheat Cereal 72

Chopra Granola 73

Blueberry Brunch Cake 74

Chocolate Chip Coffee Cake 76

Orange-Raisin Tea Bread 77

Easy Huevos Rancheros

270 Calories

—Paula Ball, Rosenburg, Oreg.

" Once in a while, I treat myself with this simplified version of my favorite egg dish. It's especially quick, and everything (except for poaching the eggs) is done right on the baking sheet that goes under the broiler. "

4 large eggs
4 corn tortillas (6" diameter)
1 cup canned refried beans
½ cup salsa
¼ cup (1 ounce) shredded reduced-fat Cheddar cheese

Preheat the broiler. Lightly coat a baking sheet with nonstick spray. In a medium skillet or saucepan, heat 1½" water to boiling. Reduce heat to low. Gently break the eggs into the simmering water. Cook 3 to 5 minutes, or until whites are set.

Meanwhile, place tortillas on the prepared baking sheet and heat under the broiler 1 minute, or until slightly crisp but not brown. Flip tortillas and spread untoasted sides with refried beans. Return to the broiler and cook 1 minute, or just until heated through. Top each tortilla with a poached egg, 2 tablespoons salsa, and 1 tablespoon cheese.

Return to the broiler and cook 30 seconds, or just until the cheese melts.

Makes 4 servings

Per serving: *270 calories, 16 g protein, 31 g carbohydrates, 9 g fat, 223 mg cholesterol, 677 mg sodium, 3 g fiber*

Diet Exchanges: *0 milk, 0 vegetable, 0 fruit, 2 bread, 1½ meat, 0 fat*

(Meatless Mexican Chorizo recipe on page 56)

Meatless Mexican Chorizo

—Mary Esther Ruiz, Houston

"Chorizo is a kind of spicy sausage used in many Latin dishes. It can be very fatty. My version is fat-controlled, yet as spicy as the real thing. Use it as a filling for burritos, an addition to stews, or as an accompaniment to breakfast eggs."

1 **pound meatless sausage links**
½ **onion, chopped**
1 **can (14½ ounces) vegetable or chicken broth**
¼ **cup chili powder**
1 **tablespoon ground cinnamon**
2 **teaspoons ground cumin**
2 **teaspoons dried oregano**
2 **teaspoons dried thyme**
¾ **teaspoon salt or to taste**
½ **teaspoon paprika**
½ **cup red wine vinegar**
½ **cup tequila or nonalcoholic beer**
8 **peppercorns**
6 **garlic cloves**
2 **bay leaves**

Cook sausage in a large nonstick skillet according to package directions. Finely chop and set aside.

In the same skillet, cook onion in 2 tablespoons broth over medium heat 5 minutes, or until tender. Add chili powder, cinnamon, cumin, oregano, thyme, salt, and paprika. Cook 1 minute. Add cooked sausage, vinegar, tequila or beer, peppercorns, garlic, bay leaves, and remaining broth.

Heat to boiling. Reduce heat to low and simmer, uncovered, 30 minutes. Remove garlic and bay leaves. Refrigerate 24 hours before using.

Makes 8 servings

Per serving: *187 calories, 12 g protein, 12 g carbohydrates, 11 g fat, 0 mg cholesterol, 954 mg sodium, 2 g fiber*

Diet Exchanges: *0 milk, 0 vegetable, 0 fruit, 1 bread, 1½ meat, 0 fat*

(Photograph on page 55)

Roasted Home Fries

271 Calories

—Karen C. Gray, San Leandro, Calif.

"For extra-crispy, run the baking dish under the broiler for the last 5 minutes."

4 large potatoes, cut into ½" pieces
1 green or red bell pepper, chopped
1 red onion, thinly sliced
2 teaspoons olive oil
1½ teaspoons seasoned salt
1 teaspoon ground black pepper
½ teaspoon garlic powder (optional)

Preheat the oven to 425°F. Coat a large baking dish with nonstick spray.

Toss the potatoes, bell pepper, onion, oil, seasoned salt, black pepper, and garlic powder, if using, in the pan until well-coated. Bake, stirring occasionally, 35 to 40 minutes, or until potatoes are fork-tender and golden.

Makes 4 servings

Per serving: *271 calories, 6 g protein, 58 g carbohydrates, 3 g fat, 0 mg cholesterol, 589 mg sodium, 7 g fiber*

Diet Exchanges: *0 milk, 0 vegetable, 0 fruit, 3 bread, 0 meat, ½ fat*

(Photograph on page 61)

Fat-Free Skillet Home Fries

334 Calories

—Mrs. Kara Kelly, Ellwood City, Pa.

"I make home fries without any added fat. I use chicken broth instead of butter."

1½ cups chicken or vegetable broth
6 potatoes, thinly sliced
3 scallions, chopped
½ teaspoon onion salt
¼ teaspoon garlic powder
¼ teaspoon ground sage
¼ teaspoon ground black pepper
¼ teaspoon paprika

In a large, heavy nonstick skillet, heat ½ cup broth to boiling. Add potatoes, scallions, onion salt, garlic powder, sage, pepper, and paprika. Cover and cook over high heat 5 minutes, or until liquid is absorbed, turning potatoes occasionally. Reduce heat to low and cook 10 minutes, adding broth as needed until potatoes are tender and browned.

Makes 4 servings

Per serving: *334 calories, 9 g protein, 75 g carbohydrates, 1 g fat, 0 mg cholesterol, 430 mg sodium, 6 g fiber*

Diet Exchanges: *0 milk, 0 vegetable, 0 fruit, 4 bread, 0 meat, 0 fat*

Easy Ham and Cheese "Soufflé"

304 Calories

—Sandie Robinson, South Burlington, Vt.

"This mock soufflé is a trimmed-down version of a one-dish brunch favorite. It's healthier than most other breakfast foods and easier, too. Just assemble in the morning and bake when you are ready."

2 eggs

4 egg whites

1½ cups fat-free milk

1 cup (4 ounces) shredded reduced-fat extra-sharp Cheddar cheese

6 slices whole-wheat bread, cubed

1 can (4 ounces) sliced mushrooms, drained

2 ounces lean smoked ham, diced

½ teaspoon dried Italian seasoning

Preheat the oven to 350°F. Coat a 2-quart baking dish with nonstick spray.

In a large bowl, beat eggs and egg whites until frothy. Stir in milk, cheese, bread, mushrooms, ham, and Italian seasoning. Pour into the prepared baking dish.

Bake 45 minutes, or until golden and a knife inserted in the center comes out clean.

Makes 4 servings

Per serving: *304 calories, 26 g protein, 28 g carbohydrates, 11 g fat, 136 mg cholesterol, 814 mg sodium, 5 g fiber*

Diet Exchanges: *0 milk, 0 vegetable, 0 fruit, 2 bread, 2 meat, 0 fat*

Breakfast in a Cup

107 Calories

—Dinah Burnette, Lewisville, N.C.

" These egg 'muffins' make a hearty breakfast and can be eaten on the run. Make them ahead and warm them in the microwave oven for a fast breakfast treat. Try them between English muffins, too. "

4 ounces reduced-fat loose breakfast sausage

¼ cup chopped green bell pepper

¼ cup chopped onion

1 cup liquid egg substitute or 4 eggs

1 large egg

1 can (4 ounces) sliced mushrooms, drained

½ cup (2 ounces) shredded reduced-fat Cheddar cheese

Coat a 6-cup muffin pan with nonstick spray. Preheat the oven to 350°F.

In a medium nonstick skillet over medium-high heat, cook the sausage, pepper, and onion 5 minutes, or until sausage is browned. Spoon mixture into a bowl and cool slightly. Stir in egg substitute or eggs, egg, and mushrooms. Spoon mixture evenly into the prepared muffin pan. Sprinkle with cheese. Bake 20 minutes, or until egg is set.

Makes 6 servings

Per serving: *107 calories, 12 g protein, 4 g carbohydrates, 5 g fat, 49 mg cholesterol, 318 mg sodium, 1 g fiber*

Diet Exchanges: *0 milk, 0 vegetable, 0 fruit, 0 bread, 1½ meat, 0 fat*

(Roasted Home Fries recipe on page 57)

Savory Hash-Browned Potatoes

157 Calories

—Marcie Lehman, St. Helena, Calif.

"My secret to crispy hash browns is to cook the potatoes without peeling them. The skins give a rustic flavor and add fiber, too."

1 tablespoon vegetable oil
2 baking potatoes, coarsely grated
1 small onion, coarsely grated
1 garlic clove, minced
¾ teaspoon salt
¼ teaspoon ground black pepper

Warm oil in a large nonstick skillet over medium heat.

In a large bowl, combine potatoes, onion, garlic, salt, and pepper.

Spread potato mixture into the skillet. Top with a 9" or 10" plate or cake pan weighted down with something heavy, such as cans of soup. Cook 4 minutes, or until browned. Turn potatoes over and cook 4 minutes, or until browned.

Makes 4 servings

Per serving: *157 calories, 3 g protein, 29 g carbohydrates, 4 g fat, 0 mg cholesterol, 409 mg sodium, 1 g fiber*

Diet Exchanges: *0 milk, 0 vegetable, 0 fruit, 1½ bread, 0 meat, 1 fat*

TIP: You can use a flat-sided waffle iron in place of the skillet and weights. Coat the griddle (flat) surfaces of the waffle iron with nonstick spray and warm on the medium setting. Spread a quarter to half of the mixture onto the waffle iron and cook for 4 minutes, or until crispy. Remove to a plate and keep warm. Repeat with remaining mixture.

NINE HANDHELD BREAKFASTS

Sometimes breakfast means rushing out the door, sitting behind the wheel of a car, or sitting at a desk and wolfing down a bagel with jelly. Why jelly instead of cream cheese? To save on fat grams, right? Well, not quite. The choice of jelly may seem noble, but that choice will leave you drooping way before noon. A good breakfast is based on carbohydrates (like the bagel, or bread, or cereal), but it should also contain some protein and fat. Yes, some fat. Meals that contain only carbohydrate and very little protein and fat (like a bagel with jelly or cereal with skim milk) won't stay with you long. Within about 45 minutes, you'll be hungry again. But a meal that contains all three nutrients will keep you satisfied throughout the morning.

So go for the reduced-fat cream cheese instead of jelly. Or grab one of the portable breakfasts below. They make great lunches, too. The best beverage choice? A handy carton of low-fat milk or juice.

Beyond PB & J. Make a sandwich with two slices of whole-wheat toast. Spread one slice with orange marmalade and the other with a thin layer of chunky peanut butter. Sprinkle with raisins.

Salmon Sandwich. Mix canned salmon with reduced-fat cream cheese. Season with dried dill and black pepper. Sandwich between two slices of cracked-wheat bread with a layer of sprouts.

More Than a Muffin. Spread a bran muffin with reduced-fat ricotta cheese. Drizzle with honey and sprinkle with wheat germ.

Smooth Sailing. In a blender, combine low-fat yogurt (plain, lemon, or vanilla), chopped canned peaches, orange juice, ground ginger, cinnamon, and ice cubes. Pour the smoothie into a portable mug.

Go-Go Gazpacho. In a blender, combine a tomato, half of a peeled cucumber, a little sweet onion, some olive oil, tomato juice, and ice cubes. (To wake up your taste buds, add a few drops of hot-pepper sauce.) Pulse until slightly chunky. Pour into a portable mug. Enjoy with a cheese stick.

Egg Salad on a Bagel. Mix a chopped hard-cooked egg with low-fat mayonnaise (and some Dijon mustard, if you like). Spread on a bagel.

Pizza Pick-Me-Up. There's nothing wrong with cold leftover pizza, especially if you top it with some vegetables.

Go-gurt. Grab a small container of low-fat yogurt (plain, lemon, or vanilla) and stir in a serving of all-bran cereal. Top with some apple slices or berries. Bring a spoon.

Waffle Sandwich. Toast two low-fat frozen waffles. Layer with a slice of turkey, a slice of low-fat cheese, and some cranberry sauce.

Good Morning Muffins

—Christine Finnigan, Lakewood, Wash.

207 Calories

"The apples, raisins, and nuts pack lots of flavor into these muffins. I like them on lazy weekend mornings with a cup of coffee. They keep in the refrigerator for about 5 days and in the freezer up to 4 months."

1¼ cups unbleached or all-purpose flour

2 teaspoons baking soda

½ teaspoon salt

½ teaspoon ground cinnamon

¼ teaspoon ground nutmeg

⅓ cup sugar

2 large eggs

⅓ cup vegetable oil

1 cup grated carrots

1 small Granny Smith apple, grated with peel

½ cup golden raisins

½ cup chopped dates

⅓ cup sliced almonds

⅓ cup unsweetened coconut (optional)

Preheat the oven to 350°F. Coat a 12-cup muffin pan with nonstick spray or line with paper liners.

In a small bowl, combine flour, baking soda, salt, cinnamon, and nutmeg.

In a large bowl, combine sugar, eggs, and oil. Stir sugar mixture into flour mixture just until moistened. Stir in carrots, apple, raisins, dates, almonds, and coconut, if using.

Spoon batter into the prepared pan until each muffin cup is three-quarters full. Bake 20 minutes, or until a wooden pick inserted into the center of a muffin comes out clean.

Makes 12

Per muffin: *207 calories, 4 g protein, 29 g carbohydrates, 9 g fat, 36 mg cholesterol, 313 mg sodium, 2 g fiber*

Diet Exchanges: *0 milk, 0 vegetable, 1 fruit, 1 bread, 0 meat, 1½ fat*

Quick Breakfast Crisp

351 Calories

—Dixie Lunderville, Merrillan, Wis.

"Now here's an easy breakfast dish. It doubles as a dessert or snack, too. Use apples, pears, or peaches or a mixture of all three. This single-serve recipe cooks in its serving dish. To make several for friends, cook each dish one at a time in the microwave oven—it takes only a moment."

1 apple or pear, cored and sliced
2 tablespoons packed brown sugar
2 tablespoons quick-cooking oats
2 tablespoons unbleached or all-purpose flour
1/8 teaspoon ground cinnamon
1 tablespoon reduced-fat margarine or butter, softened

Preheat the oven to 350°F. Place fruit in a small baking dish.

In a small bowl, combine brown sugar, oats, flour, and cinnamon. Rub in margarine or butter with your fingertips or a fork until mixture resembles coarse crumbs. Sprinkle over fruit. Bake 15 to 20 minutes, or until fruit is tender when pierced.

Makes 1 serving

Per serving: *351 calories, 5 g protein, 68 g carbohydrates, 8 g fat, 0 mg cholesterol, 143 mg sodium, 6 g fiber*

Diet Exchanges: *0 milk, 0 vegetable, 1 fruit, 3 bread, 0 meat, 1 fat*

Blueberry-Pecan Pancakes

—Melissa Welch, Portland, Maine

"June in Maine is wild blueberry time. That's when we enjoy these pancakes most. But it's not the only time. I make them with frozen blueberries, too. But there's one thing that never varies: We always eat them with real maple syrup."

1 cup unbleached or all-purpose flour

½ cup whole-wheat flour

½ cup oat bran

½ cup chopped pecans

1 teaspoon baking soda

¼ teaspoon salt

¼ cup molasses

1 cup boiling water

1 cup fat-free vanilla yogurt

2 large eggs

1 tablespoon canola oil

1 cup fresh or frozen blueberries, rinsed and drained

Coat a large nonstick skillet with nonstick spray and set over medium heat.

In a small bowl, combine unbleached or all-purpose flour, whole-wheat flour, oat bran, pecans, baking soda, and salt.

In a large bowl, combine molasses and water. Stir in yogurt, eggs, and oil. Pour molasses mixture into flour mixture. Mix just until moistened. Gently stir in blueberries. Pour batter by ⅓ cupfuls into the skillet, making a few at a time. Cook 2 to 3 minutes, or until bubbly and edges look dry. Turn and cook 1 minute, or until underside is golden. Serve immediately.

Makes 12

Per pancake: *159 calories, 5 g protein, 22 g carbohydrates, 5 g fat, 36 mg cholesterol, 180 mg sodium, 1 g fiber*

Diet Exchanges: *0 milk, 0 vegetable, ½ fruit, 1 bread, 0 meat, 1 fat*

Jumbo Cinnamon-Raisin Muffins

313 Calories

—Marsha and Katy Fleer, Smithville, Tenn.

" These muffins are big on flavor but not on fat. To make smaller muffins, use a regular-size 12-cup muffin pan and reduce the cooking time to about 25 minutes. "

1½ **cups whole-wheat pastry flour or unbleached flour**

½ **cup unbleached flour**

½ **cup packed brown sugar**

2 **teaspoons baking powder**

1 **teaspoon ground cinnamon**

½ **teaspoon salt**

¼ **teaspoon baking soda**

½ **teaspoon ground nutmeg**

¾ **cup raisins**

2 **large egg whites**

1 **cup low-fat plain or vanilla yogurt**

1 **tablespoon maple syrup**

1 **teaspoon vanilla extract**

Preheat the oven to 350°F. Coat a 6-cup jumbo muffin pan with nonstick spray.

In a large bowl, combine flour, brown sugar, baking powder, cinnamon, salt, baking soda, and nutmeg. Stir in raisins.

In a small bowl, beat egg whites slightly. Add yogurt, maple syrup, and vanilla extract. Mix well. Stir egg white mixture into flour mixture just until flour is moistened. Spoon batter into the prepared pan until muffin cups are about two-thirds full.

Bake 35 minutes, or until a wooden pick inserted into the center of a muffin comes out clean. Remove muffins from the pan immediately. Cool on racks.

Makes 6

Per muffin: *313 calories, 10 g protein, 64 g carbohydrates, 3 g fat, 73 mg cholesterol, 420 mg sodium, 6 g fiber*

Diet Exchanges: *0 milk, 0 vegetable, 1 fruit, 3 bread, 0 meat, 0 fat*

Lemon Scones

170 Calories

—Joyce Dickerman, Covington, Wash.

"Most scones are loaded with fat, but not these, which means that I can still 'live it up' without putting into jeopardy the 35 pounds I've lost. To keep the fat and calories down, I serve these with all-fruit strawberry preserves instead of butter or margarine."

2 cups unbleached or all-purpose flour

1 tablespoon baking powder

1 teaspoon ground cardamom or coriander

½ teaspoon salt

3 tablespoons sugar

1 tablespoon canola oil

3 egg whites

½ cup (4 ounces) low-fat plain or lemon yogurt

1 tablespoon grated lemon peel

Preheat the oven to 400°F. Coat a baking sheet with nonstick spray.

In a large bowl, combine flour, baking powder, cardamom or coriander, salt, and 2 tablespoons sugar. Drizzle with oil and mix with a fork until evenly distributed.

Reserve 1 tablespoon egg whites.

Stir yogurt, lemon peel, and remaining egg whites into flour mixture. Stir gently with a fork until mixture holds together. Turn onto lightly floured surface. Knead about 8 strokes to mix dough thoroughly. Pat out dough to form 8" circle. With a sharp knife, cut evenly into 8 wedges. Arrange wedges, about 1" apart, on the prepared baking sheet. Brush with reserved egg whites. Sprinkle with remaining 1 tablespoon sugar. Bake 15 minutes, or until golden brown.

Makes 8

Per scone: *170 calories, 6 g protein, 31 g carbohydrates, 2 g fat, 1 mg cholesterol, 314 mg sodium, 0 g fiber*

Diet Exchanges: *0 milk, 0 vegetable, 0 fruit, 2 bread, 0 meat, 0 fat*

Hot Banana-Wheat Cereal

245 Calories

—Dawn Morrow, Elyria, Ohio

"This is a very satisfying breakfast that keeps me going all morning. I vary it by using apples, peaches, or berries in place of the bananas. Look for cracked wheat in the grain or international aisle of your supermarket."

1¼ cups water
½ cup cracked wheat
¼ teaspoon ground cinnamon
2 bananas, mashed
1 tablespoon packed brown sugar
2 tablespoons walnuts, chopped (optional)

In a medium saucepan, heat water to boiling. Stir in wheat and cinnamon. Reduce heat to low. Simmer, uncovered, 7 minutes, stirring occasionally. Stir in bananas. Cook 5 minutes, stirring occasionally. Add brown sugar and walnuts, if using. Cereal will thicken as it cools.

Makes 2 servings

Per serving: *245 calories, 6 g protein, 56 g carbohydrates, 1 g fat, 0 mg cholesterol, 8 mg sodium, 3 g fiber*

Diet Exchanges: *0 milk, 0 vegetable, 1½ fruit, 2 bread, 0 meat, 0 fat*

Deepak Chopra, M.D.

Fruits, vegetables, and grains are featured at the Chopra Center for Well-Being in La Jolla, California, headed by Deepak Chopra, M.D. This breakfast cereal gives guests a healthy start to their day. Tuck a few handfuls into a plastic bag for a snack, to stir into yogurt, or to sprinkle on fruit. Ghee is a type of clarified butter used in Indian cooking. You can also use butter.

CHOPRA GRANOLA

195 Calories

2 cups rolled oats
½ cup sliced almonds
½ cup flaked coconut
¼ cup sunflower seeds
¼ cup pine nuts
¼ cup flax seeds
¼ cup sesame seeds
2 tablespoons poppy seeds
1 tablespoon ground cinnamon
1 teaspoon ground nutmeg
1 teaspoon ground allspice
½ cup maple syrup
¼ cup ghee or melted butter
2 teaspoons vanilla extract
½ cup currants
¼ cup dried cranberries

Preheat the oven to 350°F.

In a large bowl, combine oats, almonds, coconut, sunflower seeds, pine nuts, flax seeds, sesame seeds, poppy seeds, cinnamon, nutmeg, and allspice.

In a medium bowl, combine maple syrup, ghee or butter, and vanilla extract. Drizzle over oat mixture and toss to coat. Spread on a baking sheet and bake 20 minutes, stirring occasionally. Add currants and cranberries. Bake 15 to 20 minutes, being careful granola does not burn. Cool completely. Store in an airtight container for up to 2 months.

Makes 16 servings

Per serving: *195 calories, 4 g protein, 24 g carbohydrates, 10 g fat, 5 mg cholesterol, 13 mg sodium, 3 g fiber*

Diet Exchanges: *0 milk, 0 vegetable, 1 fruit, 0 bread, 0 meat, 2 fat*

Blueberry Brunch Cake

280 Calories

—Janice Mester, Nashville, Tenn.

"My interest in healthy cooking goes back many years. I have raised two children who have achieved highly in college, and I attribute much of their success to a good foundation of nutritious food."

CAKE

1½ cups unbleached or all-purpose flour

1 teaspoon baking soda

¼ teaspoon salt

½ cup sugar

1 large egg

1 cup (8 ounces) fat-free plain yogurt

2 tablespoons vegetable oil

1 teaspoon vanilla extract

1 cup fresh or frozen blueberries, rinsed and drained

TOPPING

½ cup unbleached or all-purpose flour

¼ cup sugar

2 tablespoons butter or margarine, softened

1 teaspoon ground cinnamon

To make the cake:

Preheat the oven to 350°F. Coat an 8" × 8" baking dish with nonstick spray.

In a large bowl, combine flour, baking soda, salt, and sugar.

In a medium bowl, combine egg, yogurt, oil, and vanilla extract. Stir egg mixture into flour mixture, just until moist. Stir in blueberries. Spoon batter into the prepared baking dish.

To make the topping:

In a small bowl, using a fork, combine flour, sugar, butter or margarine, and cinnamon until mixture resembles coarse crumbs. Sprinkle over cake. Bake 40 to 45 minutes, or until a wooden pick inserted into the center comes out clean.

Makes 8 servings

Per serving: *280 calories, 6 g protein, 49 g carbohydrates, 7 g fat, 8 mg cholesterol, 181 mg sodium, 0 g fiber*

Diet Exchanges: *0 milk, 0 vegetable, 1 fruit, 2 bread, 0 meat, 1 fat*

Chocolate Chip Coffee Cake

207 Calories

—Sandy Jee, New York City

"I can assemble this heavenly treat in less than 10 minutes. Then, it just cooks in the oven. Leftovers freeze well for up to 2 months."

1 cup unbleached or all-purpose flour

½ cup quick-cooking oats

½ cup wheat germ

2 teaspoons baking powder

½ teaspoon baking soda

1 teaspoon instant coffee granules or vanilla extract

⅛ teaspoon ground cinnamon

⅛ teaspoon ground nutmeg

1 cup (8 ounces) low-fat coffee or vanilla yogurt

½ cup sugar

½ cup packed brown sugar

1 egg

1 egg white

1 tablespoon fat-free milk

1 tablespoon vanilla extract

½ cup mini semi-sweet chocolate morsels

Preheat the oven to 350°F. Coat a 6-cup Bundt pan or 10" pie pan with nonstick spray.

In a large bowl, combine flour, oats, wheat germ, baking powder, baking soda, coffee or vanilla extract, cinnamon, and nutmeg.

In a medium bowl, combine yogurt, sugar, brown sugar, egg, egg white, milk, and vanilla extract. Stir yogurt mixture into flour mixture. Mix well. Stir in chocolate morsels. Spoon batter evenly into the prepared pan.

Bake 45 minutes, or until a wooden pick inserted into the center comes out clean.

Makes 12 servings

Per serving: *207 calories, 5 g protein, 39 g carbohydrates, 4 g fat, 19 mg cholesterol, 146 mg sodium, 1 g fiber*

Diet Exchanges: *0 milk, 0 vegetable, 0 fruit, 2 bread, 0 meat, 1 fat*

TIP: To make a chocolate glaze, mix together 1 cup confectioners' sugar, 2 tablespoons unsweetened cocoa powder, 1 teaspoon instant espresso coffee powder (optional), 1 teaspoon vanilla extract, and 1½ tablespoons hot water.

Orange-Raisin Tea Bread

92 Calories

—Charles M. Paugh, Valparaiso, Ind.

"I make this quick bread using dairy-free ingredients and a sugar alternative called Sucanat, which is available in health food stores. But you don't have to. Dairy and sugar amounts are also given. The calories for sugar and Sucanat are roughly the same."

CAKE

- 2 teaspoons baking powder
- ½ teaspoon salt
- 1 cup unbleached or all-purpose flour
- ¼ cup nondairy margarine or butter, softened
- ⅓ cup Sucanat or sugar
- ⅓ cup orange juice
- ¼ cup cashew milk (see tip) or fat-free milk
- 2 teaspoons grated orange peel
- ½ cup raisins

TOPPING

- 3 tablespoons Sucanat or sugar
- 2 tablespoons unbleached or all-purpose flour
- 1 tablespoon nondairy margarine or butter, softened

To make the cake:

Preheat the oven to 350°F. Coat a 9" × 5" loaf pan with nonstick spray.

In a large bowl, combine baking powder, salt, and flour. Set aside.

In a medium bowl, beat together margarine or butter and Sucanat or sugar. Add orange juice, milk, and orange peel. Beat well. Stir in raisins. Stir into flour mixture, just until moistened. Spoon batter into the prepared loaf pan.

To make the topping:

In a small bowl, using a fork, combine Sucanat or sugar, flour, and margarine or butter until mixture resembles coarse crumbs. Sprinkle evenly over batter in loaf pan. Bake 25 minutes, or until a wooden pick inserted into the center comes out clean. Remove from the pan and cool on a wire rack.

Makes 1 loaf (18 slices)

Per slice: *92 calories, 1 g protein, 14 g carbohydrates, 3 g fat, 0 mg cholesterol, 161 mg sodium, 0 g fiber*

Diet Exchanges: *0 milk, 0 vegetable, 0 fruit, ½ bread, 0 meat, ½ fat*

TIP: To make cashew milk, combine ½ cup cashews and ½ cup water in a blender. Blend until smooth. Add 1½ cups more water, ¾ teaspoon sugar or Sucanat, and ⅛ teaspoon salt. Blend 30 seconds. Makes about 2 cups. Keeps in refrigerator for 2 weeks.

Lickety-Split Lunches

Roasted Vegetable Wraps 80

Green Salad Roll-Up 82

Vegetable Quesadillas 84

Tofu Burgers 86

Baked Black Beans with Orzo 87

Quick Chicken Pasta Salad 90

Feta Farfalle Salad 91

Debra's Vegetable-Shrimp Stir-Fry 93

Broccoli Soup 94

Creamy Carrot-Potato Soup 96

Garden Vegetable Soup 97

Salmon Chowder 98

Canyon Ranch Burgers 100

Sweet Potato and Leek Soup 101

Roasted Vegetable Wraps

267 Calories

—Janie Clark, Eureka Springs, Ark.

"These were just what the doctor ordered when I was pregnant and wanted something healthy, not fattening. The wraps are full of flavor and much needed calcium."

4 large portobello mushrooms, sliced ¼" thick

2 red bell peppers, cut into ¼" strips

2 small zucchini, sliced ¼" thick

2 small yellow squash, sliced ¼" thick

2 carrots, sliced ¼" thick

2 tablespoons olive oil

2 tablespoons balsamic vinegar

½ teaspoon salt

½ cup dry-pack sun-dried tomatoes

1 cup (8 ounces) fat-free plain yogurt

⅓ cup reduced-fat ricotta cheese

2 garlic cloves, minced

1 teaspoon ground black pepper

6 flour tortillas (8" diameter)

¼ cup chopped fresh basil

Preheat the oven to 400°F.

In a large roasting pan, combine mushrooms, bell peppers, zucchini, yellow squash, carrots, oil, vinegar, and salt. Toss to coat. Bake, stirring occasionally, 20 to 30 minutes, or until vegetables are tender and browned.

Meanwhile, soak tomatoes in hot water 10 minutes, or until soft. Drain and finely chop.

In a medium bowl, combine tomatoes, yogurt, ricotta, garlic, and black pepper.

Warm tortillas in a microwave oven 15 to 20 seconds. Spread one-sixth of yogurt mixture onto a flour tortilla. Spoon one-sixth of vegetable mixture along the center of tortilla. Sprinkle vegetables with some basil. Fold like an envelope to form a closed package. Cut in half on the diagonal. Repeat with remaining ingredients.

Makes 6

Per wrap: *267 calories, 11 g protein, 39 g carbohydrates, 8 g fat, 2 mg cholesterol, 511 mg sodium, 4 g fiber*

Diet Exchanges: *0 milk, 3 vegetable, 0 fruit, 2 bread, 0 meat, 1 fat*

Green Salad Roll-Up

202 Calories

—Marjorie Mitchell, Brighton, Colo.

"I call this 'salad on the run.' No plate, no fork, no added fat. (If you like creamy salad dressing, use fat-free ranch instead of Italian.)"

1 **cup torn romaine leaves or other lettuce**

¼ **cup alfalfa or mung bean sprouts**

2 **radishes, sliced**

¼ **cup canned chickpeas, rinsed and drained**

2 **tablespoons grated carrots**

1 **tablespoon fat-free Italian dressing**

1 **teaspoon red wine vinegar**

1 **large flour or vegetable-flavored tortilla (12" diameter)**

In a medium bowl, combine lettuce, sprouts, radishes, chickpeas, and carrots.

In a small bowl, combine dressing and vinegar. Pour over salad and toss to coat. Spoon greens onto one side of tortilla. Roll like a cone.

Makes 1

Per roll-up: *202 calories, 7 g protein, 35 g carbohydrates, 4 g fat, 0 mg cholesterol, 648 mg sodium, 5 g fiber*

Diet Exchanges: *0 milk, 2 vegetable, 0 fruit, 2 bread, 0 meat, 0 fat*

Vegetable Quesadillas

282 Calories

—Madelynne Brown, Salt Lake City, Utah

*"I like to cut these into wedges for dipping into salsa.
For extra zip, use seasoned refried beans."*

1 small onion, chopped

1 small zucchini, thinly sliced

1 small yellow squash, thinly sliced

1 garlic clove, minced

1 can (11 ounces) fat-free refried beans

8 whole-wheat tortillas (8" diameter)

½ cup (2 ounces) shredded reduced-fat
Cheddar cheese

1 cup no-salt-added salsa

Coat a large skillet with nonstick spray. Warm over medium-high heat. Add onion, zucchini, yellow squash, and garlic. Cook, stirring occasionally, 7 minutes, or until vegetables are tender.

Spread beans evenly onto each tortilla. Spoon vegetables evenly onto 4 of the bean-covered tortillas. Sprinkle cheese over vegetables. Top with remaining bean-covered tortillas.

Place a quesadilla in the skillet. Cover and cook over low heat 5 minutes, turning once, or until heated through. Repeat with remaining quesadillas. Cut into wedges. Serve with salsa.

Makes 4

Per quesadilla: *282 calories, 14 g protein, 48 g carbohydrates, 3 g fat, 10 mg cholesterol, 839 mg sodium, 21 g fiber*

Diet Exchanges: *0 milk, 1 vegetable, 0 fruit, 3 bread, 0 meat, 0 fat*

Splurge Meal

1 serving Vegetable Quesadillas

2 tablespoons salsa

¼ avocado with orange slices and balsamic vinaigrette

612 calories

FROM THE PROS

Deepak Chopra, M.D.

Deepak Chopra, M.D., integrates the best of Western medicine and natural healing traditions at the Chopra Center for Well Being in La Jolla, California. There, executive chef Leanne Backer features freshly prepared natural foods made with whole grains, herbs, vegetables, and fruits. At the Chopra Center, ghee, which is similar to clarified butter, is the preferred cooking fat. You have to make it at home, but you can use melted butter instead. Tamari is a flavorful type of soy sauce. Serve these burgers with your favorite toppings.

TOFU BURGERS

343 Calories

1 tablespoon ghee or melted butter

1 onion, chopped

1 pound firm tofu, drained and crumbled

1 carrot, grated

1 zucchini, grated

¼ cup pine nuts, sunflower seeds, or chopped walnuts

1 tablespoon tamari or soy sauce

1 teaspoon chopped fresh basil or ½ teaspoon dried

1 teaspoon chopped fresh oregano or ½ teaspoon dried

1 teaspoon chopped fresh thyme or ½ teaspoon dried

1 teaspoon chopped fresh tarragon or ½ teaspoon dried

½ teaspoon ground black pepper

1 small garlic clove, minced

½ cup dry bread crumbs

4 hamburger buns

Preheat the oven to 350°F. Warm ½ teaspoon ghee or butter in a large skillet over medium heat. Add onion and cook 5 minutes, or until tender. Place in a large bowl. Add tofu, carrot, zucchini, nuts or seeds, tamari or soy sauce, basil, oregano, thyme, tarragon, pepper, and garlic. Mix well. Shape into 4 patties. Coat each with bread crumbs.

Heat remaining 2½ teaspoons ghee or butter in the skillet. Add patties and cook 8 minutes, or until golden, turning once. Place on a baking sheet and bake 10 minutes. Serve on buns.

Makes 4

Per burger: *343 calories, 17 g protein, 43 g carbohydrates, 13 g fat, 5 mg cholesterol, 658 mg sodium, 1 g fiber*

Diet Exchanges: *0 milk, 0 vegetable, 0 fruit, 2 bread, 2 meat, 1 fat*

Baked Black Beans with Orzo

332 Calories

—Jenna Finley, Stevens Point, Wis.

*"This hot lunch is ready quick. It doubles as a Super Bowl dip with chips.
If you have time, substitute cooked brown rice for the orzo.
(Orzo is ready in 8 minutes; brown rice takes 45.)"*

1 cup orzo

1 can (16 ounces) black beans, rinsed and drained

1 can (16 ounces) low-sodium tomatoes, drained and finely chopped

1 can (4 ounces) chopped green chile peppers, drained

1 garlic clove, minced

½ teaspoon ground cumin

½ teaspoon ground black pepper

1 cup (4 ounces) shredded reduced-fat Cheddar cheese

¼ cup (2 ounces) fat-free sour cream

¼ cup low-sodium salsa

1 scallion, chopped

Preheat the oven to 325°F. Coat a 1½-quart baking dish with nonstick spray.

Cook orzo according to package directions; drain. In the same pan, combine orzo with beans, tomatoes, chile peppers, garlic, cumin, and black pepper. Spoon into the prepared baking dish. Top with cheese.

Bake 15 minutes, or until bubbly and cheese is melted. Serve with sour cream, salsa, and scallion.

Makes 4 servings

Per serving: *332 calories, 19 g protein, 48 g carbohydrates, 7 g fat, 20 mg cholesterol, 718 mg sodium, 5 g fiber*

Diet Exchanges: *0 milk, 1 vegetable, 0 fruit, 2 bread, 1 meat, 1 fat*

Slimming Meal

1 serving Baked Black Beans with Orzo

1 cup steamed kale with ½ teaspoon olive oil

1 serving Corn Crepes with Strawberry Sauce (page 301)

485 calories

LUNCHING LIGHT

Portion control is tough when you're eating out and trying to lose weight. Most restaurants think that "value" to the customer means offering big portions at low prices. We're used to buying soda in 16-ounce "small" cups, 12-ounce cans, and 20-ounce plastic bottles. No wonder the recommended 8-ounce serving of soft drinks looks skimpy in a glass at home. And consider a trip to the movie theater. The amount of popcorn that the cineplex calls "small" is actually four or five servings, according to the U.S. Department of Agriculture.

Add to these oversized servings the fact that piling on fat is the easiest way to pack in flavor, and you can see why Americans are getting fatter. Fat is an inexpensive ingredient, and deep-fat frying is a no-brainer cooking technique. That's one of the reasons why fast foods are often fried and the cuisine offered at top-notch restaurants is not.

Keeping portions controlled and fat content to a minimum is especially difficult to avoid when lunching out. Unless you're treating yourself to a splurge meal, check out the best choices that follow.

In General

Most restaurants don't include nutritional analyses on their menus. But they do include words that can tip you off to the nutritional content of the food you're ordering. Here's what to look for.

Best choices: *Broiled, grilled* (on an open grill, not a griddle), *braised, baked, poached, roasted, pan-seared,* and *steamed* or *Regular, Appetizer, Child Size, Kiddie Size, Luncheon, Petite,* and *Salad Size.*

Think twice about: *Alfredo, basted, batter-dipped, breaded, buttery, creamy, crisp* (except for raw produce), *crunchy* (except for raw produce), *deep-fried, pan-fried, rich,* and *sautéed* or *Combo, Feast, Grande, Jumbo, King Size,* and *Supreme.*

Deli and Sandwich Shops

Outrageous portion sizes will be the biggest problem here. The good news? Sandwiches are generally made to order, so order exactly what you want. Or go to lunch with a friend and split a sandwich. You could even get an extra roll, make two sandwiches from one, and take the second home for dinner.

Best choices: Small bagels, baked or boiled ham, beet salad, breads made with whole grains, carrot and raisin salad, extra veggies on sandwiches, mustard instead of mayonnaise, pickles, roasted or smoked turkey, salami, sliced chicken (not chicken salad), plain tuna

Think twice about: Bologna, corned beef, eggplant or chicken parmigiana, extra cheese, pastrami, knockwurst, liverwurst, meatballs, Reuben sandwich, any sandwich buttered and cooked on a griddle

At the Mall

There is very little variation from one mall to another across the country. Once you've figured out the best food choices, you can avoid traps and surprises at any food court.

Best choices: Baked potatoes, grilled chicken, fat-free or low-fat milk, fat-free salad dressing, salad with dressing on the side, single burgers (regular or kid size), small fries

Think twice about: Cheese sauce, chicken nuggets (often made with fatty skin), croissants, fish sandwich (usually fried), fried chicken, large and jumbo sizes, onion rings, salad dressing (unless it's fat-free), chili sauce, tartar sauce

Italian Restaurants

Watch out for extras on the table—especially bread dipped in oil (each dunk adds about 40 calories). Salads with just a bit of dressing are a good way to take the edge off your appetite.

Best choices: Marinara sauce, strand pasta or shaped pasta, pasta stuffed with vegetables, white or red clam sauce, wine sauces, piccata

Think twice about: Alfredo, alla panna, carbonara, cheese-stuffed pasta, fried eggplant, fried zucchini, frito misto, parmigiana

Mexican Restaurants

Get friendly with salsa. Eat as much as you like. Fried tortillas, however, are another story. Instead, ask the server for healthy dippers such as *fresh* tortilla strips or a plate of cut-up fresh vegetables. Also go easy on other deep-fried foods. Bean dishes make a good choice if they're not slathered in cheese, sour cream, and guacamole. Even so, you can eat your way around the excess fatty toppings.

Best choices: Black bean soup, seviche (fresh raw fish marinated in citrus), chili, enchiladas, burritos, soft tacos, fajitas, gazpacho

Think twice about: Chimichangas, extra cheese, refried beans, sour cream, fried tortillas

Pizza Joints

Newfangled pizza restaurants are a real treat for waist watchers. Instead of the same old pepperoni and sausage toppings, lower-fat options are cropping up everywhere, like shrimp, grilled chicken, and tuna. The wealth of vegetables that you can add would put any salad bar to shame. Look for interesting cheeses, too. Why settle for mild, boring mozzarella when you can choose high-flavor feta, goat, and blue cheeses?

Best choices: Canadian bacon, grilled chicken, reduced-fat and strongly flavored cheeses, shrimp, tuna, vegetables

Think twice about: Bacon, extra cheese, extra olive oil, meatballs, pepperoni, sausage

Quick Chicken Pasta Salad

402 Calories

—Tammy Krick, Greenville, N.C.

"Remember this recipe when time is short and the cupboards are almost bare. I serve it on lettuce leaves with some crunchy bread and call it lunch."

4 ounces bow-tie pasta

½ pound cooked cut-up chicken breast or 1 can (7 ounces) white chunk chicken, drained

1 cup canned white beans, rinsed and drained

½ cup fat-free Italian dressing

3 Italian tomatoes, chopped

2 tablespoons chopped fresh basil or parsley

Cook pasta according to package directions. Drain and place in a large bowl. While noodles are warm, stir in chicken, beans, Italian dressing, tomatoes, and basil or parsley. Chill until ready to serve.

Makes 4 servings

Per serving: *402 calories, 29 g protein, 54 g carbohydrates, 8 g fat, 116 mg cholesterol, 707 mg sodium, 5 g fiber*

Diet Exchanges: *0 milk, 0 vegetable, 0 fruit, 3 bread, 2 meat, 0 fat*

Splurge Meal

1 serving Quick Chicken Pasta Salad

2 slices whole-wheat bread dipped in 1 teaspoon olive oil

1 baked apple dusted with ground cinnamon

717 calories

Feta Farfalle Salad

290 Calories

—Donna Logue, Havertown, Pa.

" Kidney beans turn this pasta salad into a protein-rich dish. I especially enjoy it in the summer, but it's good any time of year. "

6 ounces bow-tie pasta

1 can (16 ounces) red kidney beans, rinsed and drained

2 small bunches scallions, chopped

2 garlic cloves, minced

¼ cup (1¼ ounces) crumbled feta cheese

¼ cup dry-cured olives, pitted

3 tablespoons olive oil

2 tablespoons lemon juice

2 tablespoons chopped fresh basil or parsley

½ teaspoon salt

¼ teaspoon ground black pepper

Cook pasta according to package directions. Drain and place in a large bowl. Add beans, scallions, garlic, cheese, and olives.

In a small bowl, mix oil, lemon juice, basil or parsley, salt, and pepper. Pour over pasta and toss. Serve at room temperature or refrigerate and serve cold.

Makes 8 servings

Per serving: *290 calories, 10 g protein, 39 g carbohydrates, 10 g fat, 56 mg cholesterol, 465 mg sodium, 4 g fiber*

Diet Exchanges: *0 milk, 0 vegetable, 0 fruit, 3 bread, 0 meat, 1 fat*

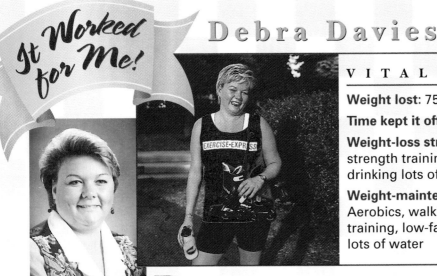

It Worked for Me!

Debra Davies

VITAL STATS

Weight lost: 75 pounds

Time kept it off: 2 years

Weight-loss strategies: Walking, strength training, low-fat diet, drinking lots of water

Weight-maintenance strategies: Aerobics, walking, strength training, low-fat diet, drinking lots of water

Dropping lots of weight made big changes in Debra Davies's body, but her spirit improved, too. And that's what keeps her motivated.

"I was one of those lucky people who never worried about my weight. That is, until my first child was born. That's when I started gaining. I struggled for 15 years with diet after diet. You name it, I tried it. But the scale continued to creep up. Exercise was never a part of my diets, which I now know is why they didn't work.

"One night, something clicked. I was in the bowling alley and looked in a mirror and didn't recognize myself because I had gotten so big. At that moment, I wanted to look better and feel better. I was determined to stick with it.

"On the first day of my new diet, I walked 2 miles. And I kept it up. I walked rain or shine, sleet or snow. The daily commitment kept me motivated. In a year, I was walking 2 miles and jogging 2 miles.

"I also decided to make some changes to what I was eating. I immediately cut out fried foods. Instead, I ate lots of fish, rice, and pasta. My cooking methods changed, too. Now, I bake, broil, or steam. Trading my sodas for water helped a lot. And veggies and fruits replaced sweets and chips.

"My biggest challenges were parties and weddings. I have to stay away from the dips. In the old days, I could empty a bowl by myself. It's not all nose to the grindstone, though. I do indulge occasionally. But the next day, I'm back on track or I exercise a little more.

"These days, I go to the gym 3 days a week. I love step aerobic classes and weight training. I also belong to a walking club. I feel better than I have in years. I feel better from the inside. I have a healthier attitude about myself and spend a lot of time around healthy people. Most healthy people are happy and positive. That keeps me motivated." ■

Debra's Vegetable-Shrimp Stir-Fry

229 Calories

"To keep my weight down, I stay away from fatty meats and dairy products. Seafood is one of my main protein sources."

⅓ cup water
2 tablespoons soy sauce
2 tablespoons cornstarch
1 teaspoon sugar
2 tablespoons vegetable oil
½ small head green cabbage, shredded
1 red bell pepper, cut into 2" pieces
4 green onions, cut into 1" pieces
½ pound asparagus, cut into 2" pieces
2 garlic cloves, minced
1 pound peeled and deveined shrimp
2 tablespoons minced fresh ginger
½ teaspoon crushed red pepper
2 tablespoons dry sherry (optional)

In a small bowl, combine water, soy sauce, cornstarch, and sugar.

Warm 1 tablespoon oil in a large nonstick skillet or wok over medium heat. Add cabbage, bell pepper, onions, asparagus, and garlic. Cook, stirring frequently, 3 minutes, or until vegetables are crisp-tender. Stir in 1 tablespoon of soy-sauce mixture. Cook until mixture is thickened and coats vegetables. Spoon vegetables onto a platter and keep warm.

Warm remaining 1 tablespoon oil in the same skillet. Add shrimp, ginger, and red pepper. Cook, stirring frequently, 5 minutes, or until shrimp are just opaque. Stir in sherry, if using, and remaining soy-sauce mixture. Cook until mixture is thickened and coats shrimp. Spoon shrimp over vegetables.

Makes 4 servings

Per serving: *229 calories, 22 g protein, 16 g carbohydrates, 8 g fat, 175 mg cholesterol, 739 mg sodium, 2 g fiber*

Diet Exchanges: *0 milk, 3 vegetable, 0 fruit, ½ bread, 1½ meat, 0 fat*

Slimming Meal

1 serving Debra's Vegetable-Shrimp Stir-Fry
½ cup brown rice
1 serving The Duchess's Chocolate Mousse Tartlets (page 289)

435 calories

Broccoli Soup

117 Calories

—Sheri Ghaby, Redondo Beach, Calif.

" This is my favorite way to cook broccoli. For Broccoli-Cheddar Soup, add ½ cup shredded reduced-fat extra-sharp Cheddar cheese along with the evaporated milk. "

1 tablespoon butter or margarine

1 onion, chopped

1 small bunch broccoli, coarsely chopped

1 can (14½ ounces) chicken or vegetable broth

1 bay leaf

¼ cup 1% milk

1 tablespoon unbleached or all-purpose flour

¾ cup fat-free evaporated milk

⅛ teaspoon ground nutmeg

¼ cup grated Parmesan cheese (optional)

Warm butter or margarine in a large saucepan over medium heat. Add onion and cook 5 minutes, or until tender. Set aside 6 to 8 broccoli florets. Add broth, bay leaf, and remaining broccoli to the saucepan. Heat to boiling. Cover, reduce heat to low, and simmer 10 minutes.

Remove from heat. Cool slightly and remove and discard bay leaf. Puree soup in a blender or food processor. Return to the pan.

In a small bowl, combine 1% milk and flour. Stir into soup along with evaporated milk and nutmeg. Cook over medium heat, stirring, until soup simmers and thickens. Add reserved broccoli florets. Cook 2 minutes. Serve sprinkled with cheese, if using.

Makes 4 servings

Per serving: *117 calories, 7 g protein, 14 g carbohydrates, 4 g fat, 10 mg cholesterol, 534 mg sodium, 2 g fiber*

Diet Exchanges: *½ milk, 1 vegetable, 0 fruit, 0 bread, 0 meat, ½ fat*

Slimming Meal

1 serving Broccoli Soup

3 stone-ground wheat crackers

½ cup fat-free fruit yogurt

1 pear

346 calories

(Multigrain Bread recipe on page 245)

Creamy Carrot-Potato Soup

186 Calories

—Debbie Liban, Greendale, Wis.

"Pair this soup with a sandwich for large appetites. Or enjoy it alone with bread. Sometimes I add celery for more veggie power. The carrots make this soup rich in beta-carotene."

1 tablespoon olive oil
½ onion, chopped
1 teaspoon chili powder
2 carrots, sliced
2 potatoes, peeled and chopped small
1 can (14½ ounces) reduced-sodium chicken broth
1½ cups fat-free milk
1 teaspoon soy sauce
2 tablespoons sesame seeds

Warm oil in a large saucepan over medium heat. Add onion and chili powder. Cook 5 minutes, or until onion is tender. Add carrots, potatoes, and broth. Heat to boiling. Reduce heat to low, cover, and simmer 10 minutes, or until vegetables are tender.

Remove from heat and cool slightly. Puree soup in a blender or food processor. Return to the pan. Stir in milk and soy sauce. Cook over medium heat just until the soup is heated through. Do not boil. Serve sprinkled with sesame seeds.

Makes 4 servings

Per serving: *186 calories, 7 g protein, 26 g carbohydrates, 7 g fat, 3 mg cholesterol, 205 mg sodium, 3 g fiber*

Diet Exchanges: *½ milk, 1 vegetable, 0 fruit, 1 bread, 0 meat, 1 fat*

Slimming Meal

1 serving Creamy Carrot-Potato Soup
1 cup mixed salad greens with low-calorie dressing
1 whole-wheat roll
¼ cantaloupe

347 calories

Garden Vegetable Soup

345 Calories

—Mark Ballard, Macon, Ga.

"This veggie soup is chock-full of goodies, and the servings are generous. Tamari, a type of rich-tasting soy sauce, gives it a shot of big flavor. Beets add a pleasant rosy color."

2 tablespoons vegetable oil

1 large onion, chopped

3 cans (14½ ounces each) reduced-sodium chicken broth

2 carrots, sliced

2 celery ribs, finely chopped

2 potatoes, cut into 1" cubes

2 beets, peeled and cut into 1" cubes

1 cup green beans, cut into 1" pieces

¼ head green cabbage, shredded

2 garlic cloves, minced

1 bay leaf

1 tablespoon tamari or soy sauce

1 cup fresh or frozen green peas

Warm oil in a large soup pot over medium heat. Add onion and cook 5 minutes, or until tender. Add broth, carrots, celery, potatoes, beets, beans, cabbage, garlic, bay leaf, and tamari or soy sauce. Heat to boiling. Reduce heat to low and simmer 15 minutes. Stir in peas and cook 10 minutes. Remove and discard bay leaf before serving.

Makes 4 servings

Per serving: *345 calories, 11 g protein, 55 g carbohydrates, 11 g fat, 0 mg cholesterol, 417 mg sodium, 12 g fiber*

Diet Exchanges: *0 milk, 4 vegetable, 0 fruit, 2 bread, 0 meat, 2 fat*

Salmon Chowder

256 Calories

—The Rev. Aaron S. Peters, Paola, Kans.

"Yogurt and buttermilk add creaminess to this chunky chowder. The salmon makes it flavorful and gives it an attractive color."

1 large potato, peeled and cut into small cubes

1 turnip, peeled and cut into small cubes

1 small onion, chopped

1 celery rib, chopped

1 teaspoon dill seed

1 bay leaf

2 cups water

1 can (12 ounces) pink salmon, drained

1 cup 1% buttermilk

1 cup (8 ounces) low-fat plain yogurt

1 tablespoon butter or margarine

2 teaspoons hot-pepper sauce

¼ teaspoon salt

½ teaspoon ground black pepper

¼ teaspoon dried tarragon

In a large saucepan, combine potato, turnip, onion, celery, dill seed, bay leaf, and water. Heat to boiling over high heat. Reduce heat to medium. Simmer, uncovered, 12 minutes, or until vegetables are tender.

Reduce heat to low. Stir in salmon, buttermilk, yogurt, butter or margarine, hot-pepper sauce, salt, black pepper, and tarragon. Cook 5 minutes, or just until heated through. Remove and discard bay leaf before serving.

Makes 4 servings

Per serving: *256 calories, 24 g protein, 21 g carbohydrates, 9 g fat, 57 mg cholesterol, 861 mg sodium, 3 g fiber*

Diet Exchanges: *0 milk, 1 vegetable, 0 fruit, 1 bread, 2 meat, 0 fat*

FROM THE PROS

Canyon Ranch Health Resorts

You probably don't need a recipe to learn how to grill burgers. But at Canyon Ranch Health Resorts, located in Tuscon and in Lenox, Massachusetts, this recipe demonstrates that calorie-wise portion control goes hand in hand with great taste.

CANYON RANCH BURGERS

288 Calories

1 pound extra-lean ground beef
8 small whole-wheat hamburger buns
⅓ cup low-fat Thousand Island dressing
8 tomato slices
8 onion slices
8 lettuce leaves

Coat a grill rack or broiler pan with non-stick spray. Preheat the grill or broiler. Form the meat into 8 patties and place on the prepared rack or pan. Grill over coals or broil until a thermometer inserted in center registers 160°F and meat is no longer pink.

Spread each bun with 2 teaspoons dressing. Place 1 patty on each bun and garnish with tomato, onion, and lettuce.

Makes 8

Per burger: *288 calories, 17 g protein, 34 g carbohydrates, 11 g fat, 36 mg cholesterol, 558 mg sodium, 1 g fiber*

Diet Exchanges: *0 milk, 0 vegetable, 0 fruit, 2 bread, 2 meat, 0 fat*

Sweet Potato and Leek Soup

170 Calories

—S. D. Freedman, Absecon, N.J.

"White potatoes are the classic choice for this soup, but I like the flavor and color of sweet potatoes."

3 leeks

2 tablespoons unsalted butter

1 tablespoon olive oil

1 large onion, chopped

1½ pounds sweet potatoes or yams, peeled and diced

3 cans (14¾ ounces) reduced-sodium chicken broth

¼ teaspoon ground red pepper

Cut off and discard dark green leaves and roots from leeks. Cut each lengthwise, up to the core. Rinse under running water, fanning leaves to remove any grit. Slice the leeks.

In a large soup pot, melt butter with oil over medium heat. Add onion and leeks. Cover and cook, stirring occasionally, 7 minutes, or until soft. Add sweet potatoes or yams and broth. Heat to boiling. Reduce heat to low, cover, and simmer, stirring occasionally, 20 to 25 minutes, or until potatoes are fork-tender. Cool slightly. Puree soup in a blender or food processor. Blend in pepper.

Makes 8 servings

Per serving: *170 calories, 3 g protein, 28 g carbohydrates, 6 g fat, 8 mg cholesterol, 26 mg sodium, 1 g fiber*

Diet Exchanges: *0 milk, 1 vegetable, 0 fruit, 1 bread, 0 meat, 1 fat*

Snacks, Nibbles, and Mini-Meals

Spicy Dipper Rolls 104

Spinach Squares .105

Portobellos and Goat Cheese 106

Pita Pizza 109

Tomato-Crab Bake 110

Dinah's Shredded Chicken Spread 113

Roasted Garlic Spread 114

Herbed Cheese Spread 115

Hot Black Bean Dip 116

Quick Black Bean and Artichoke Dip . . .118

Salsa Mexicana .119

Buttermilk Fruit Smoothie 120

Peanut Butter and Banana Shake 122

Purple Power Shake 123

Spicy Dipper Rolls

229 Calories

—Stacey Carpenter, Excelsior, Minn.

" I use this recipe whenever I need party food. It doubles easily to handle a crowd and it keeps in the refrigerator for up to a week. "

1 package (8 ounces) reduced-fat cream cheese, softened

1 cup (8 ounces) reduced-fat sour cream

6 scallions, minced

1 can (4 ounces) chopped green chile peppers, drained

6 flour tortillas (12" diameter)

1 jar (16 ounces) salsa

In a large bowl, combine cream cheese, sour cream, scallions, and peppers.

Spread one-sixth of mixture onto 1 side of a tortilla. Roll up tortilla, jelly-roll style. Wrap with plastic wrap. Repeat with remaining tortillas.

Refrigerate rolls overnight. To serve, remove plastic wrap. With a sharp knife, cut rolls into 1" slices on the diagonal. Serve with salsa.

Makes 6 servings (about 72 slices)

Per serving (about 12 slices): *229 calories, 11 g protein, 33 g carbohydrates, 5 g fat, 12 mg cholesterol, 943 mg sodium, 3 g fiber*

Diet Exchanges: *0 milk, 0 vegetable, 0 fruit, 2 bread, 0 meat, 1½ fat*

Spinach Squares

105 Calories

—Lisa Keys, Middlebury, Conn.

"With two children who love sports, getting enough exercise is no problem for me. But I still have to be extra careful about following a low-fat diet. These spinach squares are one of my favorite ways to do it. I sometimes serve this as a main dish for four."

1 tablespoon olive oil

1 onion, chopped

3 ounces chopped mushrooms

1 red bell pepper, chopped

4 cups chopped fresh spinach

4 ounces reduced-fat cream cheese

1 cup liquid egg substitute or 4 eggs

¼ cup seasoned dry bread crumbs

2 tablespoons sesame seeds

2 tablespoons grated Parmesan cheese

¼ teaspoon salt

Preheat the oven to 350°F. Coat a 9" × 9" baking dish with nonstick spray.

Warm oil in a large skillet over medium-high heat. Add onion, mushrooms, and pepper. Cook 5 minutes, or until pepper is tender. Add spinach and cook 1 to 2 minutes, or until wilted. Remove from heat. Cool slightly.

In a large bowl, beat cream cheese until smooth. Stir in egg substitute or eggs, bread crumbs, 1 tablespoon sesame seeds, 1 tablespoon Parmesan, and salt. Stir in spinach mixture. Spoon into the prepared baking dish. Sprinkle with remaining 1 tablespoon sesame seeds and 1 tablespoon Parmesan. Bake 30 minutes, or until edges are golden brown.

Makes 8 servings

Per serving: *105 calories, 9 g protein, 8 g carbohydrates, 5 g fat, 2 mg cholesterol, 369 mg sodium, 2 g fiber*

Diet Exchanges: *0 milk, 2 vegetable, 0 fruit, 0 bread, 1 meat, 0 fat*

Portobellos and Goat Cheese

175 Calories

—Janet Fry, West Jordan, Utah

" I'll dig into this mini-meal almost any time of day. For a summer lunch or supper, serve it with a fresh green salad and crusty bread. "

1 cup prepared marinara sauce

4 large portobello mushroom caps

1 package (4 ounces) mild goat cheese (chèvre or Montrachet), cut into 4 pieces

2 tablespoons finely chopped pitted black olives

1 tablespoon chopped parsley

Preheat the oven to 375°F.

Spread sauce in the bottom of a 9" × 9" baking dish. Arrange mushroom caps, gill side up, on top. Place a piece of goat cheese on each mushroom. Sprinkle evenly with olives. Bake 30 minutes, or until hot and bubbly.

Makes 4 servings

Per serving: *175 calories, 9 g protein, 10 g carbohydrates, 11 g fat, 22 mg cholesterol, 622 mg sodium, 2 g fiber*

Diet Exchanges: *0 milk, 3 vegetable, 0 fruit, 0 bread, 0 meat, 2 fat*

It Worked for Me!

Richard Simmons

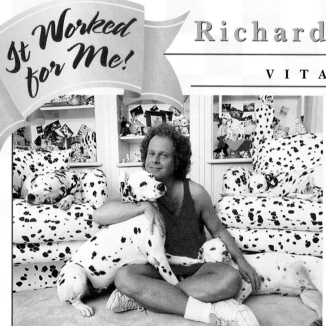

VITAL STATS

Weight lost: 137 pounds

Time kept it off: 25 years

Weight-loss strategies: Exercise, low-calorie diet

Weight-maintenance strategies: Has a 5-pound gain/loss window, low-calorie diet, daily exercise, finds comfort in things other than food, helps others lose weight

The Prince of Weight Loss is so successful at encouraging others to drop pounds because he constantly battles with his own weight.

"I've been on diets since I was 8," says Richard Simmons. He tried scores of movie-magazine reducing plans, counting and juggling calories, all the way to a liquid diet. He even admits that he had his own subscription to *Cosmopolitan* magazine because, at the time, they ran a different diet each month. By age 12, he went on a liquid diet and lost 75 pounds. It was a short-lived loss. By the time he was in high school, Richard had reached his highest weight: 268 pounds. Then he tried starvation, having nothing but water for 2½ months. It worked. Richard lost 127 pounds; but it landed him in the hospital.

"In 1974, when I opened my exercise studio in Beverly Hills, I made up my mind that I had to stay on a strict eating plan. I also realized that I have to exercise every day. I have to do it in the morning. Later in the day, I'll make excuses and put it off.

"I eat 1,600 to 1,800 calories a day and no more than 30 grams of fat. I divide those calories among three meals a day. I often make breakfast and lunch fat-free so that I can have the fat to play with for dinner.

"Now, it's a way of life for me," he says. His diet and exercise habits have become automatic. He has also gotten real about the weight that is right for him. "I've been obese. I've been bone thin. I've settled on a weight of about 150 pounds. I had to starve to stay at 138, but at 150, I feel just right." ∎

Pita Pizza

247 Calories

—Rachel Povse, Cary, N.C.

"This is an update of the English muffin mini-pizzas from the 1950s. Nothing is easier or tastier."

- 4 small whole-wheat or regular pitas
- ½ cup spaghetti or tomato sauce
- 2 cups sliced vegetables (mushrooms, green peppers, tomatoes, onions)
- ½ cup (4 ounces) shredded mozzarella cheese
- ½ teaspoon dried oregano
- 2 teaspoons extra-virgin olive oil

Preheat the oven to 450°F.

Split each pita into 2 thin rounds. Place, crust side down, on a large baking sheet. Bake 10 minutes, or just until crisp.

Remove from the oven and top each round evenly with sauce, vegetables, cheese, and oregano. Drizzle each with olive oil. Bake 5 to 8 minutes, or just until cheese melts.

Makes 4 servings

Per serving: *247 calories, 14 g protein, 43 g carbohydrates, 5 g fat, 0 mg cholesterol, 689 mg sodium, 7 g fiber*

Diet Exchanges: *0 milk, 2 vegetable, 0 fruit, 1½ bread, ½ meat, 1 fat*

Tomato-Crab Bake

212 Calories

—Majeda Casciano, Santa Anna, Calif.

"These crab cakes make an elegant lunch or appetizer. No one will guess that they're not high-fat. For brunch, top each with a poached egg."

½ cup dry bread crumbs

2 large tomatoes, cut into ½" slices

1 cup fresh lump crabmeat, well-drained

1 cup (4 ounces) shredded low-fat mozzarella cheese

½ cup finely chopped black olives

½ cup (1¼ ounces) finely chopped mushrooms

½ cup finely chopped parsley

1 garlic clove, minced

½ teaspoon dried oregano

½ teaspoon dried basil

Preheat the oven to 350°F. Coat a baking sheet with nonstick spray.

Place bread crumbs on a plate. Coat both sides of tomato slices with nonstick spray. Dip tomato slices in bread crumbs to coat well. Place tomato slices on the prepared baking sheet.

In a large bowl, combine crabmeat, cheese, olives, mushrooms, parsley, garlic, oregano, and basil. Spoon crab mixture evenly onto tomato slices.

Bake 15 minutes, or until hot.

Makes 4 servings

Per serving: *212 calories, 16 g protein, 16 g carbohydrates, 9 g fat, 50 mg cholesterol, 607 mg sodium, 1 g fiber*

Diet Exchanges: *0 milk, 1 vegetable, 0 fruit, 0 bread, 2 meat, 1 fat*

It Worked for Me!

Dinah Burnette

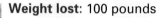

VITAL STATS

Weight lost: 100 pounds

Time kept it off: 2 years

Weight-loss strategies: Low-fat diet, drinks lots of water, walks and strength trains

Weight-maintenance strategies: Has a 5-pound gain/loss window, drinks lots of water, avoids elastic waistbands

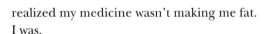

*D*inah Burnette dropped 100 pounds, got out of her size 24 clothing, and got into a size 10. She continues to take control of her life.

"I was one of those people everybody hates because I could eat anything. Fast foods and chocolate chip cookies were my staples. I never thought about my weight because it never changed.

"Then, my doctor prescribed medication for anxiety, which caused me to gain weight. I admit that I used my medication to some extent as an excuse to let myself get out of shape. My afternoon snacks were two peanut butter and jelly sandwiches with chocolate milk. And I never exercised.

"Of course, the weight crept up. I didn't realize how serious my problem had become until I saw a photo of myself: 245 pounds stuffed into a size 24 dress. It was then that I realized my medicine wasn't making me fat. I was.

"It was time to take control. When I finally admitted that I was responsible for my current weight, I also realized that I could change it, too. I drank a gallon of water every day. I also started walking—just a ½ mile at first. After 2 or 3 weeks, I was walking a mile. Then, I added a daily 20-minute jog in the backyard pool. I joined the YMCA and started lifting weights. I learned how breakfast kick-starts the metabolism, so I began each day with a slice of whole-grain bread, a box of raisins, and a glass of fat-free milk. I'd snack on fruit, low-fat yogurt, cereal, or raw veggies throughout the day.

"Within 6 months, I lost 50 pounds and was down to a size 16. Even my shoes and rings were too big. And my double chin was disappearing. I loved the way I felt. I rediscovered energy that I hadn't had in years. Exactly one year later, I hit my goal.

"Today, good nutrition and exercise are central to my life. Every day, I run or walk 3 miles and lift weights every other day. Great

nutrition isn't monotonous either, since I've learned to make my favorite recipes healthier.

"One trick I use to stay slim is that I refuse to wear any clothing with elastic waistbands. I'm also very careful about what I eat on weekdays, and I don't worry about the weekends. I don't want to ever be fat again. I want to stay healthy. I didn't like myself when I gained weight. I like myself so much more now." ■

Dinah's Shredded Chicken Spread

"This makes a great sandwich on pumpernickel bread. Or serve it on lettuce with your favorite raw vegetables and sliced fruit."

¾ **pound boneless, skinless chicken breast**

1 **package (8 ounces) fat-free or reduced-fat cream cheese, softened**

1 **small onion, minced**

1 **celery rib, minced**

1 **jar (2 ounces) chopped pimiento**

½ **teaspoon salt**

½ **teaspoon cracked black pepper**

Combine chicken and enough water to cover in a 4-quart saucepan over high heat. Heat to boiling. Reduce heat to low and cook 10 minutes, or until a thermometer inserted in the thickest breast registers 160°F and

juices run clear. Remove chicken to a plate to cool. With 2 forks, pull chicken into shreds.

In a large bowl, combine chicken, cream cheese, onion, celery, pimiento, salt, and pepper. Cover and refrigerate at least 2 hours to meld flavors.

Makes 4 servings

Per serving: *178 calories, 23 g protein, 16 g carbohydrates, 2 g fat, 34 mg cholesterol, 666 mg sodium, 3 g fiber*

Diet Exchanges: *0 milk, 0 vegetable, 0 fruit, 1 bread, 1½ meat, 0 fat*

Roasted Garlic Spread

79 Calories

—Barb Pomaville, Pincoming, Mich.

"Garlic changes completely when you roast it. It takes on a sweet, almost buttery flavor and becomes soft and spreadable. I like this spread on melba toast. It's also good as a dip with cut-up vegetables."

1 whole garlic bulb

1 package (8 ounces) reduced-fat cream cheese, softened

1/3 cup fat-free mayonnaise

Preheat the oven to 350°F.

Discard papery skin from garlic, but leave bulb intact. Sprinkle with a little water and wrap in foil. Place on a baking sheet and bake 45 minutes.

Squeeze each clove of garlic from its skin into a medium bowl. Discard skin. Add cream cheese and mayonnaise. Mix well.

Makes 1½ cups

Per 2 tablespoons: *79 calories, 3 g protein, 6 g carbohydrates, 5 g fat, 10 mg cholesterol, 286 mg sodium, 0 g fiber*

Diet Exchanges: *0 milk, 0 vegetable, 0 fruit, ½ bread, 0 meat, ½ fat*

Herbed Cheese Spread

32 Calories

—Marjorie Mitchell, Brighton, Colo.

"Why give up cheese? There's no need when you have this easy spread recipe on hand. Serve with soda crackers or Belgian endive. I usually make this a day ahead to let the flavors develop."

1 cup (8 ounces) fat-free sour cream

1 cup (4 ounces) shredded reduced-fat Cheddar cheese

1 scallion, minced

2 tablespoons chopped parsley

½ teaspoon dried thyme

½ teaspoon dried rosemary, crushed

½ teaspoon ground black pepper

In a medium bowl, combine sour cream, cheese, scallion, parsley, thyme, rosemary, and pepper. Cover and refrigerate up to 4 days.

Makes 2 cups

Per 2 tablespoons: *32 calories, 3 g protein, 2 g carbohydrates, 2 g fat, 5 mg cholesterol, 45 mg sodium, 0 g fiber*

Diet Exchanges: *0 milk, 0 vegetable, 0 fruit, 0 bread, ½ meat, 0 fat*

Hot Black Bean Dip

64 Calories

—Adriane Lockwood, Lawrenceville, Ga.

"Need something easy to please the kids? Or a quick party dip? This one's a hit every time. It's excellent with chips or fresh vegetables. It's best hot, but good cold, too."

1 can (16 ounces) fat-free refried black or pinto beans

1 cup (8 ounces) reduced-fat sour cream

1 cup salsa

½ teaspoon salt

1 teaspoon ground black pepper

½ cup (2 ounces) shredded reduced-fat Cheddar cheese (optional)

Preheat the oven to 325°F.

In a large bowl, combine beans, sour cream, salsa, salt, and pepper. Spoon into a 3- to 4-cup shallow baking dish. Top with cheese, if using. Bake 10 to 15 minutes, or until heated through.

Makes 3 cups

Per ¼ cup: *64 calories, 3 g protein, 10 g carbohydrates, 1 g fat, 6 mg cholesterol, 403 mg sodium, 3 g fiber*

Diet Exchanges: *0 milk, 0 vegetable, 0 fruit, 1 bread, ½ meat, 0 fat*

Quick Black Bean and Artichoke Dip

61 Calories

—Margaret Blakely, New Philadelphia, Ohio

"For me, a sensible approach to health is simple: regular exercise and a diet of vegetables, fruits, grains, and low-fat meats and dairy. And avoiding fad diets. This easy dip fits perfectly into my approach. I serve it with baked tortilla chips or crackers."

1 garlic clove

2 jalapeño chile peppers, seeded (wear plastic gloves when handling)

1 can (16 ounces) black beans, rinsed and drained

1 can (14 ounces) artichoke hearts, drained

3 ounces reduced-fat cream cheese, softened

2 tablespoons lemon juice

1 tablespoon chopped parsley

½ teaspoon salt

In a food processor, chop garlic and peppers. Add beans, artichoke hearts, cream cheese, lemon juice, parsley, and salt. Process until smooth.

Makes 3 cups

Per ¼ cup: *61 calories, 3 g protein, 9 g carbohydrates, 1 g fat, 2 mg cholesterol, 338 mg sodium, 1 g fiber*

Diet Exchanges: *0 milk, 1 vegetable, 0 fruit, ½ bread, 0 meat, 0 fat*

FROM THE PROS

Rancho la Puerta

Rancho la Puerta is a health and fitness spa located just outside
of San Diego in Tecate, Baja California, Mexico. It serves the best-tasting
salsa north or south of the border. Look for New Mexican and arbol chile peppers in
your supermarket's produce section. Or try your favorite dried chiles.
For more heat, leave the seeds in the chiles.

SALSA MEXICANA

17 Calories

2 dried New Mexican chile peppers,
  seeded and rinsed (wear plastic
  gloves when handling)

1 dried arbol chile, seeded and rinsed
  (wear plastic gloves when handling)

4 tomatoes, chopped

1 onion, chopped

2 cups water

1 tablespoon chopped fresh oregano
  or 1 teaspoon dried

2 garlic cloves, chopped

¼ cup chopped fresh cilantro

Place peppers in a medium saucepan.
Toast over low heat for 2 minutes, or until
fragrant. Add tomatoes, onion, water, and
oregano. Heat to boiling over high heat.
Reduce heat to low, cover, and simmer 10
minutes, or until tomatoes are soft. Drain.

Puree in a blender. Add garlic and
blend until smooth. Stir in cilantro.

Makes 1½ cups

Per 2 tablespoons: *17 calories, 1 g protein,
4 g carbohydrates, 0 g fat, 0 mg cholesterol,
23 mg sodium, 1 g fiber*

Diet Exchanges: *0 milk, 1 vegetable, 0 fruit,
0 bread, 0 meat, 0 fat*

Buttermilk Fruit Smoothie

243 Calories

—Michelle Keller, Bisbee, N.Dak.

"The refreshing creaminess of this shake comes from the buttermilk. But it's also good made with fat-free milk or low-fat soy milk. Use your favorite frozen fruit or a combination of fruits."

2 cups low-fat buttermilk

1 ripe banana, cut into chunks

1 cup frozen unsweetened strawberries or peaches

2 tablespoons honey

1 cup ice cubes

In a blender, combine buttermilk, banana, strawberries or peaches, honey, and ice. Blend until frothy.

Makes 2

Per smoothie: *243 calories, 9 g protein, 49 g carbohydrates, 3 g fat, 9 mg cholesterol, 264 mg sodium, 3 g fiber*

Diet Exchanges: *1 milk, 0 vegetable, 2 fruit, 0 bread, 0 meat, 0 fat*

50 LOW-CALORIE SNACKS

The need to nibble can strike at any time. Below are snacks to satisfy your craving for any kind of sweet or salty nibble (even chocolate!). Each food listed contains about 50 calories. For a 150-calorie snack, choose three, including one from the "Protein-and-Just-a-Little-Fat Snacks" list. Stash these in your car, handbag, desk drawer, or anywhere you might nosh. There are plenty that don't need a fridge.

Carbohydrate Snacks

1 cup strawberries
½ small orange
½ banana
1 melon wedge
½ cup dried fruit
½ cup cherries
½ cup blueberries
½ baked apple
2 prunes
½ cup orange juice
2 frozen juice bars (2½ ounces each)
2 sesame breadsticks
5 baked tortilla chips with 1 tablespoon salsa
1 mini bagel (2" diameter)
⅓ small whole-wheat bagel (3½" diameter)
3 (2") pretzels
1 slice unbuttered whole-wheat toast
1 mini pita (4½" diameter)
3 stone-ground wheat crackers
2 rye crackers
25 goldfish crackers
6 graham crackers (1½ two-inch squares)
⅓ cup oatmeal
2 tablespoons low-fat granola
1 tablespoon trail mix
1½ cups unbuttered air-popped popcorn
⅓ cup caramel popcorn
1½ rice cakes
1⅓ popcorn cakes
1 fig bar
½ small unbuttered baked potato
1 cup gazpacho
1 tablespoon chocolate morsels
15 plain M & M's

Protein-and-Just-a-Little-Fat Snacks

1 slice (¾ ounce) reduced-fat Cheddar cheese
⅔ cheese stick
⅓ cup 1% cottage cheese
½ cup 1% milk
¼ cup low-fat yogurt
1 small hard-cooked egg
¼ cup refried beans
1½ teaspoons peanut butter
1 tablespoon peanuts
1 tablespoon almonds
½ cup miso soup
⅓ cup canned shrimp
¼ cup water-packed light tuna
1 ounce turkey salami
2 slices turkey breast
1 fat-free hot dog

Peanut Butter and Banana Shake

366 Calories

—Linda Quinonez, Burbank, Calif.

"Here's a smoothie with a new twist! Kids love it. Drink the whole thing for breakfast or lunch. I keep bananas in the freezer so they are ready to go. The peels darken, but the fruit is still fine."

1 cup (8 ounces) fat-free plain yogurt
1 frozen banana
1 tablespoon creamy peanut butter
1 teaspoon vanilla extract
1 teaspoon honey
½ teaspoon ground cinnamon

In a blender, combine yogurt, banana, peanut butter, vanilla extract, honey, and cinnamon. Blend until smooth.

Makes 1

Per shake: *366 calories, 18 g protein, 55 g carbohydrates, 9 g fat, 4 mg cholesterol, 252 mg sodium, 3 g fiber*

Diet Exchanges: *1½ milk, 0 vegetable, 2 fruit, 0 bread, 1 meat, 0 fat*

Purple Power Shake

381 Calories

—Britt Isaac, Tampa, Fla.

"For an energy boost, my fiancé has one of these shakes before his tennis matches. I like it because it's a good source of calcium, fruit, vitamins, and soy protein. Even my most tofu-phobic friends love this shake. Use your favorite fruit and berries."

½ cup chopped fresh fruit (bananas, peaches, mangos)

½ cup fresh or frozen berries (blueberries, strawberries, raspberries)

⅓ cup frozen orange juice concentrate

4 ounces (½ cup) silken tofu, drained

1 cup fat-free milk or fat-free soy milk

In a blender, combine fruit, berries, orange juice concentrate, tofu, and milk. Blend until smooth.

Makes 1

Per shake: *381 calories, 17 g protein, 71 g carbohydrates, 4 g fat, 4 mg cholesterol, 141 mg sodium, 4 g fiber*

Diet Exchanges: *1 milk, 0 vegetable, 4 fruit, 0 bread, 0 meat, 0 fat*

TIP: Silken tofu has a creamier consistency than regular tofu and is sometimes packaged in an aseptic box. Look for it near the regular tofu in the refrigerated produce section at your supermarket.

Snappy Weeknight Suppers

Chicken and Rice Italiano 126

Chicken Fiesta Mexicana 127

Unfried Crunchy Chicken 128

Big-Flavor Chicken 129

Greek Island Chicken 130

Mango Chicken 132

Chicken Therese 133

Marlene's Chicken and
    Vegetable Stir-Fry 135

Orange-Almond Chicken 136

Skillet Chicken with Tomatoes 138

Slow-Cooker Lemon Chicken 139

Chicken Fajitas 142

Confetti Enchiladas 144

Beef 'n' Macaroni Skillet Supper 145

Tomatoes and Zucchini with Meatballs . .146

Taco Bake 148

Red Chile Steak Burritos 150

Slow-Cooked Pork Stew 152

Tuscan Bean Soup with Sausage 154

Fettuccine with Pot-Lickin'
    Chicken Sauce 156

Lamb Chops with Herbed
    Apricot Sauce 157

Spicy Spaghetti Marinara 158

Easy Rigatoni .159

Linguine Montecatini 160

Mushroom and Tofu Fettuccine 161

Mediterranean Pasta 162

Angel Hair Pasta with Clam Pesto 164

Salmon Teriyaki 165

Crab Cakes 166

Norma's Grilled Garlicky Salmon 169

Baked Catfish with Dill Sauce 170

Flounder Dijon 171

Salmon with Lemon-Caper
    Cream Sauce 172

Shrimp Creole 174

Brown Rice Vegetable Stir-Fry 176

Quick Black Bean Enchiladas 177

Black Bean and Corn Burritos 178

Ensalada Mexicana Vegetariana 179

Chicken and Rice Italiano

381 Calories

—Erin Ruocco, Poway, Calif.

" Here's my Italian twist on the Spanish arroz con pollo. For variety, serve the saucy chicken over cooked pasta instead of rice. "

4 boneless, skinless chicken breast halves

1 jar (16 ounces) pasta sauce with garlic and peppers

2 tablespoons (½ ounce) grated Parmesan cheese

½ teaspoon dried Italian seasoning

1 can (14½ ounces) fat-free, reduced-sodium chicken broth

¾ cup Arborio or regular long-grain white rice

Preheat the oven to 450°F.

Place chicken in a shallow baking dish. Spoon sauce evenly over the top. Sprinkle with cheese and Italian seasoning. Cover dish with foil and bake 18 to 22 minutes, or until a thermometer inserted in thickest portion registers 160°F and juices run clear.

Meanwhile, in a medium saucepan, heat broth to boiling. Stir in rice. Cover and reduce heat to low. Simmer 15 minutes, or until rice is tender and liquid is absorbed.

Divide rice among 4 plates. Top with chicken and sauce.

Makes 4 servings

Per serving: *381 calories, 24 g protein, 51 g carbohydrates, 7 g fat, 48 mg cholesterol, 602 mg sodium, 3 g fiber*

Diet Exchanges: *0 milk, 0 vegetable, 0 fruit, 3 bread, 2 meat, 0 fat*

Chicken Fiesta Mexicana

284 Calories

—Betty Jimenez, Houston

" My family loves this simple chicken dish, especially when served with Spanish rice. When it's in season, I add corn on the cob to the menu. "

4 boneless, skinless chicken breast halves

2 tablespoons ground cumin

2 tablespoons garlic powder or minced garlic

½ teaspoon salt

¼ teaspoon ground black pepper

1 cup salsa

¾ cup (3 ounces) shredded reduced-fat extra-sharp Cheddar cheese

¾ cup (3 ounces) shredded reduced-fat Monterey Jack cheese

1 small avocado, pitted, peeled, and sliced (optional)

Preheat the oven to 350°F.

Place chicken in a medium nonstick baking dish. Coat both sides of chicken with nonstick spray. Sprinkle both sides evenly with cumin, garlic powder or minced garlic, salt, and pepper. Top with salsa. Bake 20 minutes.

Remove from the oven and sprinkle with Cheddar and Monterey Jack. Bake 10 minutes, or until cheese is melted and a thermometer inserted in thickest portion registers 160°F and juices run clear. Serve with avocado, if using.

Makes 4 servings

Per serving: *284 calories, 32 g protein, 12 g carbohydrates, 12 g fat, 76 mg cholesterol, 924 mg sodium, 5 g fiber*

Diet Exchanges: *0 milk, 0 vegetable, 0 fruit, 0 bread, 4 meat, 0 fat*

Unfried Crunchy Chicken

408 Calories

—Penny Lewis, St. Croix, U.S. Virgin Islands

" I learned to cut out extraneous fat from my foods and replace the flavor with seasonings and spices. Now, I have a toned and firmed body, atop which sits a head full of positive and happy wishes. "

Preheat the oven to 375°F.

In a small bowl, mix garlic, lime juice, 1 tablespoon soy sauce, and ¼ teaspoon pepper. Rub into chicken and refrigerate 30 minutes.

In a shallow bowl, combine yogurt, flour, garlic powder, milk, remaining 1 tablespoon soy sauce, and remaining ¼ teaspoon pepper. Spread bread crumbs on waxed paper.

Dredge chicken in yogurt mixture, then press into bread crumbs on all sides. Place on the rack of a roasting pan and coat generously with nonstick spray.

Bake 45 minutes, or until a thermometer inserted in thickest portion registers 170°F and juices run clear.

Makes 4 servings

Per serving: *408 calories, 38 g protein, 49 g carbohydrates, 6 g fat, 74 mg cholesterol, 760 mg sodium, 0 g fiber*

Diet Exchanges: *½ milk, 0 vegetable, 0 fruit, 2 bread, 2 meat, 0 fat*

(Asian Slaw recipe on page 252)

  4 **garlic cloves, crushed**
  1 **tablespoon lime juice**
  2 **tablespoons reduced-sodium soy sauce**
 ½ **teaspoon ground black pepper**
  4 **skinless bone-in chicken breasts or thighs**
  1 **cup (8 ounces) fat-free plain yogurt**
 ½ **cup unbleached or all-purpose flour**
 ½ **teaspoon garlic powder**
  2 **tablespoons fat-free milk**
1½ **cups dry bread crumbs**

Big-Flavor Chicken

237 Calories

—Amy S. Hutchins, Charlotte, N.C.

"We like to serve this dish with brown rice and a big green salad. It's a filling meal, yet easy enough to make on busy weeknights."

½ cup (4 ounces) reduced-fat sour cream

1 envelope (1¼ ounces) Hollandaise sauce mix

⅓ cup dry white wine or nonalcoholic wine

2 tablespoons Worcestershire sauce

1 tablespoon Dijon mustard

4 boneless, skinless chicken breast halves

4 slices (¾ ounce each) reduced-fat American cheese

⅓ cup dry bread stuffing mix

Preheat the oven to 350°F. Coat a 9" × 9" baking dish with nonstick spray.

In a medium bowl, combine sour cream, Hollandaise sauce mix, wine, Worcestershire sauce, and mustard. Spoon one-third of mixture evenly into the prepared baking dish. Arrange chicken in baking dish. Top each piece of chicken with a slice of cheese. Spoon remaining sour-cream mixture over chicken. Top with stuffing mix. Bake 30 to 40 minutes, or until a thermometer inserted in thickest portion registers 160°F and juices run clear.

Makes 4 servings

Per serving: *237 calories, 23 g protein, 8 g carbohydrates, 10 g fat, 73 mg cholesterol, 649 mg sodium, 0 g fiber*

Diet Exchanges: *0 milk, 0 vegetable, 0 fruit, ½ bread, 2½ meat, 0 fat*

Slimming Meal

1 serving Big-Flavor Chicken

1 cup broccoli rabe with lemon and garlic

½ cup couscous with 1 teaspoon grated Parmesan cheese

⅛ honeydew or Crenshaw melon

415 calories

Greek Island Chicken

350 Calories

—Paige Morehouse, Sonora, Calif.

*"*I serve this high-flavor dinner over cooked rice to soak up the savory sauce.*"*

1 tablespoon olive oil

4 boneless, skinless chicken breast halves

1 onion, chopped

2 garlic cloves, minced

3 ounces mushrooms, sliced

1 cup dry white wine or nonalcoholic wine

1 jar (8 ounces) marinated artichoke hearts, drained

⅓ cup coarsely chopped dry-pack sun-dried tomatoes

¼ cup pitted Greek olives, halved

1 teaspoon lemon-pepper seasoning

1 teaspoon honey

¼ teaspoon salt

½ teaspoon dried oregano

½ teaspoon ground cinnamon

½ cup (2½ ounces) crumbled feta cheese

4 lemon wedges or slices

Warm oil in a large nonstick skillet over medium-high heat. Add chicken and cook 5 minutes on each side, or until browned. Remove to a plate.

Reduce heat to medium and add onion and garlic to the same skillet. Cook 5 minutes, or until onion is tender. Stir in mushrooms. Cook 10 minutes, or until mushrooms render their juices. Add wine, artichokes, tomatoes, olives, lemon-pepper seasoning, honey, salt, oregano, cinnamon, and chicken. Reduce heat to low, cover, and cook 15 minutes.

Uncover and cook 5 minutes, or until sauce thickens slightly and a thermometer inserted in thickest portion registers 160°F and juices run clear. Sprinkle with cheese. Serve with lemon for squeezing.

Makes 4 servings

Per serving: *350 calories, 23 g protein, 19 g carbohydrates, 19 g fat, 74 mg cholesterol, 949 mg sodium, 3 g fiber*

Diet Exchanges: *0 milk, 1 vegetable, 0 fruit, 0 bread, 3 meat, 2 fat*

Mango Chicken

272 Calories

—Pamela Valois, Piedmont, Calif.

"Depending on what's in the house, I serve this over brown rice, couscous, or pasta. If you can't find fresh mango, look for frozen or jarred or substitute fresh papaya."

1 teaspoon vegetable oil

1 pound boneless, skinless chicken breasts, cubed

8 scallions, chopped

2 tomatoes, seeded and chopped

2 ripe mangos, peeled, pitted, and chopped (see tip)

¾ teaspoon ground cumin

¾ teaspoon ground coriander

½ teaspoon salt

½ teaspoon ground black pepper

1 cup (8 ounces) fat-free plain yogurt

1 cup reduced-fat unsweetened coconut milk

½ cup chopped fresh cilantro

Warm oil in a nonstick skillet or wok over medium-high heat. Add chicken and scallions. Cook 5 minutes, or until chicken is browned. Add tomatoes, mangos, cumin, coriander, salt, and pepper. Cook 3 minutes. Add yogurt and milk. Reduce heat to low and cook 10 to 15 minutes, or until sauce thickens and chicken is fork-tender and no longer pink. Sprinkle with cilantro.

Makes 4 servings

Per serving: *272 calories, 22 g protein, 27 g carbohydrates, 9 g fat, 46 mg cholesterol, 363 mg sodium, 4 g fiber*

Diet Exchanges: *0 milk, 1 vegetable, 1 fruit, 0 bread, 2½ meat, 0 fat*

TIP: To peel, pit, and chop a mango, stand it on end and slice off two "fillets" from the flat sides of the fruit, cutting as close to the pit as possible. Cut crisscross diamond patterns into the flesh of the fillets, but don't cut through the peel. Use your thumbs to push the fruit from the peel side, turning the fillet inside out and exposing the cubes. Cut the cubes away from the peel. Discard the pit and peel.

Chicken Therese

202 Calories

—Therese Meyer, Blaine, Minn.

"Fresh ingredients like mushrooms and flavor boosters like sherry and dry mustard really kick up the flavor of this skillet chicken. You'd never guess that the sauce base is a reduced-fat canned soup. Serve over rice or noodles."

 4 boneless, skinless chicken breast halves
 1 teaspoon garlic salt
¼ teaspoon ground black pepper
⅛ teaspoon ground red pepper
 1 tablespoon olive oil
10 mushrooms, sliced
 1 onion, chopped
 1 can (10¾ ounces) reduced-fat cream of chicken soup
 2 tablespoons dry sherry
¾ teaspoon mustard powder
¼ teaspoon ground nutmeg

Rub each chicken breast half with garlic salt, black pepper, and red pepper.

Warm oil in a large nonstick skillet over medium-high heat. Add chicken and cook until browned on both sides, turning once. Remove chicken to a plate and keep warm.

Add mushrooms and onion to the same skillet. Cook 5 minutes, or until tender. Stir in soup, sherry, mustard powder, and nutmeg. Heat to boiling and add chicken. Reduce heat to low, cover, and simmer 20 minutes, or until a thermometer inserted in thickest portion registers 160°F and juices run clear.

Makes 4 servings

Per serving: *202 calories, 20 g protein, 11 g carbohydrates, 8 g fat, 55 mg cholesterol, 885 mg sodium, 2 g fiber*

Diet Exchanges: *0 milk, 0 vegetable, 0 fruit, 1 bread, 1½ meat, 0 fat*

It Worked for Me!

Marlene Dropp

V I T A L   S T A T S

Weight lost: 60 pounds

Time kept it off: 12 years

Weight-loss strategies: Walking; weight training; low-fat diet; small, frequent meals

Weight-maintenance strategies: Has a 5- to 7-pound gain/loss window, walks 5 miles a day, skis cross-country, uses clothing fit as a gauge

Daily exercise and eating several small meals a day got Marlene Dropp, mother of four kids, lean, energized, and de-stressed.

"After I had my first two children in my 20s, I was back in pre-pregnancy clothes in no time. But in my 30s, after my second two children, I gave in to munching on junk food. That left me at the 200-pound mark. I tried dieting, but that didn't work. And between my family and my job, I had no time for exercise. It was a last priority.

"I was a blimp. To cheer me up and get me out of the house, my oldest daughter suggested we go for a walk. We only walked around the block but, to my amazement, it felt great! Just the act of moving lifted my spirits and chased the blues away. I thought, 'If it worked once, it will work again.' I walked the next day and the next. Each time, I came home full of energy and feeling good about myself. That's when I decided that a morning walk would be a number one priority, every day.

"My first goal was a 5-mile walk. There are lots of half-mile circular roads in my neighborhood, so every week I'd add another loop to the route. Afterward, I'd measure the distance with my car, then note my progress on the fridge calendar. Within 2 months, I'd reached my goal.

"My next goal was to increase my speed and do a 13-minute mile. I didn't do as well with this goal. I thought that my diet might be the reason, so I cut out junk food and started eating four or five small, low-fat meals a day. After about a year of healthy eating habits and more walking, I finally hit a 13-minute mile. Best of all, just 2 years after my first walk around the block, I had shed 60 pounds.

"Walking every day has become a habit for me. It's what took the weight off and what keeps it off. I walk 5 miles every day and still watch my fat and calorie intake. I also started cross-country skiing. When I work out, I feel better physically and emotionally." ∎

Marlene's Chicken and Vegetable Stir-Fry

410 Calories

*"For this dish, I let the chicken marinate while I go for a walk.
When I return, it's ready to stir-fry."*

3 tablespoons soy sauce

2 tablespoons cornstarch

1 garlic clove, minced

1 pound boneless, skinless chicken breast, cut into 1" pieces

1 cup long-grain white rice

2 tablespoons peanut or vegetable oil

1 package (16 ounces) frozen mixed vegetables, thawed

¼ cup dry roasted peanuts (optional)

In a large bowl, combine soy sauce, cornstarch, and garlic. Add chicken and toss to coat. Cover and refrigerate 20 minutes or overnight.

Cook rice according to package directions. Keep warm.

Warm 1 tablespoon of oil in a large skillet or wok over medium-high heat. Add chicken, reserving marinade. Cook 5 minutes, or until browned, stirring frequently. Remove chicken to a plate. Add remaining 1 tablespoon oil to the pan. Stir in vegetables. Cook 5 minutes, or until vegetables are tender.

Return chicken to the pan. Add reserved marinade and cook 1 minute, or until sauce is thickened and chicken is no longer pink. Serve over rice. Sprinkle with peanuts, if using.

Makes 4 servings

Per serving: *410 calories, 24 g protein, 53 g carbohydrates, 11 g fat, 46 mg cholesterol, 852 mg sodium, 5 g fiber*

Diet Exchanges: *0 milk, 2 vegetable, 0 fruit, 1½ bread, 3 meat, 0 fat*

Splurge Meal

1 serving Marlene's Chicken and Vegetable Stir-Fry

½ cup rice noodles sautéed with scallions in ½ teaspoon sesame oil

½ cup baby corn

1 coconut macaroon

½ cup orange sorbet

744 calories

Orange-Almond Chicken

265 Calories

—Lisa Pettit, Tavernier, Fla.

"When I'm craving Chinese-style sweet-and-sour but don't want the calories or fat, I turn to this recipe."

¼ cup sliced almonds
1 tablespoon peanut or vegetable oil
4 boneless, skinless chicken breast halves
½ cup chopped shallots
3 ounces mushrooms, sliced
⅓ cup orange marmalade
3 tablespoons soy sauce
¼ teaspoon ground black pepper
Orange slices (optional)

Place almonds in a large nonstick skillet. Toast over medium heat, shaking the pan often, 5 minutes, or until fragrant. Remove to a plate and set aside.

Warm oil in the same skillet over medium-high heat. Add chicken and cook 5 minutes, or until no longer pink, turning occasionally. Remove to a plate.

Add shallots to the pan and cook 5 minutes, or until soft. Add mushrooms and cook 5 minutes, or until mushrooms render their juices. Stir in marmalade, soy sauce, and pepper. Return chicken to the pan. Reduce the heat to low, cover, and simmer 10 minutes, or until a thermometer inserted in thickest portion registers 160°F and juices run clear. Top with almonds and orange slices, if using.

Per serving: *265 calories, 20 g protein, 26 g carbohydrates, 10 g fat, 46 mg cholesterol, 818 mg sodium, 1 g fiber*

Diet Exchanges: *0 milk, 0 vegetable, 0 fruit, 1½ bread, 2 meat, 0 fat*

Skillet Chicken with Tomatoes

156 Calories

—Caroline B. Hurley, Honolulu

"On days when you're tired but want both a tasty and filling meal, this dish can't be beat. I serve it on aromatic jasmine rice, but any rice or pasta will do."

4 boneless, skinless chicken breast halves
½ cup fat-free Italian salad dressing
1 tablespoon olive oil
1 can (14½ ounces) Italian-style stewed tomatoes

In a resealable plastic bag, combine chicken and salad dressing. Set aside in refrigerator 20 minutes. Remove chicken from marinade, reserving marinade.

Warm oil in a medium skillet over medium-high heat. Add chicken and cook 5 minutes, or until no longer pink, turning occasionally. Stir in reserved marinade and tomatoes (with juice). Heat to boiling. Reduce heat to low, cover, and simmer 15 minutes, or until a thermometer inserted in thickest portion registers 160°F and juices run clear.

Makes 4 servings

Per serving: *156 calories, 18 g protein, 6 g carbohydrates, 5 g fat, 46 mg cholesterol, 679 mg sodium, 1 g fiber*

Diet Exchanges: *0 milk, 2 vegetable, 0 fruit, 0 bread, 1½ meat, 0 fat*

Slimming Meal

1 serving Skillet Chicken with Tomatoes

½ cup cooked egg noodles

½ cup steamed baby carrots with dill

½ cup blueberries with ½ cup low-fat lime yogurt

451 calories

Slow-Cooker Lemon Chicken

—Leighanne C. Hersey, Waycross, Ga.

"This meal is perfect for workdays or any time you're busy in the evening. Just start the recipe in the morning (it only takes a moment) and let the Crock-Pot do the cooking while you're at work or doing other things."

4 boneless, skinless chicken breast halves

1 tablespoon lemon-pepper seasoning

1 bag (16 ounces) fresh soup vegetables, chopped

1 can (10¾ ounces) reduced-fat cream of chicken soup

1 teaspoon dried rosemary, crushed

Coat chicken with lemon-pepper seasoning. Coat a medium nonstick skillet with nonstick spray and warm over medium-high heat. Add chicken and cook 5 minutes, or until browned on both sides, turning once.

Place chicken in slow cooker. Add vegetables.

In a medium bowl, combine soup, half a soup can of water, and rosemary. Pour over vegetables and chicken. Cover and cook on low 8 hours or high 4 hours.

Makes 4 servings

Per serving: *205 calories, 21 g protein, 18 g carbohydrates, 4 g fat, 55 mg cholesterol, 940 mg sodium, 3 g fiber*

Diet Exchanges: *0 milk, 1 vegetable, 0 fruit, 1 bread, 1½ meat, 0 fat*

Slimming Meal

1 serving Slow-Cooker Lemon Chicken

½ cup steamed green beans with 1 teaspoon slivered almonds

1 whole sliced tomato with ½ ounce crumbled feta cheese

1 serving Black Cherry Baked Apples (page 302)

454 calories

SIX SIMPLE SAUCES FOR CHICKEN

On a busy night, nothing's easier than broiled, grilled, or poached chicken breasts. And nothing more boring! Wake up your next chicken dinner with these super-quick, low-calorie sauces. Each mini-recipe makes 4 servings, enough to generously sauce four boneless, skinless chicken breasts cooked your favorite way.

Caribbean Salsa

Combine 1 finely chopped mango or papaya, ¹/₂ cup finely chopped pineapple, 2 tablespoons chopped fresh mint, 2 tablespoons chopped white onion, ¹/₄ teaspoon salt, and ¹/₄ teaspoon ground red pepper. Let rest 1 hour to develop flavors.

Per serving: *47 calories, 0 g protein, 12 g carbohydrates, 0 g fat, 0 mg cholesterol, 135 mg sodium, 2 g fiber*

Diet Exchanges: *0 milk, 0 vegetable, 1 fruit, 0 bread, 0 meat, 0 fat*

Lemon Goat Cheese

Brown 1 tablespoon butter in a small skillet. Stir in 1 tablespoon unbleached or all-purpose flour. Cook 1 minute. Whisk in 1¹/₂ cups chicken broth and cook, stirring constantly, until sauce boils. Blend in 4 to 6 ounces mild goat cheese (such as chèvre

or Montrachet) and ¹/₂ teaspoon grated lemon peel.

Per serving: *141 calories, 7 g protein, 2 g carbohydrates, 12 g fat, 30 mg cholesterol, 272 mg sodium, 0 g fiber*

Diet Exchanges: *0 milk, 0 vegetable, 0 fruit, 0 bread, 1 meat, 1 fat*

Mushroom

Warm 1 teaspoon olive oil in a medium nonstick skillet over medium heat. Add 1¹/₂ cups sliced mushrooms and ¹/₄ cup finely chopped onion. Cook until mushrooms are soft. Stir in 2 tablespoons soy sauce or balsamic vinegar and 1 tablespoon crushed fresh rosemary or thyme. Cover and cook 2 minutes. Uncover and boil until sauce reduces by half. Season with ¹/₄ teaspoon salt and a pinch of ground black pepper.

Per serving: *25 calories, 1 g protein, 3 g carbohydrates, 1 g fat, 0 mg cholesterol, 649 mg sodium, 1 g fiber*

Diet Exchanges: *0 milk, 1 vegetable, 0 fruit, 0 bread, 0 meat, 0 fat*

Pepperonata

Warm 1 teaspoon olive oil in a medium nonstick skillet over medium heat. Add ¹/₄ cup diced cooked ham and ¹/₄ cup chopped onion. Cook 4 minutes. Add $\frac{1}{2}$ cup red and/or green bell pepper strips, $\frac{1}{4}$ teaspoon dried thyme, and $\frac{1}{2}$ cup chicken broth. Cover and cook until peppers are tender. Serve with chopped parsley.

Per serving: *42 calories, 3 g protein, 3 g carbohydrates, 2 g fat, 5 mg cholesterol, 229 mg sodium, 1 g fiber*

Diet Exchanges: *0 milk, 1 vegetable, 0 fruit, 0 bread, $\frac{1}{2}$ meat, 0 fat*

Santa Fe

In a dry medium nonstick skillet, toast $\frac{3}{4}$ teaspoon dried oregano, $\frac{1}{2}$ teaspoon chili powder, and $\frac{1}{4}$ teaspoon ground cinnamon just until fragrant. Stir in 1 chopped tomato and $\frac{1}{2}$ cup cooked or drained canned black beans. Heat to boiling. Stir in $\frac{1}{4}$ cup chopped fresh cilantro. Serve with lime wedges and fat-free sour cream.

Per serving: *27 calories, 2 g protein, 6 g carbohydrates, 0 g fat, 0 mg cholesterol, 137 mg sodium, 2 g fiber*

Diet Exchanges: *0 milk, 0 vegetable, 0 fruit, $\frac{1}{2}$ bread, 0 meat, 0 fat*

Sesame

In a small saucepan, warm $\frac{1}{2}$ teaspoon peanut oil and $\frac{1}{2}$ teaspoon sesame oil. Add 1 minced garlic clove and cook 2 minutes over medium heat. Add $\frac{1}{2}$ teaspoon grated fresh ginger, $\frac{3}{4}$ cup chicken broth, $\frac{1}{2}$ teaspoon soy sauce, and $\frac{1}{8}$ teaspoon crushed red-pepper flakes. Heat to boiling. In a small cup, stir together 1 teaspoon cornstarch and 2 tablespoons water until smooth. Blend into sauce and cook, stirring constantly, until thickened and boiling. Serve with toasted sesame seeds.

Per serving: *22 calories, 1 g protein, 1 g carbohydrates, 1 g fat, 0 mg cholesterol, 189 mg sodium, 0 g fiber*

Diet Exchanges: *0 milk, 0 vegetable, 0 fruit, 0 bread, 0 meat, $\frac{1}{2}$ fat*

Chicken Fajitas

417 Calories

—Kelly Stack, Fenton, Mich.

"When you start with boneless, skinless chicken breasts, dinner is only minutes away. This Mexican dish is a family favorite any night of the week."

½ **pound boneless, skinless chicken breast, cut into strips**

1 **bag (16 ounces) frozen peppers and onions**

1 **envelope (1.12 ounces) fajita seasoning mix**

8 **flour tortillas (12" diameter)**

½ **cup (4 ounces) fat-free sour cream**

1 **large tomato, finely chopped**

1 **cup shredded reduced-fat Cheddar cheese (optional)**

Coat a large skillet with nonstick spray. Add chicken and cook, stirring occasionally, 5 to 7 minutes, or until no longer pink. Add vegetables and cook until heated through. Add fajita mix and cook 5 minutes more. Spoon into each tortilla and top with sour cream, tomato, and cheese, if using. Roll up each fajita like a cone.

Makes 4 servings

Per serving: *417 calories, 21 g protein, 70 g carbohydrates, 7 g fat, 23 mg cholesterol, 989 mg sodium, 5 g fiber*

Diet Exchanges: *0 milk, 1 vegetable, 0 fruit, 4 bread, 1 meat, 0 fat*

Confetti Enchiladas

301 Calories

—Sharon Swindle, Fort Worth, Tex.

" Traditionally, corn tortillas are fried before filling for enchiladas. I soften them in broth instead. It saves not only fat and calories but also time and mess. Sometimes, I make two casseroles and freeze one by replacing the 13" × 9" dish with two 8" × 8" dishes. "

1 can (12½ ounces) white chunk chicken, drained, or ¾ pound cubed cooked chicken

1 can (14½ ounces) diced tomatoes, drained

1 can (4½ ounces) chopped green chile peppers, drained

1 cup fresh or frozen corn kernels

6 scallions, chopped

4 tomatillos, chopped

½ cup chopped red bell pepper

½ cup (4 ounces) low-fat plain yogurt

1 teaspoon salt

1 teaspoon chili powder

½ teaspoon ground red pepper

1½ cups (6 ounces) shredded reduced-fat Colby and Monterey Jack cheese mixture

1 can (16 ounces) fat-free chicken broth

16 corn tortillas (6" diameter)

Preheat the oven to 350°F. Spray a 13" × 9" baking dish with nonstick spray.

In a large bowl, mix chicken, tomatoes, chile peppers, corn, scallions, tomatillos, bell pepper, yogurt, salt, chili powder, ground red pepper, and ¾ cup cheese.

Warm broth in a large skillet over low heat. Add tortillas (in batches, if necessary) and cook 2 to 3 minutes, or until softened.

Remove tortillas to a paper towel. Spoon ⅓ cup filling along the middle of each tortilla. Roll up tightly and place, seam side down, in the prepared baking dish. Sprinkle with remaining ¾ cup cheese. Cover with foil and bake 25 to 30 minutes, or until hot and bubbly.

Makes 8 servings

Per serving: *301 calories, 21 g protein, 33 g carbohydrates, 10 g fat, 40 mg cholesterol, 833 mg sodium, 1 g fiber*

Diet Exchanges: *0 milk, 2 vegetable, 0 fruit, 1 bread, 2 meat, 0 fat*

TIP: Tomatillos are a type of small green tomato with a papery husk. Look for them near the red tomatoes in your supermarket's produce section.

Beef 'n' Macaroni Skillet Supper

476 Calories

—Carole Plaza-O'Connell, Wayne, N.J.

" We updated this old family favorite to use less fat. Evaporated milk makes it creamy without having to use high-fat heavy cream. It's still a bit high in fat, so we save it for nights when we're celebrating. "

- 1 cup elbow macaroni
- ¾ pound extra-lean ground beef
- 1 garlic clove, minced
- 1 can (3½ ounces) fat-free evaporated milk
- 1 envelope (2.1 ounces) chicken noodle soup mix
- ¾ cup water
- ¾ teaspoon ground black pepper
- ½ teaspoon dried Italian seasoning
- 1 cup (4 ounces) shredded reduced-fat extra-sharp Cheddar cheese

Cook macaroni according to package directions. Drain.

In a large skillet over medium-high heat, cook beef and garlic 10 minutes, or until beef is no longer pink. Stir to break beef into small pieces. Drain and discard fat. Stir in evaporated milk, soup mix, water, pepper, Italian seasoning, 2 tablespoons cheese, and cooked macaroni. Top with remaining cheese. Cover and cook over low heat 10 minutes, or until hot and bubbly.

Makes 4 servings

Per serving: *476 calories, 37 g protein, 31 g carbohydrates, 21 g fat, 93 mg cholesterol, 1,479 mg sodium, 1 g fiber*

Diet Exchanges: *0 milk, 0 vegetable, 0 fruit, 2 bread, 4 meat, 2 fat*

Splurge Meal

- 1 serving Beef 'n' Macaroni Skillet Supper
- 1 serving multigrain bread
- 1 cup chilled cooked green beans on shredded romaine lettuce with fat-free Italian dressing
- ½ cup vanilla frozen yogurt with 1 tablespoon chocolate syrup and 1 teaspoon chopped peanuts

935 calories

Tomatoes and Zucchini with Meatballs

357 Calories

—Kim Mustill, Parker, Colo.

" I use this one-dish meal to sneak in a few servings of vegetables. Serve it in bowls with crusty Italian bread or spoon it over fettuccine. "

½ **pound extra-lean ground beef or ground turkey**

¼ **cup dry seasoned bread crumbs**

¼ **cup liquid egg substitute or 1 egg**

¾ **teaspoon ground black pepper**

6 **tablespoons (1½ ounces) grated Parmesan cheese**

1 **tablespoon olive oil**

1 **small onion, finely chopped**

2 **garlic cloves, minced**

2 **small zucchini, halved lengthwise and sliced**

1 **small yellow squash, halved lengthwise and sliced**

1 **can (16 ounces) Italian-style cut tomatoes**

1 **can (16 ounces) crushed tomatoes**

¼ **teaspoon sugar**

¼ **cup chopped fresh basil leaves**

In a large bowl, combine beef or turkey, bread crumbs, egg substitute or egg, ½ teaspoon pepper, and 4 tablespoons cheese. Form into balls the size of walnuts.

Warm oil in a large nonstick skillet over medium-high heat. Add meatballs, several at a time, and cook 15 minutes, or until browned and no longer pink inside. Remove to a bowl, leaving drippings in the skillet.

In the same skillet in warm drippings over medium-high heat, add onion and garlic. Cook 5 minutes, or until onion is tender. Stir in zucchini, yellow squash, cut tomatoes (with juice), crushed tomatoes, sugar, remaining 2 tablespoons Parmesan, remaining ¼ teaspoon pepper, and meatballs. Heat to boiling. Reduce heat to low, cover, and cook 20 minutes. Stir in basil.

Makes 4 servings

Per serving: *357 calories, 21 g protein, 27 g carbohydrates, 14 g fat, 43 mg cholesterol, 935 mg sodium, 4 g fiber*

Diet Exchanges: *0 milk, 3 vegetable, 0 fruit, 0 bread, 2½ meat, 1 fat*

Taco Bake

440 Calories

—Grace Schefter, Yakima, Wash.

"When I make this recipe ahead and store it covered in the refrigerator, the kids just cut squares and warm them in the microwave. Serve with chips (the baked kind) and enjoy!"

½ **pound extra-lean ground beef**

½ **pound ground turkey breast**

1 **can (15½ ounces) pinto beans, rinsed and drained**

1 **can (4 ounces) chopped green chile peppers, drained**

1 **envelope (1¼ ounces) reduced-sodium taco seasoning mix**

1 **cup (8 ounces) fat-free sour cream**

1 **cup (4 ounces) shredded reduced-fat Cheddar cheese**

Baked tortilla chips (optional)

Preheat the oven to 350°F. Coat a 9" × 9" baking dish with nonstick spray.

Warm a large nonstick skillet over medium-high heat. Add beef and turkey, stirring to break meat into pieces. Cook 10 minutes, or until no longer pink. Stir in beans, peppers, and taco seasoning mix. Spoon into the prepared baking dish. Spread sour cream evenly over the top. Sprinkle with cheese. Bake 30 minutes, or until heated through and cheese is bubbly. Serve with chips, if using.

Makes 4 servings

Per serving: *440 calories, 37 g protein, 30 g carbohydrates, 20 g fat, 83 mg cholesterol, 1,152 mg sodium, 0 g fiber*

Diet Exchanges: *0 milk, 0 vegetable, 0 fruit, 2 bread, 4 meat, 0 fat*

Red Chile Steak Burritos

537 Calories

—Marie Yakes, Papillion, Nebr.

"These burritos are the real deal—steak, chiles, and tomatoes cooked up right and served in flour tortillas. If you like, add reduced-fat Cheddar cheese and fat-free sour cream."

2 teaspoons olive oil

1 onion, finely chopped

3 garlic cloves, minced

1 pound London broil or other lean steak, finely chopped

1 tablespoon unbleached or all-purpose flour

2 cans (4½ ounces each) chopped green chile peppers, drained

1 can (28 ounces) tomatoes

1 teaspoon ground black pepper

8 large flour tortillas (12" diameter)

Warm oil in a large saucepan or Dutch oven over medium heat. Add onion and garlic. Cook 10 minutes, or until tender. Toss beef with flour. Add beef to the saucepan and cook 5 minutes, or until no longer pink. Stir in chile peppers, tomatoes (with juice), and black pepper. Heat to boiling over high heat. Reduce heat to low, cover, and simmer 45 minutes, or until meat is very tender, breaking up tomatoes with the back of a spoon.

Using a slotted spoon, remove about 3 tablespoons of meat and place it on a tortilla. Roll like an envelope to make an enclosed package. Repeat with remaining meat and tortillas. Top with sauce left in the pan.

Makes 4 servings

Per serving: *537 calories, 33 g protein, 60 g carbohydrates, 18 g fat, 58 mg cholesterol, 941 mg sodium, 5 g fiber*

Diet Exchanges: *0 milk, 1 vegetable, 0 fruit, 3 bread, 3 meat, 1 fat*

Splurge Meal

1 serving Red Chile Steak Burritos

1 ear corn on the cob with 2 tablespoons Roasted Garlic Spread (page 114)

½ cup sliced mango with ½ cup chocolate frozen yogurt sprinkled with chili powder

1,040 calories

Slow-Cooked Pork Stew

538 Calories

—C. Barber, Big Spring, Tex.

"The pork and vegetables in this dish taste best when cooked slowly. The meat becomes so tender, you can tear it with a fork. I usually make it in a Crock-Pot slow cooker, but you can bake it in a covered casserole, too. Follow the recipe using a Dutch oven or large casserole instead of a slow cooker. Cover tightly and bake at 275°F for 5 hours without disturbing."

2 pounds lean pork loin, cut into 1" cubes
½ pound baby carrots
3 large potatoes, cut into 1" cubes
2 parsnips, cut into 1" cubes
2 onions, cut into wedges
3 garlic cloves, minced
2 teaspoons ground black pepper
1 teaspoon dried thyme
1 teaspoon salt
2½ cups canned vegetable juice
2 tablespoons brown sugar
1 tablespoon mustard
4 teaspoons tapioca

Place pork in a slow cooker. Add carrots, potatoes, parsnips, onions, garlic, pepper, thyme, and salt.

In a medium bowl, combine vegetable juice, brown sugar, mustard, and tapioca. Pour over meat and vegetables.

Cover and cook on low 6 hours or high 4 hours.

Makes 6 servings

Per serving: *538 calories, 39 g protein, 64 g carbohydrates, 14 g fat, 71 mg cholesterol, 865 mg sodium, 7 g fiber*

Diet Exchanges: *0 milk, 1 vegetable, 0 fruit, 3 bread, 3½ meat, 0 fat*

Splurge Meal

1 serving Slow-Cooked Pork Stew
1 small roasted sweet potato
½ cup apple slices braised in apple juice
1 cup sugar-free coffee gelatin with 2 tablespoons vanilla yogurt

1,084 calories

Tuscan Bean Soup with Sausage

252 Calories

—Jana Talbot, Nashville, Tenn.

"We serve this hearty, satisfying soup with crusty bread and a green salad and call it dinner."

1 tablespoon olive oil

¼ pound loose Italian-style turkey sausage

2 teaspoons fennel seeds (optional)

1 onion, chopped

½ head green cabbage, shredded

2 garlic cloves, minced

1 can (16 ounces) white kidney or cannellini beans, rinsed and drained

2 cans (14½ ounces each) fat-free, reduced-sodium chicken broth

1 can (14 ounces) Italian-style stewed tomatoes

Warm oil in a large nonstick saucepan over medium heat. Add sausage and fennel seeds, if using. Cook 10 minutes, or until sausage is no longer pink. Remove sausage to a small bowl, leaving drippings in the saucepan.

Add onion to drippings in the saucepan. Cook 5 minutes, or until onion is tender. Stir in cabbage and garlic. Cook 2 minutes. Stir in beans, broth, tomatoes (with juice), and sausage. Heat to boiling.

Reduce heat to low, cover, and simmer 20 minutes.

Makes 4 servings

Per serving: *252 calories, 14 g protein, 29 g carbohydrates, 9 g fat, 23 mg cholesterol, 835 mg sodium, 8 g fiber*

Diet Exchanges: *0 milk, 2 vegetable, 0 fruit, 1 bread, 1 meat, 1 fat*

Fettuccine with Pot-Lickin' Chicken Sauce

429 Calories

—Lisa Smith, Flushing, N.Y.

*"*For a healthy twist to meat sauce, I use skinless chicken pieces instead of fatty ground beef.*"*

1 tablespoon olive oil

1 pound boneless, skinless chicken breast, cubed

1 green bell pepper, chopped

1 can (28 ounces) tomatoes packed in puree, or crushed tomatoes

1 small onion, quartered

4 garlic cloves

2 teaspoons sugar

2 teaspoons dried basil

½ teaspoon ground black pepper

1 can (4 ounces) pitted, sliced black olives, drained (optional)

8 ounces dried fettuccine

Warm oil in large saucepan over medium-high heat. Add chicken and bell pepper. Cook 5 minutes, or until chicken is no longer pink.

In a blender, combine tomatoes (with juice), onion, garlic, sugar, basil, and black pepper. Blend until smooth. Add to chicken. Reduce heat to medium-low and simmer 25 minutes, or until slightly thickened. Stir in olives, if using.

Meanwhile, cook fettuccine according to package directions. Drain.

Serve fettuccine topped with chicken sauce.

Makes 4 servings

Per serving: *429 calories, 28 g protein, 64 g carbohydrates, 6 g fat, 46 mg cholesterol, 534 mg sodium, 6 g fiber*

Diet Exchanges: *0 milk, 1 vegetable, 0 fruit, 3 bread, 2 meat, 0 fat*

FROM THE PROS

Canyon Ranch Health Resorts

Canyon Ranch Health Resorts, located in Tuscon and in Lenox, Massachusetts, have the good fortune of having menu consultant and low-fat cooking guru Jeanne Jones on board. She created this herb-infused spa favorite.

LAMB CHOPS WITH HERBED APRICOT SAUCE

238 Calories

4 boneless sirloin lamb chops ($\frac{1}{4}$ pound each), trimmed of all visible fat and skewered

$\frac{1}{2}$ teaspoon garlic salt

$\frac{1}{2}$ teaspoon ground black pepper

$\frac{1}{2}$ pound dried apricot halves

1 can (14$\frac{1}{2}$ ounces) chicken broth

$\frac{1}{2}$ teaspoon balsamic vinegar

$\frac{1}{2}$ teaspoon dried oregano

$\frac{1}{2}$ teaspoon dried thyme

$\frac{1}{4}$ teaspoon dried rosemary, crushed

$\frac{1}{4}$ teaspoon salt

$\frac{1}{8}$ teaspoon ground nutmeg

Sprinkle both sides of lamb evenly with garlic salt and pepper. Warm a large non-stick skillet over medium heat until hot. Add lamb and brown well on both sides.

In a medium saucepan, combine apricots and broth. Heat to boiling over high heat. Reduce heat to low and simmer 5 minutes, or until apricots are very soft. Transfer half of apricots and all of liquid to a blender or food processor. Add vinegar, oregano, thyme, rosemary, salt, and nutmeg. Puree. Pour over lamb. Sprinkle with remaining cooked apricots. Reduce heat to low, cover, and simmer 10 minutes, or until a thermometer inserted in center of a chop registers 160°F and juices run clear.

Makes 4 servings

Per serving: *238 calories, 25 g protein, 13 g carbohydrates, 9 g fat, 74 mg cholesterol, 638 mg sodium, 4 g fiber*

Diet Exchanges: *0 milk, 0 vegetable, 0 fruit, 1 bread, 2 meat, 0 fat*

Spicy Spaghetti Marinara

—Bonnie Voight, Weatogue, Conn.

"This very simple sauce can be doubled to serve later over tortellini or ravioli. Refrigerate the sauce for up to a week or freeze for up to 6 months. For a spicier sauce, add more red-pepper flakes."

1 pound spaghetti
2 tablespoons olive oil
1 small onion, chopped
3 garlic cloves, minced
1 cup red wine or nonalcoholic wine
1 can (28 ounces) plum tomatoes, chopped
2 teaspoons dried basil
½ teaspoon red-pepper flakes

Cook spaghetti according to package directions. Drain.

Meanwhile, warm oil in a large saucepan over medium-high heat. Add onion and cook 5 minutes. Stir in garlic and cook 1 minute. Stir in wine and cook 2 minutes. Add tomatoes (with juice), basil, and red-pepper flakes. Cook, uncovered, 20 minutes, or until reduced by one-third. Serve with spaghetti.

Makes 4 servings

Per serving: *583 calories, 18 g protein, 97 g carbohydrates, 9 g fat, 0 mg cholesterol, 467 mg sodium, 6 g fiber*

Diet Exchanges: *0 milk, 2 vegetable, 0 fruit, 5 bread, 0 meat, 2 fat*

Splurge Meal

1 serving Spicy Spaghetti Marinara

1 cup escarole with garlic croutons and 1 chopped hard-cooked egg

1 slice whole-wheat Italian bread rubbed with garlic and ½ teaspoon olive oil

1 serving Roasted Fruit Wraps with Dipping Sauce (page 308)

1,061 calories

Easy Rigatoni

427 Calories

—Lori Varney, Thunder Bay, Ontario

"This is a good make-ahead-and-freeze recipe. I often make a double batch. It's reassuring to know that I have it in the freezer to rescue me on busy nights! It's very filling, but not fattening."

2 tablespoons olive oil

1 onion, chopped

3 garlic cloves, crushed

1 can (6 ounces) tomato paste

1 can (28 ounces) crushed tomatoes

1 teaspoon sugar

1½ teaspoons dried oregano

1½ teaspoons dried basil

1 teaspoon salt

½ teaspoon ground black pepper

8 ounces rigatoni

2 tablespoons (½ ounce) grated Parmesan cheese

Warm oil in a medium skillet over medium heat. Add onion and garlic. Cook 10 minutes, or until tender. Add tomato paste and cook 3 minutes. Stir in tomatoes, sugar, oregano, basil, salt, and pepper. Heat to boiling. Reduce heat to medium-low, cover, and cook, stirring occasionally, 30 minutes.

Meanwhile, cook rigatoni according to package directions. Drain. Toss with sauce. Serve with cheese.

Makes 4 servings

Per serving: *427 calories, 16 g protein, 65 g carbohydrates, 11 g fat, 68 mg cholesterol, 938 mg sodium, 6 g fiber*

Diet Exchanges: *0 milk, 4 vegetable, 0 fruit, 3 bread, 0 meat, 2 fat*

The Spa at Doral

Guests of the Spa at Doral in Miami enjoy great-tasting food. The secret to intensifying the flavor of tomatoes is to remove some of the water. Add a pinch of crushed red-pepper flakes for a little extra kick.

LINGUINE MONTECATINI

295 Calories

8 plum tomatoes, cut in half
2 teaspoons olive oil
8 garlic cloves, peeled and thinly sliced
¼ pound fresh spinach
8 ounces linguine

Preheat the oven to 200°F. Place tomatoes, cut side up, on a rack in a large baking dish and bake 20 minutes, or until slightly dry. Coarsely chop.

Warm oil in a large nonstick skillet over medium heat. Add garlic, spinach, and tomatoes and cook until spinach is wilted.

Cook linguine according to package directions. Drain, add to the skillet, and toss well.

Makes 4 servings

Per serving: *295 calories, 10 g protein, 57 g carbohydrates, 4 g fat, 0 mg cholesterol, 43 mg sodium, 3 g fiber*

Diet Exchanges: *0 milk, 2 vegetable, 0 fruit, 3 bread, 0 meat, ½ fat*

Mushroom and Tofu Fettuccine

375 Calories

—George Toro, Phoenix

"Evaporated milk adds richness without fat in this creamy pasta dish. The tofu adds protein without the cholesterol of meat and eggs."

8 ounces dried fettuccine or 6 ounces fresh

1 tablespoon olive oil

4 ounces low-fat firm tofu, drained and cut into small cubes

3 ounces shiitake or button mushrooms, chopped

2 garlic cloves, minced

1 can (7 ounces) fat-free evaporated milk

¼ cup chopped fresh parsley

2 tablespoons finely chopped pitted black olives

2 tablespoons finely chopped fresh chives

¾ teaspoon salt

½ teaspoon ground black pepper

⅓ cup (1½ ounces) grated Parmesan cheese

Cook fettuccine according to package directions. Drain.

Warm oil in a large skillet over medium-high heat. Add tofu and cook 5 minutes, or until lightly browned. Add mushrooms and cook 5 minutes, or until golden. Add garlic and cook 1 minute. Reduce heat to low and add evaporated milk, parsley, olives, chives, salt, and pepper. Cook 5 minutes, stirring occasionally. Add pasta and toss to mix. Cook 2 minutes, or until heated through. Serve with cheese.

Makes 4 servings

Per serving: *375 calories, 17 g protein, 56 g carbohydrates, 10 g fat, 8 mg cholesterol, 763 mg sodium, 2 g fiber*

Diet Exchanges: *0 milk, 0 vegetable, 0 fruit, 3 bread, 2 meat, 0 fat*

Mediterranean Pasta

—Tina Groves, Kanata, Ontario

"Bring home the flavors of the sun-drenched islands with this easy dish."

½ cup dry-pack sun-dried tomatoes

8 ounces angel hair pasta or thin spaghetti

1 tablespoon olive oil

2 onions, chopped

1 teaspoon dried oregano

1 package (10 ounces) fresh spinach, chopped, or 2 packages frozen chopped spinach, thawed and squeezed dry

2 tablespoons chopped pitted kalamata olives or black olives

1 cup (5 ounces) crumbled feta cheese

Soak tomatoes in hot water 10 minutes, or until soft. Drain and chop.

Cook pasta according to package directions. Drain.

Meanwhile, warm oil in a large nonstick skillet over medium heat. Add onions and oregano. Cook 10 minutes, or until onions are tender. Add spinach, cover, and cook 5 minutes, or until spinach is wilted. Add olives, tomatoes, and pasta. Toss to mix. Sprinkle with cheese.

Makes 4 servings

Per serving: *471 calories, 19 g protein, 59 g carbohydrates, 19 g fat, 50 mg cholesterol, 908 mg sodium, 5 g fiber*

Diet Exchanges: *0 milk, 2 vegetable, 0 fruit, 3 bread, 1 meat, 3 fat*

EYES ON THE SIZE

Knowing and doing are two different things. You may know that you want to eat 1 cup of pasta with your pork dinner, but dishing out 1 cup is another matter entirely. That doesn't mean you have to pull out the measuring cups. Use a few visual cues instead. Picture the following objects when serving up your favorite foods. (To see what counts as a serving and how many servings to eat, see pages 11, 16, 17, and 20.)

- Light bulb = 1 cup
- Closed fist = 1 cup
- Tennis ball = ½ cup
- Ping-Pong ball = 2 tablespoons
- Deck of cards = 3 ounces (of cooked meat, fish, or chicken, for instance)
- Woman's palm = 3 ounces
- Top of thumb (from tip to 2nd joint) = 1 teaspoon
- Top of thumb (from tip to 2nd joint) = 1 ounce (of cheese, for instance)

Angel Hair Pasta with Clam Pesto

509 Calories

—Tracy Viselli, Annandale, Va.

"Classic pesto recipes are made with lots of olive oil, and that means lots of calories. Adding bread crumbs cuts the fat and calories way back without losing body. The herbal taste is still intense and fresh. I sometimes add finely chopped tomatoes for more flavor."

8 ounces angel hair pasta

2 cans (8 ounces each) minced clams

1 slice white bread, crust removed

1 cup loosely packed fresh basil

3 tablespoons pine nuts

2 garlic cloves

½ teaspoon salt

2 tablespoons olive oil

½ cup finely chopped tomatoes (optional)

2 tablespoons (½ ounce) grated Parmesan cheese

Cook pasta according to package directions. Drain and place in a large bowl.

Meanwhile, drain clams, reserving ¼ cup liquid.

Tear bread into large pieces and place in a food processor or blender. Process or blend to fine crumbs. Add basil, pine nuts, garlic, salt, oil, and clam liquid. Process until a smooth paste forms.

Add clams, basil mixture, and tomatoes (if using) to hot pasta. Toss to mix. Serve with cheese.

Makes 4 servings

Per serving: *509 calories, 40 g protein, 53 g carbohydrates, 15 g fat, 78 mg cholesterol, 488 mg sodium, 2 g fiber*

Diet Exchanges: *0 milk, 0 vegetable, 0 fruit, 4 bread, 2½ meat, 0 fat*

Splurge Meal

1 Virgin Mary (spiced tomato juice)

1 serving Angel Hair Pasta with Clam Pesto

½ cup chilled steamed green beans

½ cup vanilla frozen yogurt splashed with warm espresso

1,028 calories

Canyon Ranch Health Resorts

Salmon is high in heart-healthy omega-3 fatty acids, which is why it's often featured at Canyon Ranch Health Resorts, located in Tuscon and in Lenox, Massachusetts. This marinade convinces even non-fish-eaters that good-for-you food tastes great, too.

SALMON TERIYAKI *448 Calories*

½ cup reduced-sodium soy sauce

2 tablespoons rice vinegar

3 garlic cloves, cut in half

1 tablespoon finely chopped fresh ginger

1½ cups (12 ounces) frozen unsweetened apple juice concentrate, undiluted and thawed

½ cup finely chopped scallions

6 salmon steaks (6 ounces each)

In a blender, combine soy sauce, vinegar, garlic, ginger, and apple juice. Puree until smooth. Pour into a large glass baking dish. Add scallions and salmon. Cover tightly and refrigerate at least 8 hours, turning fish occasionally.

Preheat the oven to 350°F. Uncover and bake salmon in its marinade 8 to 10 minutes, or until fish is just opaque.

Makes 4 servings

Per serving: *448 calories, 39 g protein, 48 g carbohydrates, 10 g fat, 65 mg cholesterol, 1,306 mg sodium, 0 g fiber*

Diet Exchanges: *0 milk, 0 vegetable, 2 fruit, 0 bread, 4 meat, 0 fat*

Splurge Meal

1 serving Salmon Teriyaki

1 serving Lentil-Rice Salad (page 272)

1 small baked sweet potato

1 serving Chocolate-Pecan Meringues (page 294)

1,017 calories

Crab Cakes

232 Calories

—Kathy Fruendt, East Stroudsburg, Pa.

"When I make these crab cakes, I use chowder crackers because they are unsalted. But unsalted saltines work, too. Serve with low-fat coleslaw."

12 chowder or soda crackers, crushed (1 cup)

2 egg whites

1 tablespoon Worcestershire sauce

2 teaspoons crab-boil seasoning, such as Old Bay

¼ teaspoon crushed red-pepper flakes

6 tablespoons reduced-fat mayonnaise

1 pound lump crabmeat

1 teaspoon pickle relish

1 teaspoon minced onion

4 lemon wedges

In a large bowl, combine crackers, egg whites, Worcestershire sauce, crab-boil seasoning, red-pepper flakes, and 2 tablespoons mayonnaise. Gently fold in crabmeat. Form into 4 patties.

Coat a large skillet with nonstick spray and warm over medium heat. Add crab cakes and cook 20 minutes, turning once, or until crispy.

In a small bowl, combine relish, onion, and remaining 4 tablespoons mayonnaise. Serve crab cakes with sauce and lemon wedges.

Makes 4 servings

Per serving: *232 calories, 23 g protein, 13 g carbohydrates, 10 g fat, 121 mg cholesterol, 894 mg sodium, 0 g fiber*

Diet Exchanges: *0 milk, 0 vegetable, 0 fruit, 1 bread, 2 meat, 0 fat*

Slimming Meal

1 serving Crab Cakes

1 serving Asian Slaw (page 252)

1 whole-wheat roll

½ broiled peach with 2 tablespoons low-fat vanilla yogurt

425 calories

It Worked for Me!

Norma Abler

V I T A L   S T A T S

Weight lost: 48 pounds

Time kept it off: 11 years

Weight-loss strategies: Weight training, cycling, running, low-fat diet

Weight-maintenance strategies: Has a 7-pound gain/loss window, weighs in every 2 weeks, jogs

Ten years ago, Norma Abler was an overweight housewife who turned to a crash diet to lose 30 pounds. After adding exercise to her routine, she went from saggy to shapely. She has since competed in 30 triathlons.

"Losing 30 pounds in 6 weeks sounds great to most people, but it left me looking like a deflated balloon. I had saggy, loose skin hanging everywhere. I looked so bad that I hid under long sleeves and long pants and even considered gaining the weight back. I really believed that I'd need surgery to get rid of the flabby skin, but a friend convinced me that what I needed was exercise to rebuild the muscle that I'd lost on the crash diet.

"I found a friend to walk with, and we started with only a half-mile. We eventually worked up to 3 miles a day. Then, scheduling conflicts kept me from meeting my friend, so I joined a fitness center. There, I started riding a stationary bike. That's when I real-

ized how out of shape I was. Despite my regular walking, I could do only 3 minutes on the bike before I was exhausted. Luckily, encouragement from other club members kept me going. Within a few months, I was riding the bike for 30 minutes.

"Then, I began lifting weights. It was really a struggle at first because I was so weak. But gradually, I started getting stronger. I loved it. After about 9 months, I noticed that the back part of my arms that used to wobble and wag when I waved had turned into strong, firm muscle. But because I was lifting too much too fast, I injured my lower back. My doctor recommended that I get hooked up with a personal trainer. I found Rhonda, who showed me that by moving slowly through exercise and concentrating on what I was doing, I could isolate different muscle groups and make my workouts more intense and effective. That made a huge difference in my appearance. The toned, shapely muscles filled out all the saggy skin.

"Rhonda also suggested that I keep a log of everything I eat. She showed me all the fat in my diet—doughnuts, cheese, fried chicken. She encouraged me to replace these high-fat foods with complex carbohydrates such as pasta, potatoes, and rice; fruits and vegetables; and lean meats like chicken, turkey, and fish. The diet and exercise changes resulted in big changes in my body.

"But I didn't stop there. I continued to challenge myself and have since completed 30 triathlons! In the last one I completed, I came in first in my age group (60 to 69 years) and 142nd out of 286 participants. I was the oldest woman in my age group, but I beat both men and women. I'm getting better all the time." ◼

Norma's Grilled Garlicky Salmon

268 Calories

"A basil vinaigrette gives this summery salmon great aroma. Grilling over hot coals intensifies the taste. You can also broil it 3" to 4" from the heat."

2 tablespoons red wine vinegar

2 tablespoons finely chopped fresh basil leaves

1 tablespoon olive oil

2 garlic cloves, minced

4 salmon steaks or fillets (6 ounces each)

In a large baking dish, combine vinegar, basil, oil, and garlic. Add salmon and turn to coat. Cover and refrigerate at least 15 minutes or up to 2 hours.

Coat a grill rack with nonstick spray. Preheat the grill. Grill salmon 10 minutes per inch of thickness, turning halfway through cooking time.

Makes 4 servings

Per serving: *268 calories, 33 g protein, 1 g carbohydrates, 14 g fat, 91 mg cholesterol, 73 mg sodium, 0 g fiber*

Diet Exchanges: *0 milk, 0 vegetable, 0 fruit, 0 bread, 3½ meat, 0 fat*

Baked Catfish with Dill Sauce

293 Calories

—Judy Allen, Melrose, Mass.

" I've been fond of catfish since childhood, when my brother fished for it in our Massachusetts ponds and lakes. (We called it horned pout back then!) I sometimes use this recipe for bluefish, too. "

¼ **cup fat-free milk**

2 **catfish fillets (1½ pounds), cut into 4 pieces**

1 **cup (8 ounces) fat-free plain yogurt**

1 **tablespoon dried dill**

1 **slice whole-wheat bread**

1 **tablespoon melted butter or margarine**

1 **tablespoon Dijon mustard**

¼ **teaspoon salt**

Preheat the oven to 325°F.

Pour milk into a shallow baking dish. Add catfish.

In a cup, combine yogurt and dill. Spread on top of fish. Bake, uncovered, 15 minutes.

Meanwhile, place bread in a food processor or blender and chop to make fine crumbs. Pour into a small bowl and stir in butter or margarine, mustard, and salt.

Sprinkle bread-crumb mixture over fish. Bake 10 minutes, or until fish flakes easily and crumbs are browned.

Makes 4 servings

Per serving: *293 calories, 36 g protein, 10 g carbohydrates, 11 g fat, 107 mg cholesterol, 475 mg sodium, 2 g fiber*

Diet Exchanges: *½ milk, 0 vegetable, 0 fruit, 0 bread, 3 meat, 0 fat*

Carolina Wellness Retreat

To make lifestyle changes that last, food should be easy to make and delicious. That's the approach of Colleen Wracker, R.D., a nutritionist at the Carolina Wellness Retreat in Hilton Head, South Carolina. This simple recipe is like a breath of fresh air.

FLOUNDER DIJON

184 Calories

4 large carrots, cut into matchsticks
2 tablespoons chopped parsley
1 teaspoon olive oil
⅛ teaspoon salt
⅛ teaspoon ground black pepper
4 flounder or cod fillets (¼ pound each)
2 teaspoons stone-ground Dijon mustard
1 teaspoon honey

In an 11" × 7" microwaveable dish, combine carrots, parsley, oil, salt, and pepper. Cover with waxed paper. Microwave on high power 5 minutes, stirring once. Fold thin fillets to make each an even thickness. Place on top of carrots in the corners of the dish with the thickest parts toward the outside.

In a small bowl, combine mustard and honey. Spread over fish. Cover with waxed paper. Microwave on high power 2 minutes. Rotate fillets, placing cooked parts toward the center, and cook 1 to 3 minutes more, or just until fish flakes easily. Let stand, covered, 2 minutes.

Makes 4 servings

Per serving: *184 calories, 28 g protein, 9 g carbohydrates, 3 g fat, 77 mg cholesterol, 283 mg sodium, 2 g fiber*

Diet Exchanges: *0 milk, 1 vegetable, 0 fruit, 0 bread, 2 meat, 0 fat*

Slimming Meal

1 serving Flounder Dijon
½ cup boiled red potatoes tossed with Dijon mustard and chopped chives
½ cup peas with chopped mint
1 chocolate wafer cookie
1 cup orange sections

407 calories

Salmon with Lemon-Caper Cream Sauce

—Michael Ostrowsky, Riverton, Utah

"A sinfully rich tasting lemony sauce makes salmon a real treat. I sometimes serve this with almond green beans and roasted potatoes."

2 teaspoons olive oil
1 garlic clove, minced
¼ cup lemon juice
2 tablespoons capers
1 teaspoon lemon-pepper seasoning
½ cup (4 ounces) fat-free sour cream
4 salmon steaks (6 ounces each)

Coat a broiler pan with nonstick spray. Preheat the broiler.

In a small saucepan, warm oil over medium heat. Add garlic and cook 1 minute. Reduce heat to low. Stir in lemon juice, capers, and lemon-pepper seasoning. Cook 5 minutes. Add sour cream and cook 5 minutes, or until heated through.

Meanwhile, place salmon on the prepared broiler pan. Broil 4" from the heat 5 minutes. Turn and broil 5 minutes more, or until fish is just opaque. Serve with sauce.

Makes 4 servings

Per serving: 319 calories, 43 g protein, 3 g carbohydrates, 14 g fat, 76 mg cholesterol, 338 mg sodium, 0 g fiber

Diet Exchanges: 0 milk, 0 vegetable, 0 fruit, 0 bread, 4 meat, 0 fat

Shrimp Creole

166 Calories

—Sara D. Gullett, Fayette, Ala.

"In Alabama, we enjoy fresh seafood from our coast. And we think the best way to serve shrimp is a la Creole. *Here's a lower-fat and quicker way to enjoy the traditional dish. Serve over hot cooked rice."*

2 bacon strips
1 onion, chopped
½ green bell pepper, chopped
1 celery rib, chopped
1 garlic clove, minced
1 can (16 ounces) chopped tomatoes
1 bay leaf
½ teaspoon salt
¼ teaspoon ground black pepper
¼ teaspoon Worcestershire sauce
¼ teaspoon hot-pepper sauce
1 pound fresh or thawed frozen medium shrimp, peeled and deveined

Cook bacon in a large skillet over medium heat until crisp. Remove bacon to paper towels. Crumble when cool. Remove and discard all but 1 tablespoon drippings from the skillet.

In hot drippings over medium heat, cook onion, bell pepper, and celery 5 minutes, or until tender. Stir in garlic and cook 1 minute. Add tomatoes (with juice), bay leaf, salt, black pepper, Worcestershire sauce, and hot-pepper sauce. Heat to boiling. Reduce heat to low and simmer 20 minutes. Add shrimp and bacon. Cook 10 minutes, or until shrimp are opaque. Remove and discard bay leaf before serving.

Makes 4 servings

Per serving: *166 calories, 22 g protein, 12 g carbohydrates, 3 g fat, 178 mg cholesterol, 820 mg sodium, 3 g fiber*

Diet Exchanges: *0 milk, 3 vegetable, 0 fruit, 0 bread, 1 meat, 0 fat*

Slimming Meal

1 serving Shrimp Creole
½ cup brown rice
1 cup curly endive with 1 tablespoon each bacon and low-fat vinaigrette
1 wedge watermelon

394 calories

Brown Rice Vegetable Stir-Fry

273 Calories

—Conrad and Tricia Holsomback, Hodges, S.C.

"This is a great dish for using leftover rice. (One cup uncooked rice makes about 3 cups cooked.) Add bits of cooked meat, shrimp, and/or tofu for more protein. Water chestnuts, green beans, and sprouts also make great additions to the sautéed vegetables."

1 cup brown rice

2½ cups fat-free, reduced-sodium chicken broth

1 tablespoon sesame or peanut oil

2 large leeks, white part only, sliced

2 celery ribs, thinly sliced

2 carrots, thinly sliced

2 garlic cloves, minced

2 tablespoons soy sauce

1 tablespoon rice vinegar or cider vinegar

1 tablespoon oyster sauce

Cook and stir rice in a large, dry saucepan over medium heat 5 minutes, or until fragrant and toasted. Add broth. Reduce heat to low, cover, and simmer 40 to 45 minutes, or until rice is tender and liquid is absorbed.

Meanwhile, warm oil in a large skillet over medium-high heat. Add leeks, celery, carrots, and garlic. Cook 5 minutes, stirring frequently, or until vegetables are crisp-tender. Stir in rice, soy sauce, vinegar, and oyster sauce.

Makes 4 servings

Per serving: *273 calories, 7 g protein, 51 g carbohydrates, 5 g fat, 0 mg cholesterol, 679 mg sodium, 5 g fiber*

Diet Exchanges: *0 milk, 3 vegetable, 0 fruit, 2 bread, 0 meat, 1 fat*

Quick Black Bean Enchiladas

640 Calories

—Wendie Clark, Fairfax, Vt.

"Fifteen-minute meals are a godsend in my household. This one tastes like you spent more time on it. Make it as spicy or mild as you like by using more or less of the jalapeño peppers and hot or mild salsa."

1½ **cups (12 ounces) 1% low-sodium cottage cheese**

2 **cans (14 ounces each) black beans, rinsed and drained**

1–2 **jalapeño chile peppers, seeded and chopped (wear plastic gloves when handling)**

2 **cups (8 ounces) shredded reduced-fat Cheddar cheese**

8 **flour tortillas (10" diameter)**

1 **jar (16 ounces) salsa**

Preheat the oven to 350°F. Coat a 13" × 9" baking dish with nonstick spray.

In a large bowl, mix cottage cheese, beans, peppers, and 1 cup cheese. Spoon a scant cup of mixture onto a tortilla. Roll up jelly-roll style. Place, seam side down, in the prepared baking dish. Repeat with remaining filling and tortillas.

Pour salsa evenly over enchiladas. Sprinkle with remaining 1 cup cheese. Cover with foil and bake 20 minutes. Remove foil and bake 10 minutes, or until hot and bubbly.

Makes 4 servings

Per serving: *640 calories, 40 g protein, 85 g carbohydrates, 15 g fat, 30 mg cholesterol, 1,193 mg sodium, 5 g fiber*

Diet Exchanges: *0 milk, 0 vegetable, 0 fruit, 5 bread, 3 meat, 0 fat*

Splurge Meal

1 serving Quick Black Bean Enchiladas

2 tablespoons salsa

½ sliced avocado with orange sections and low-fat vinaigrette with fresh oregano

1 serving Quick Rice Pudding (page 299)

1,017 calories

Black Bean and Corn Burritos

200 Calories

—Lissa Hill, Pasadena, Calif.

" These are very messy to eat yet very satisfying. (Use a fork if necessary.) With so many tastes and textures, there's no need for lots of cheese here. "

1 teaspoon vegetable oil

¼ cup chopped red bell pepper

1 can (4 ounces) chopped green chile peppers, drained

½ cup frozen corn, thawed

½ teaspoon chili powder

¼ teaspoon ground black pepper

1 can (16 ounces) black beans, rinsed and drained

4 whole-wheat tortillas (12" diameter), warmed

½ cup (4 ounces) fat-free sour cream

½ cup salsa

¼ cup chopped red onion or scallions

½–2 jalapeño chile peppers, seeded and chopped (wear plastic gloves when handling)

2 tablespoons lime juice

¼ cup chopped fresh cilantro

Warm oil in a medium nonstick skillet over medium heat. Add bell pepper and cook 5 minutes, or until soft. Add green chile pepper, corn, chili powder, and black pepper. Cook 1 minute. Add beans, mashing them with the back of a wooden spoon until slightly creamy. Cook 8 minutes.

Spread bean mixture on tortillas and top each with sour cream, salsa, red onion or scallions, jalapeño chile peppers, lime juice, and cilantro. Roll up like an envelope to make an enclosed package.

Makes 4

Per burrito: *200 calories, 10 g protein, 41 g carbohydrates, 1 g fat, 0 mg cholesterol, 930 mg sodium, 17 g fiber*

Diet Exchanges: *0 milk, 1 vegetable, 0 fruit, 2 bread, 0 meat, 0 fat*

Slimming Meal

1 serving Black Bean and Corn Burritos

1 whole sliced tomato with red onions

1 cup lemon sorbet

1 chocolate wafer cookie

404 calories

Ensalada Mexicana Vegetariana

514 Calories

—Stephanie Goddard, Athens, Ohio

"Taco salad never looked better. Look for bulgur in the grain aisle of your supermarket."

Cook bulgur according to package directions.

Warm oil in a large skillet over medium heat. Add onion and cook 5 minutes. Add garlic and cook 2 minutes, or until onion is tender. Reduce heat to low. Stir in beans, cumin, salt, and cooked bulgur. Cook 5 minutes, or until hot.

For each serving, arrange a layer of one-fourth of tortilla chips on a plate. Top each with layers of lettuce, bulgur mixture, tomatoes, cucumber, pepper, olives, and cheese. Finish each with 1 tablespoon sour cream.

Makes 4 big servings

Per serving: 514 calories, 24 g protein, 73 g carbohydrates, 18 g fat, 20 mg cholesterol, 917 mg sodium, 17 g fiber

Diet Exchanges: 0 milk, 1 vegetable, 0 fruit, 4 bread, 1 meat, 2 fat

1 cup bulgur

2 tablespoons olive oil

1 small onion, chopped

2 garlic cloves, minced

1 can (16 ounces) refried beans

1 teaspoon ground cumin

¼ teaspoon salt

3 cups crumbled baked tortilla chips

3 cups shredded lettuce

2 tomatoes, finely chopped

1 cucumber, peeled, seeded, and finely chopped

1 green bell pepper, finely chopped

½ cup olives, chopped

1 cup (4 ounces) shredded reduced-fat Cheddar cheese

¼ cup (2 ounces) fat-free sour cream

Splurge Meal

1 cup prepared gazpacho

1 corn muffin

1 serving Ensalada Mexicana Vegetariana

½ sliced mango with cinnamon sugar

798 calories

Delightful Weekend Dinners

Chicken Fettuccine 182

Chinese Chicken in a Bag 184

Secret Chicken 185

White Chicken Chili 186

Pollo Loco 188

Roast Sirloin Steak 189

Joan's Jewel of the Nile
    Chicken Kabobs 191

Confetti Meat Loaf 192

El Dorado Casserole 194

Grilled Pork Chops 196

Garbanzo-Sausage Soup 197

Spicy Pork and Beans Stew 198

Lentil-Sausage Stew 200

Lemon Red Snapper with Jalapeños 201

Seafood Chowder 202

Shrimp Risotto 205

Shrimp in Tomato Sauce over Pasta 206

Asian Veggie Wraps 208

Very Vegetable Soup 209

Vegetable Lasagna 210

Spinach Lasagna 212

Meximix 213

Jodie's Pineapple Pizza 215

Broccoli-Stuffed Shells 216

Veggie Cassoulet 218

Black-Eyed Pea Stew 220

Braised Tofu 221

Eggplant Parmesan 222

Unstuffed Cabbage 223

Mediterranean Stuffed Eggplant 224

Chicken Fettuccine

458 Calories

—Cheryl Tomasz, Amesbury, Mass.

" I save this dish for those busy weekends when I don't feel like cooking. It comes together quickly, yet still has an elegant flavor. "

1 large onion, sliced

2 garlic cloves, minced

1 cup dry white wine or nonalcoholic white wine

1 pound boneless, skinless chicken breasts, cut into thin strips

1 can (8 ounces) black olives, sliced

1 large tomato, chopped

1 can (8 ounces) low-sodium tomato sauce

1/2 teaspoon ground thyme

1/4 teaspoon ground black pepper

8 ounces dried fettuccine or 6 ounces fresh

1 bunch chives or 2 scallions, chopped

Coat a large nonstick skillet with nonstick spray and warm over medium heat. Add onion and garlic. Cook 4 minutes, or until soft. Add wine and heat to boiling over high heat. Reduce heat to medium and simmer 5 minutes.

Add chicken and simmer 10 minutes, or until no longer pink. Add olives, tomato, tomato sauce, thyme, and pepper. Heat through.

Meanwhile, cook fettuccine according to package directions. Drain.

Serve pasta topped with chicken and sauce. Sprinkle with chives or scallions.

Makes 4 servings

Per serving: *458 calories, 26 g protein, 54 g carbohydrates, 10 g fat, 46 mg cholesterol, 488 mg sodium, 2 g fiber*

Diet Exchanges: *0 milk, 3 vegetable, 0 fruit, 3 bread, 2 meat, 0 fat*

FROM THE PROS

Canyon Ranch Health Resorts

At Canyon Ranch Health Resorts, located in Tuscon and in Lenox, Massachusetts, guests have come to expect great-tasting food. Menu consultant Jeanne Jones delivers—and then some—with this simple Asian-flavored chicken.

CHINESE CHICKEN IN A BAG

229 Calories

1 **whole chicken (3 to 4 pounds)**
1 **teaspoon ground ginger**
½ **teaspoon Chinese five-spice powder**
1½ **teaspoons salt**
3 **scallions, cut into 3-inch pieces**
1 **tablespoon unbleached or all-purpose flour**
3 **tablespoons hoisin sauce**
3 **tablespoons honey**
2 **tablespoons dry sherry or apple juice**
½ **teaspoon coarsely ground black pepper**

Rinse chicken inside and out with cold water and pat dry with paper towels. In a cup, mix ginger, five-spice powder, and ½ teaspoon salt. Rub all over inside of chicken. Place scallions in cavity.

Put flour in a large (14" × 20") oven-safe cooking bag and shake to coat inside of the bag.

In a small bowl, mix hoisin sauce, honey, sherry or apple juice, pepper, and remaining 1 teaspoon salt. Rub all over outside of chicken. Place chicken in the bag with any remaining sauce. Close bag. Place the bag in a 13" × 9" baking dish. Refrigerate at least 4 hours.

Preheat the oven to 350°F.

Cut six ½" slits in the top of the bag. Place chicken in the bag in the baking dish in the oven, making sure that the bag does not overhang the dish. Bake 1 hour, or until a thermometer inserted in a breast registers 180°F and juices run clear.

Remove chicken from the oven and allow to stand 10 minutes. Carefully cut the bag open. Remove chicken from the bag and pour juices into a bowl. Place the bowl in the freezer a few minutes so that fat can congeal on top for easy removal. Cut chicken into serving pieces and serve with the defatted juices.

Makes 8 servings

Per serving: *229 calories, 23 g protein, 17 g carbohydrates, 7 g fat, 63 mg cholesterol, 558 mg sodium, 0 g fiber*

Diet Exchanges: *0 milk, 0 vegetable, 0 fruit, 1½ bread, 1½ meat, 0 fat*

Secret Chicken

269 Calories

—Roberta Handel, Delray Beach, Fla.

"The 'secret' is that this is the best, easiest, most healthful chicken recipe you will ever find. Try it once. You will use this recipe forever! It's delicious hot or cold."

3 pounds skinless chicken parts, trimmed
  of visible fat
1–1½ teaspoons seasoned salt
  1 lemon

Place chicken in a resealable plastic bag. Add salt and shake to coat the pieces. Squeeze juice from lemon and add it to chicken. Toss to coat. Seal the bag and refrigerate overnight to marinate.

Preheat the oven to 325°F. Place chicken in a large nonstick baking dish and cook 45 minutes to 1 hour, or until a thermometer inserted in thickest portion registers 170°F and juices run clear.

Makes 4 servings

Per serving: *269 calories, 50 g protein, 1 g carbohydrates, 6 g fat, 137 mg cholesterol, 499 mg sodium, 0 g fiber*

Diet Exchanges: *0 milk, 0 vegetable, 0 fruit, 0 bread, 3½ fat, 0 fat*

White Chicken Chili

357 Calories

—Debbie Wilson, Flowery Branch, Ga.

"I serve this Crock-Pot chili with a small amount of fat-free sour cream or fat-free yogurt. If you don't have a Crock-Pot, cook it in a covered casserole in the oven set at 250°F."

1 tablespoon olive oil

¾ pound boneless, skinless chicken breast, cubed

1 large onion, chopped

2 garlic cloves, minced

1 cup dry white wine or chicken broth

2 cans (12 ounces each) navy beans, rinsed and drained

1 teaspoon mustard powder

1 teaspoon ground cumin

½ teaspoon salt

⅛ teaspoon ground black pepper

4 cups (4 ounces) baked tortilla chips

½ cup (2 ounces) shredded reduced-fat extra-sharp Cheddar cheese

Warm oil in a large skillet over medium-high heat. Add chicken and cook 10 minutes, or until chicken is no longer pink, stirring frequently. Remove and set aside. Add onion and garlic to the skillet and cook 5 minutes, or until tender.

Spoon chicken, onion, and garlic into a slow cooker. Add wine or broth, beans, mustard powder, cumin, salt, and pepper. Simmer on low 5 to 6 hours. Serve over tortilla chips and sprinkle with cheese.

Makes 6 servings

Per serving: *357 calories, 27 g protein, 43 g carbohydrates, 6 g fat, 40 mg cholesterol, 867 mg sodium, 2 g fiber*

Diet Exchanges: *0 milk, 0 vegetable, 0 fruit, 2½ bread, 2 meat, 0 fat*

Pollo Loco

224 Calories

—Kelly Gracey, Wooster, Ohio

"This is a crazy kind of chicken chili. (In Spanish, pollo means chicken and loco means crazy.) I modified my beef chili recipe. If you like your chili spicy, don't remove the seeds from the jalapeño pepper."

1 onion, chopped

2 teaspoons olive oil

1 pound ground chicken or turkey breast

2 garlic cloves, minced

1 jalapeño chile pepper, seeded and chopped (wear plastic gloves when handling)

1 tablespoon ground cumin

2 cans (14½ ounces each) Mexican-style stewed tomatoes

1 can (28 ounces) low-sodium tomato sauce

1 can (4 ounces) mushrooms, drained

1 can (15½ ounces) small white beans, rinsed and drained

1 can (15 ounces) pink beans, rinsed and drained

½ cup (2 ounces) shredded low-fat Monterey Jack cheese

Sauté onion in oil in a large saucepan over medium heat until soft. Add chicken or turkey and cook 5 minutes, or until no longer pink. Add garlic, pepper, and cumin. Cook 5 minutes longer. Add tomatoes (with juice), tomato sauce, and mushrooms. Heat to boiling. Reduce heat to low, cover, and simmer over medium-low heat 30 minutes, stirring frequently. Add beans and continue cooking another 15 minutes. Serve in a bowl and top with cheese.

Makes 8 servings

Per serving: *224 calories, 19 g protein, 30 g carbohydrates, 4 g fat, 28 mg cholesterol, 545 mg sodium, 6 g fiber*

Diet Exchanges: *0 milk, 3 vegetable, 0 fruit, 1 bread, 1 meat, 0 fat*

Roast Sirloin Steak

234 Calories

—Scott Mingus, Allentown, Pa.

"Whenever the hankering for beef strikes, I turn to this ultra-simple recipe."

1½ pounds sirloin steak (2" thick),
    trimmed of visible fat
 1 cup low-fat Italian dressing
½ teaspoon ground black pepper

Place steak in a large roasting pan. Coat completely with dressing. Cover and marinate in the refrigerator 2 hours or up to 8 hours, turning occasionally. Drain and discard marinade.

Preheat the oven to 400°F.

Uncover the pan and roast steak in the oven 35 to 40 minutes, or until a thermometer inserted in center registers 145°F for medium-rare. Remove from the oven and sprinkle with black pepper. Let stand 10 minutes before slicing.

Makes 4 servings

Per serving: *234 calories, 33 g protein, 4 g carbohydrates, 7 g fat, 97 mg cholesterol, 912 mg sodium, 0 g fiber*

Diet Exchanges: *0 milk, 0 vegetable, 0 fruit, 0 bread, 3 meat, 0 fat*

TIP: This dish tastes great with vegetables added to the roasting pan. While the steak is roasting, place another ¼ cup Italian dressing in a medium bowl. Add 2 cups chopped vegetables, such as halved and sliced zucchini, red onion wedges, and halved cherry tomatoes. Toss to coat. Let sit 5 minutes. Remove steak from oven after 20 minutes of cooking time and place vegetables in the roasting pan around steak. Roast 15 to 20 minutes, or until vegetables are soft.

(Twice-Baked Potatoes recipe on page 229)

It Worked for Me!

Joan Lunden

VITAL STATS

Weight lost: 50 pounds

Time kept it off: 10 years

Weight-loss strategies: Kept food diary, low-fat foods, daily exercise

Weight-maintenance strategies: Healthy eating, exercise, stress reduction through meditation and visualization

One of television's most versatile reporters and former early morning host has found inspiration, balance, and health in her new life.

"I chose to make a life change at age 39. I was 50 pounds overweight, unhappy with my life, and downright frightened about my health. One thing I knew for sure, in the deepest part of my soul, was that if I got healthy, I would get happy. So I changed the way I ate, and I changed the way I thought about and perceived food and exercise."

Joan tried every diet out there, but she soon realized that dieting is a false state of living that she could not maintain. Joan is a great example of the principle that changes come slowly if they are going to be permanent. "There's no magic bullet. It takes time, effort, desire, and the right information and strategy to make the change," she explains. "Once you've learned the ground rules, they will become second nature. And eating healthfully can become an integral and painless part

of your lifestyle." She has the same lifelong approach to her exercise commitment.

Joan admits that the idea of going to the gym to get into shape was a drag at first. Then, her pal and trainer suggested that she look at working out the way an athlete does: as training for a particular goal. That was good advice for Joan. Once she figured out what sport she was training for (mountain climbing) and set a date for her event (6 months out), she had a goal to work toward. Going to the gym became exciting and fun. "Exercise isn't about suffering," she says. "Exercise is about finding something you enjoy doing that also happens to protect your health, lift your mood, and give your energy level a kick in the butt."

Joan realized that being physically fit and eating healthy was only part of the equation. She found that lasting health also meant taking care of her mind and spirit. She learned about the mind-body connection and used this concept to improve her overall well-being. "I have been on the most fantastic journey, seeking out great adventures for my mind, body, and spirit," she smiles. "I'm constantly reaching for a happier, healthier life." ◾

Joan's Jewel of the Nile Chicken Kabobs

230 Calories

"These kabobs are always a hit with the family. The colorful vegetables are like jewels on a skewer and the marinade gives them a Middle Eastern flavor. They make great party fare, too."

¼ **cup chopped parsley**

¼ **cup (2 ounces) fat-free plain yogurt**

¼ **cup lemon juice**

2 **tablespoons olive oil**

1 **tablespoon chopped fresh cilantro**

1 **tablespoon paprika**

1 **tablespoon curry powder**

2 **teaspoons ground cumin**

2 **small garlic cloves, minced**

½ **teaspoon salt**

½ **teaspoon ground black pepper**

1 **pound boneless, skinless chicken breasts, cubed**

1 **small yellow or orange bell pepper, cut into 1" pieces**

1 **yellow summer squash, sliced ¼" thick**

8 **cherry tomatoes**

1 **onion, cut into ½" wedges**

In a large bowl, combine parsley, yogurt, lemon juice, oil, cilantro, paprika, curry powder, cumin, garlic, salt, and black pepper. Add chicken and toss to coat. Cover and refrigerate at least 20 minutes or up to 2 hours.

Heat a large saucepan of lightly salted water to boiling. Drop in bell pepper and cook 2 minutes. Remove with a slotted spoon and drain. Drop in squash and cook 1 minute. Remove with a slotted spoon and drain. Thread a cherry tomato on each of 4 skewers, then alternately thread marinated chicken, bell pepper, squash, and onion, ending with a cherry tomato.

Coat a grill rack or broiler pan with non-stick spray. Preheat the grill or broiler. Grill kabobs 4" to 6" from heat for 3 to 4 minutes per side, or until chicken is no longer pink and juices run clear.

Makes 4 servings

Per serving: *230 calories, 21 g protein, 16 g carbohydrates, 10 g fat, 46 mg cholesterol, 344 mg sodium, 4 g fiber*

Diet Exchanges: *0 milk, 2 vegetable, 0 fruit, 0 bread, 2½ meat, 0 fat*

Confetti Meat Loaf

273 Calories

—Helaine Ferebee, Desert Hot Springs, Calif.

"To reduce the fat and calories in my ordinary meat loaf, I use brown rice to extend the beef. The rice also keeps the meat loaf moist and lends a nutty flavor. I keep cooked rice in the freezer for fast and easy preparation. This makes a nice meal with roasted potatoes and steamed brocoli."

½ cup brown rice

1 tablespoon olive oil or vegetable oil

1 small onion, chopped

1 cup chopped red and green bell peppers

1 pound extra-lean ground beef and/or ground turkey breast

1 cup chunky salsa

¼ cup liquid egg substitute or 1 egg

¾ teaspoon salt

½ teaspoon ground black pepper

¼ teaspoon celery seeds

Cook rice according to package directions. Preheat the oven to 350°F.

Warm oil in a small skillet over medium heat. Add onion and bell peppers. Cook 5 minutes, or until tender.

In a large bowl, combine meat, salsa, egg substitute or egg, salt, black pepper, and celery seeds. Stir in vegetables and rice. Place mixture in a round baking dish and pat into an oblong loaf. Bake 45 to 50 minutes, or until thermometer inserted in center registers 160°F and meat is no longer pink.

Makes 6 servings

Per serving: *273 calories, 17 g protein, 21 g carbohydrates, 13 g fat, 47 mg cholesterol, 597 mg sodium, 3 g fiber*

Diet Exchanges: *0 milk, 1 vegetable, 0 fruit, 1 bread, 2 meat, 0 fat*

El Dorado Casserole

339 Calories

—Kelly Tinsley, Cottage Grove, Oreg.

"This healthier version of the popular Mexican-style casserole is hearty and satisfying. It's easy to make ahead, too. It's still a bit high in fat, so I like to save it for times when I want to splurge."

1 pound extra-lean ground beef or ground turkey breast

1 onion, chopped

1 cup (8 ounces) fat-free ricotta cheese

1 package (8 ounces) reduced-fat cream cheese

2 cans (4 ounces each) chopped green chile peppers

1 can (4 ounces) black olives, drained and chopped

4 cups coarsely broken baked tortilla chips

¾ cup (3 ounces) shredded reduced-fat Monterey Jack cheese

¾ cup (3 ounces) shredded reduced-fat Cheddar cheese

Salsa (optional)

Preheat the oven to 375°F. Coat a 13" × 9" baking dish with nonstick spray.

In a large nonstick skillet over medium-high heat, cook beef or turkey and onion, stirring occasionally, 10 minutes, or until meat is no longer pink and onion is tender. Drain off any fat.

In a large bowl, combine ricotta, cream cheese, peppers (with liquid), and olives.

Spoon half of meat into the prepared baking dish. Top with half of ricotta mixture. Top with 2 cups tortilla chips. Sprinkle with half of Monterey Jack and half of Cheddar. Repeat layers with remaining meat mixture, ricotta mixture, chips, and shredded cheeses.

Cover and bake 20 minutes. Uncover and bake 10 minutes, or until hot and bubbly. Serve with salsa, if using.

Makes 8 servings

Per serving: *339 calories, 24 g protein, 16 g carbohydrates, 19 g fat, 71 mg cholesterol, 659 mg sodium, 2 g fiber*

Diet Exchanges: *0 milk, 0 vegetable, 0 fruit, 1 bread, 2 meat, 2 fat*

Grilled Pork Chops

175 Calories

—Lori Carillo, Wailuku, Hawaii

"To cook pork chops evenly without becoming too browned and tough on the outside, I turn them often. Grill vegetables and a few chunks of pineapple to round out the meal."

4 boneless center-cut pork loin chops, trimmed of visible fat (each about 3 ounces and 1½" thick)

1 tablespoon Worcestershire sauce

2 garlic cloves, minced

½ teaspoon salt

½ teaspoon paprika

⅛ teaspoon ground black pepper

Sprinkle pork chops all over with Worcestershire sauce, garlic, salt, paprika, and pepper. Cover and refrigerate at least 20 minutes or up to 2 hours.

Coat a grill rack or broiler pan with nonstick spray. Preheat the grill or broiler. Cook 4" from the heat, turning once halfway through cooking time, 10 to 12 minutes, or until a thermometer inserted in the center of a chop registers 160°F and juices run clear.

Makes 4 servings

Per serving: *175 calories, 19 g protein, 1 g carbohydrates, 10 g fat, 63 mg cholesterol, 353 mg sodium, 0 g fiber*

Diet Exchanges: *0 milk, 0 vegetable, 0 fruit, 0 bread, 2½ meat, 0 fat*

Slimming Meal

1 serving Grilled Pork Chops

1 cup grilled sliced eggplant, zucchini, and potatoes

2 rings grilled pineapple drizzled with 1 teaspoon honey

415 calories

(Herbed Rice recipe on page 236)

Garbanzo-Sausage Soup

317 Calories

—Janet Fry, West Jordan, Utah

" Here's my favorite soup—satisfying yet calorie-savvy. The sausage is drained, so you get the spice but not much fat. I use chorizo, a type of spicy Mexican sausage, but you can also use turkey sausage. Sometimes I vary the vegetables to get different flavors. "

1 package (16 ounces) dried garbanzo beans

4 ounces chorizo, thinly sliced, or spicy bulk turkey sausage, crumbled

3 leeks, white part only, chopped

2 celery ribs, chopped

2 shallots, minced

2 garlic cloves, minced

1 can (6 ounces) tomato paste

3 cans (16 ounces) fat-free, reduced-sodium chicken broth

2 teaspoons dried Italian seasoning

1 can (15¼ ounces) yellow corn, drained

1 can (14½ ounces) sliced carrots, drained

Wash beans and discard any stones or shriveled beans. Place beans in a large saucepan with enough water to cover. Let soak 12 hours or overnight. Drain. (Or, use the quick-soak method: Instead of soaking 12 hours, heat beans and water to boiling. Boil 2 minutes. Remove from the heat, cover, and let stand 1 hour. Drain.)

In a large saucepan over medium-high heat, cook sausage until no longer pink. Remove to a bowl with a slotted spoon. Drain and discard all but 1 tablespoon of the fat from the pan. Stir in leeks, celery, and shallots. Cook 5 minutes. Stir in garlic and cook 1 minute. Stir in tomato paste, broth, Italian seasoning, and beans. Heat to boiling. Reduce heat to low and simmer 2 hours, or until beans are tender. Add corn and carrots. Cook 5 minutes.

Makes 8 servings

Per serving: *317 calories, 19 g protein, 60 g carbohydrates, 9 g fat, 11 mg cholesterol, 360 mg sodium, 4 g fiber*

Diet Exchanges: *0 milk, 2 vegetable, 0 fruit, 3 bread, 1 meat, 0 fat*

TIP: To clean leeks, trim off the white roots and dark green tops. Slice the leeks from top to bottom and rinse thoroughly under running water to remove any grit trapped between the leaf layers.

Spicy Pork and Beans Stew

542 Calories

—Valorie Rogers, Ponca City, Okla.

"I love to cook, and I indulge in this hobby every chance I get. At work, I always find that my co-workers are willing taste-testers. They absolutely loved this stew. Serve it over rice or noodles. Or, have it with cornbread on the side."

1 tablespoon olive oil

¾ pound lean pork tenderloin, cut into 1" cubes

1 green bell pepper, chopped

1 large onion, chopped

6 garlic cloves, minced

2 jalapeño chile peppers, seeded and finely chopped (wear plastic gloves when handling)

3 tablespoons chili powder

1 tablespoon ground cumin

½ teaspoon ground black pepper

¼ teaspoon ground red pepper

1 can (14½ ounces) low-sodium diced tomatoes

1 can (14½ ounces) diced tomatoes with chile peppers

2 cans (16 ounces each) red kidney beans, rinsed and drained

1 can (16 ounces) black beans, rinsed and drained

Warm oil in a large nonstick saucepan over medium heat. Add pork and cook until no longer pink. Stir in bell pepper, onion, garlic, chile peppers, chili powder, cumin, black pepper, and red pepper. Cook 8 minutes, or until vegetables are tender. Stir in diced tomatoes (with juice), diced tomatoes with chiles (with juice), kidney beans, and black beans. Cook 10 to 15 minutes, or until flavors are blended.

Makes 4 servings

Per serving: *542 calories, 42 g protein, 72 g carbohydrates, 13 g fat, 53 mg cholesterol, 1,205 mg sodium, 23 g fiber*

Diet Exchanges: *0 milk, 2 vegetable, 0 fruit, 3 bread, 3½ meat, 0 fat*

Lentil-Sausage Stew

568 Calories

—Laura A. Hansen, Maryland Heights, Mo.

"When I realized that I had gained 30 pounds, I decided to take action. I found that eating a hot dish at dinner helped me feel satisfied and motivated to keep losing."

1 tablespoon olive oil

1 onion, chopped

1 green bell pepper, chopped

1 pound turkey sausage, crumbled, or reduced-fat kielbasa, thinly sliced

3 garlic cloves, minced

2 cups dry lentils

2 cups fat-free, reduced-sodium chicken broth

1 can (14 ounces) low-sodium tomatoes

1 teaspoon fennel seeds

1/1 teaspoon dried Italian seasoning

1/2 teaspoon dried thyme

1/2 teaspoon ground black pepper

Warm oil in a large nonstick skillet over medium heat. Add onion and bell pepper. Cook 10 minutes, or until tender. Stir in sausage or kielbasa and garlic. Cook 10 minutes, stirring occasionally, or until sausage is no longer pink. Stir in lentils, broth, tomatoes (with juice), fennel seeds, Italian seasoning, thyme, and black pepper. Heat to boiling. Reduce heat to low, cover, and simmer 40 minutes, or until lentils are tender.

Makes 4 servings

Per serving: *568 calories, 48 g protein, 69 g carbohydrates, 15 g fat, 71 mg cholesterol, 1,067 mg sodium, 2 g fiber*

Diet Exchanges: *0 milk, 1 vegetable, 0 fruit, 4 bread, 3 meat, 0 fat*

Splurge Meal

1 serving Lentil-Sausage Stew

1/2 cup shredded carrots with caraway seeds

1 serving Portobellos and Goat Cheese (page 106)

1/2 cup blueberries and strawberries with 1/2 cup lime yogurt

977 calories

Lemon Red Snapper with Jalapeños

156 Calories

—Marlene Agnely, Ocean Springs, Miss.

"This is an elegant but easy dish. It's cooked in foil so that the fish stays moist and flavorful without added fat. And there are no pans to clean up!"

4 firm-flesh fish fillets (about 6 ounces each), such as snapper, cod, or halibut

¼ cup low-fat Italian salad dressing

2 scallions, cut into matchsticks

2 teaspoons lemon-pepper seasoning

1 jalapeño chile pepper, seeded and chopped (wear plastic gloves when handling)

¼ teaspoon salt

Preheat the oven to 375°F.

Cut 8 pieces of foil, each about 10" long, depending on the size of fish. Place a fillet on a piece of foil. Top with 1 tablespoon salad dressing, one-fourth of scallions, ½ teaspoon lemon-pepper seasoning, one-fourth of chile pepper, and pinch of salt. Cover with another piece of foil and crimp edges to seal. Repeat with remaining ingredients. Place on a baking sheet. Bake 10 minutes, or until fish flakes easily.

Makes 4 servings

Per serving: *156 calories, 30 g protein, 1 g carbohydrates, 3 g fat, 74 mg cholesterol, 586 mg sodium, 0 g fiber*

Diet Exchanges: *0 milk, 0 vegetable, 0 fruit, 0 bread, 2 meat, 0 fat*

Slimming Meal

1 serving Lemon Red Snapper with Jalapeños

½ cup roasted sliced red-skinned potatoes with mint

½ cup steamed sugar snap peas with roasted red peppers and basil

½ broiled peach with ½ cup vanilla frozen yogurt sprinkled with nutmeg

462 calories

Seafood Chowder

338 Calories

—Tammy L. DePriest, Tall Timbers, Md.

"In Maryland, we love our chowder milky and rich. I didn't want to give it up, so I found a way to make it low in fat and calories."

2 tablespoons butter or margarine

1 small onion, chopped

1 celery rib, chopped

1 can (14½ ounces) fat-free, reduced-sodium chicken broth

1 cup (3 ounces) small shell pasta

1 bay leaf

¼ teaspoon dried thyme

⅛ teaspoon ground nutmeg

⅛–¼ teaspoon ground red pepper

1 can (13 ounces) fat-free evaporated milk

8 ounces fresh or thawed frozen peeled and deveined shrimp and/or scallops

1 can (16 ounces) clams or oysters

8 ounces fresh or frozen and thawed fish fillets, cut into 1" cubes

2 tablespoons chopped pimiento

2 tablespoons chopped parsley

Warm butter or margarine in a large saucepan over medium heat. Add onion and celery and cook 5 minutes, or until tender. Add broth, pasta, bay leaf, thyme, nutmeg, and red pepper. Heat to boiling. Reduce heat to low and cook 15 minutes, or until pasta is tender. Stir in evaporated milk, shrimp and/or scallops, clams or oysters (with liquid), fish, pimiento, and parsley. Heat gently 10 minutes, or until fish flakes easily. Remove and discard bay leaf before serving.

Makes 4 servings

Per serving: *338 calories, 32 g protein, 35 g carbohydrates, 7 g fat, 130 mg cholesterol, 489 mg sodium, 1 g fiber*

Diet Exchanges: *1 milk, 0 vegetable, 0 fruit, 1 bread, 1½ meat, 0 fat*

EAT MORE FOOD AND FEWER CALORIES

The next time you visit a salad bar or self-service food counter, notice what's at the front of the line: iceberg lettuce, rice, pasta, and other salads. It's no accident. Chefs know that when you pile your plate with fluffy (and inexpensive) foods like lettuce, you'll have less room down the line for more expensive items like shrimp or imported ham.

Fortunately for you, giving more space to bulky foods like grains, beans, lettuce, and pasta is calorie-savvy math, too. Consider the numbers: Fatty foods like prime rib have more calories per gram than carbohydrate-rich or protein-rich foods like pasta or beans (9 calories per gram for fats versus 4 per gram for carbohydrates and proteins). The easiest way to cut calories but not volume from your meals is to cut back on the amount of fats that you eat and increase the amount of carbohydrate and protein foods.

Here are a few calorie equations that make the point. Every one of these portions has the same calories. Sure, some examples are extreme (broccoli is no substitute for ice cream), but they paint a clear picture. Notice how the portion sizes grow as you go down the list. Also notice that the higher the fiber and the lower the fat in a food, the more you can eat for the same number of calories.

Food	Calories	Fiber (g)	Fat (g)
½ cup premium ice cream	230	0	17
1⅛ cups cooked brown rice	230	4	2
1⅙ cups cooked pasta	230	2	2
1¼ cups fat-free frozen yogurt	230	0	0
1⅓ cups cooked couscous	230	3	0
2⅛ bananas	230	8	2
2⅝ apples	230	11	3
3⅓ slices whole-wheat bread	230	6	4
5¼ cups steamed broccoli	230	25	3
7⅔ carrots	230	17	1
7½ cups air-popped popcorn	230	9	3
17¾ saltine crackers	230	2	6
23 cups leaf lettuce	230	30	0
29 baked tortilla chips	230	4	2
46 animal crackers	230	1	8

Shrimp Risotto

309 Calories

—Michael Woodward, Exton, Pa.

" The secret to creamy—but not fattening—risotto is to use short-grain Italian Arborio rice and to stir it constantly while it cooks. "

3 cups chicken broth

1 cup water

1 tablespoon extra-virgin olive oil

1 small onion, chopped

1 garlic clove, minced

2 tablespoons tomato paste

2 cups Arborio rice

¾ pound medium fresh or frozen and thawed shrimp, peeled and deveined

½ cup white wine (optional)

¼ cup (1 ounce) grated Parmesan cheese

In a medium saucepan, combine broth and water. Heat to simmering. Reduce heat to low and keep warm.

Warm oil in a large shallow saucepan over medium heat. Add onion and garlic. Cook 10 minutes, or until onion is tender. Stir in tomato paste and cook 10 minutes. Stir in rice. Reduce heat to medium-low. Add about 1 cup of warm broth and cook, stirring constantly, until almost completely absorbed. Continue adding broth, 1 cup at a time, stirring constantly, until rice is barely tender. Stir in shrimp and wine, if using. Cook 5 minutes, or until rice is tender yet firm and shrimp is opaque. Serve with cheese.

Makes 8 servings

Per serving: *309 calories, 15 g protein, 48 g carbohydrates, 4 g fat, 68 mg cholesterol, 428 mg sodium, 1 g fiber*

Diet Exchanges: *0 milk, 0 vegetable, 0 fruit, 3 bread, 1 meat, 0 fat*

Shrimp in Tomato Sauce over Pasta

390 Calories

—Frances Lobiondo, Wall, N.J.

" My husband and I try to keep calories down for almost all of our home-cooked meals. Since cooking is my passion, I'm constantly creating low-fat recipes. Here's one we come back to again and again. "

1 tablespoon olive oil
1 small bunch scallions, chopped
2 garlic cloves, minced
1 can (28 ounces) crushed tomatoes
¾ cup dry white wine or nonalcoholic white wine
1 tablespoon sugar
¾ cup chopped flat-leaf parsley or basil
12 fresh or frozen and thawed jumbo shrimp, peeled and deveined
8 ounces spaghetti
¼ cup grated Parmesan cheese

Warm oil in a medium saucepan over medium heat. Add scallions and garlic. Cook 10 minutes, or just until scallions begin to turn golden.

Add tomatoes, wine, sugar, and ½ cup parsley or basil. Heat to boiling. Reduce heat to low, cover, and simmer 20 to 25 minutes, or until sauce is slightly thickened.

Add shrimp and return to a simmer. Cook 4 to 5 minutes, or until shrimp are opaque.

Meanwhile, cook spaghetti according to package directions. Drain and transfer to a large bowl. Add sauce and toss to mix.

Sprinkle with Parmesan and remaining ¼ cup parsley or basil.

Makes 4 servings

Per serving: *390 calories, 16 g protein, 60 g carbohydrates, 7 g fat, 37 mg cholesterol, 630 mg sodium, 4 g fiber*

Diet Exchanges: *0 milk, 2 vegetable, 0 fruit, 3 bread, 1 meat, 1 fat*

Asian Veggie Wraps

268 Calories

—Micara Morency, Lawrenceville, N.J.

" I've lost 50 pounds by increasing the amount of vegetables in my diet. And I'm still losing! These wraps are one of my favorite ways to eat vegetables. "

2 tablespoons vegetable oil

2 cups shredded bok choy or green cabbage

2 carrots, cut into matchsticks

1 small zucchini, cut into matchsticks

4 ounces mushrooms, sliced

5 scallions, cut into matchsticks

1 cup broccoli florets

3 tablespoons soy sauce

1 tablespoon sesame oil

4 flour tortillas or jalapeño wraps (10" diameter)

Preheat the oven to 400°F. Coat a baking sheet with nonstick spray.

Warm vegetable oil in a large skillet over medium heat. Add bok choy or cabbage, carrots, zucchini, mushrooms, scallions, and broccoli. Cook, stirring frequently, 5 minutes, or until carrots and broccoli are crisp-tender. Stir in soy sauce and sesame oil.

Spoon about 1 cup mixture along center of a tortilla and fold it like an envelope to make a package. Place, folded edges down, on the prepared baking sheet. Repeat with remaining ingredients. Bake 10 minutes, or until golden brown.

Makes 4

Per wrap: *268 calories, 7 g protein, 33 g carbohydrates, 13 g fat, 0 mg cholesterol, 977 mg sodium, 4 g fiber*

Diet Exchanges: *0 milk, 3 vegetable, 0 fruit, 1 bread, 0 meat, 2½ fat*

Very Vegetable Soup

—Debra Davies, Manchester, N.H.

*" It's easy to get your 5 servings of vegetables a day
when this stewlike soup is part of your menu. "*

2 tablespoons olive oil

1 large onion, chopped

2 green and/or red bell peppers, chopped

4 garlic cloves, minced

½ teaspoon ground cumin

½ small head green cabbage, sliced

2 large carrots, sliced

1 zucchini, chopped

1 yellow squash, chopped

1 can (14½ ounces) low-sodium stewed
   tomatoes

1 bottle (46 ounces) vegetable juice

½ teaspoon ground black pepper

¼ teaspoon crushed red-pepper flakes

Warm oil in a large saucepan over medium heat. Add onion and bell peppers. Cook 5 minutes, or until tender. Add garlic and cumin. Cook 1 minute. Add cabbage, carrots, zucchini, squash, tomatoes (with juice), vegetable juice, black pepper, and red-pepper flakes. Heat to boiling. Reduce heat to low, cover, and simmer 1 hour.

Makes 6 servings

Per serving: *170 calories, 5 g protein, 29 g carbohydrates, 5 g fat, 0 mg cholesterol, 834 mg sodium, 7 g fiber*

Diet Exchanges: *0 milk, 5 vegetable, 0 fruit, 0 bread, 0 meat, 1 fat*

Slimming Meal

1 serving Very Vegetable Soup

1 serving Warm Pepper and Pork
Salad (page 264)

1 slice whole-wheat bread

1 pear

501 calories

Vegetable Lasagna

212 Calories

—Anna Riester, River Ridge, La.

"Sure, this dish can be enjoyed right away, but like many casseroles, it tastes even better the next day!"

1 teaspoon olive oil

1 zucchini, chopped

2 cups (16 ounces) reduced-fat ricotta cheese

1 egg

1 tablespoon dried basil

¼ teaspoon salt

⅛ teaspoon ground black pepper

1 jar (16 ounces) spaghetti sauce

8 ounces no-cook lasagna (about 9 noodles)

10 ounces frozen broccoli, thawed

1 can (28 ounces) tomatoes

¼ cup (1 ounce) grated Parmesan cheese

¼ cup (1 ounce) shredded reduced-fat mozzarella cheese

Preheat the oven to 350°F. Coat a 13" × 9" baking dish with nonstick spray.

Warm oil in a medium skillet over medium heat. Add zucchini and cook 5 minutes, or until crisp-tender. Remove from heat and set aside.

In a medium bowl, mix ricotta, egg, basil, salt, and pepper. Set aside ½ cup pasta sauce.

Place 3 sheets of lasagna in the prepared baking dish. Evenly spoon half of remaining pasta sauce over lasagna. Top with half of ricotta mixture, half the broccoli, half the zucchini, half the tomatoes (with juice), and half the Parmesan. Repeat layering with 3 more sheets of lasagna and remaining ingredients. End with remaining sheets of lasagna. Spoon reserved pasta sauce over top and sprinkle with mozzarella.

Cover with foil and bake 25 minutes. Uncover and bake 20 minutes, or until hot and bubbly. Let stand 10 minutes before serving.

Makes 8 servings

Per serving: *212 calories, 15 g protein, 24 g carbohydrates, 6 g fat, 43 mg cholesterol, 881 mg sodium, 4 g fiber*

Diet Exchanges: *0 milk, 2 vegetable, 0 fruit, 1 bread, 1 meat, 0 fat*

Spinach Lasagna

253 Calories

—Carrie Wright, Boulder, Colo.

"For a less fussy lasagna, I use a no-cook sauce and no-boil lasagna noodles. If you prefer the taste and texture, use fresh noodles and cook according to package directions before assembling the lasagna."

2 cans (15 ounces each) tomato sauce

1 can (28 ounces) low-sodium tomatoes, drained

2 teaspoons dried oregano

2 teaspoons dried basil

1 teaspoon dried thyme

¼ teaspoon ground black pepper

1 package (10 ounces) fresh spinach, chopped, or 2 packages frozen chopped spinach, thawed and squeezed dry

8 ounces no-cook lasagna (about 9 noodles)

1 container (15 ounces) reduced-fat ricotta cheese

1 cup (8 ounces) shredded reduced-fat mozzarella cheese

Preheat the oven to 375°F.

In a large bowl, combine tomato sauce, tomatoes, oregano, basil, thyme, and pepper. Break up whole tomatoes with the back of a spoon. Set aside.

Coat a medium nonstick skillet with non-stick spray. Add spinach and cook 4 minutes, or until wilted.

Spread ½ cup tomato mixture into a 13" × 9" baking dish. Place 3 sheets of lasagna on top (they will not completely cover the bottom of the dish). Spread half of ricotta over noodles. Layer with half of spinach. Top with a third of remaining sauce and sprinkle with a third of mozzarella. Cover with 3 more noodles, remaining ricotta, then remaining spinach. Spoon on ¼ cup remaining sauce and ¼ cup remaining mozzarella. Cover with 3 more noodles and top with remaining sauce and mozzarella.

Cover and bake 30 minutes. Uncover and bake 15 minutes, or until hot and bubbly. Let stand 10 minutes before serving.

Makes 8 servings

Per serving: *253 calories, 17 g protein, 27 g carbohydrates, 10 g fat, 36 mg cholesterol, 863 mg sodium, 3 g fiber*

Diet Exchanges: *0 milk, 1 vegetable, 0 fruit, 2 bread, 1 meat, 0 fat*

Meximix

532 Calories

—Holly Smaill, Vancouver, British Columbia

" Call it a casserole or call it Southwest lasagna. Either way, it'll be a favorite. *"*

1 teaspoon olive oil

1 green bell pepper, seeded and chopped

1 onion, chopped

½ pound frozen ground beef substitute, thawed

1 envelope (1¼ ounces) reduced-sodium taco seasoning mix

1 can (28 ounces) low-sodium tomatoes

4 large flour tortillas (12" diameter)

1 can (16 ounces) red kidney beans, rinsed and drained

1 can (16 ounces) white cannellini beans, rinsed and drained

1 cup (4 ounces) shredded reduced-fat Cheddar or Monterey Jack cheese

Warm oil in a large nonstick skillet over medium heat. Add pepper and onion. Cook 10 minutes, or until tender. Stir in meat substitute, taco seasoning mix (also add water, if directed on seasoning label), and tomatoes (with juice). Heat to boiling. Reduce heat to low, cover, and simmer 15 to 20 minutes.

Preheat the oven to 350°F.

Lightly coat a 9" × 9" baking dish with nonstick spray. Cut tortillas into 2"-wide strips. Arrange a single layer in the bottom of the prepared baking dish and top with half of taco filling, half of kidney beans, half of cannellini beans, and one-third of cheese. Arrange another layer of tortilla strips and top with remaining taco filling, beans, and a third of cheese. Top with remaining tortilla strips and sprinkle with remaining cheese.

Cover with foil and bake 20 minutes. Uncover and bake 10 minutes, or until hot and bubbly.

Makes 4 servings

Per serving: *532 calories, 39 g protein, 82 g carbohydrates, 11 g fat, 20 mg cholesterol, 1,580 mg sodium, 17 g fiber*

Diet Exchanges: *0 milk, 3 vegetable, 0 fruit, 4 bread, 2 meat, 0 fat*

Splurge Meal

1 serving Meximix

1 corn muffin with 1 serving Herbed Cheese Spread (page 115)

½ cup brown rice

½ papaya with ½ cup lemon yogurt

1,099 calories

It Worked for Me!

Jodie Wissmiller

VITAL STATS

Weight lost: 45 pounds

Time kept it off: 2 years

Weight-loss strategies: Studying nutrition and exercise, low-fat diet, strength training, aerobics

Weight-maintenance strategies: Eating low-calorie and low-fat, daily workouts

*L*ife for a 181-pound 15-year-old was not fun. When Jodie Wissmiller realized that her weight was messing up her life, she finally did something about it. Now she's a role model for her family.

"As if adolescence weren't difficult enough, my weight added to the struggle in my teens. It seemed as though all I did was eat, sleep, cry, and complain. I was constantly being teased about my weight, which made me shy and self-conscious. At the same time, I admired my thin, outgoing friends. I wanted to look up to myself, too.

"It was spring break one year that I realized I had to do something about my weight. I read every thing I could find on weight loss and exercise. I clipped and copied everything and arranged them by subject in a binder.

"I learned that muscle burns more calories than fat, and that if I developed my muscles, it would be easier to lose weight. I began with 45 minutes of stretching and strength training twice a day. I gave up evening TV for crunches, leg lifts, and free weights.

"I read about nutrition and learned that the easiest way to cut calories was to cut down on the fat I ate. That meant giving up fatty school lunches like tacos and burgers. I packed my own lunch, which was usually a turkey sandwich with mustard, a piece of fruit, and juice. I changed my breakfast to cereal, fruit, and plain toast. While the rest of my family was eating Mexican take-out or burgers and fries, I cooked my own meals. At first, I made steamed vegetables and poached chicken breast. Then, I started collecting recipes. Within a few weeks, the pounds started dropping. Eventually, my mom started to change the way she cooked, and she started exercising with me. She has lost 14 pounds so far and has helped me convince Dad to start walking and riding his bike.

"I will graduate soon, and I no longer want to hide my body. I'll be happy and confident to walk across the stage. I can't tell you how good that feels." ■

Jodie's Pineapple Pizza

551 Calories

"This is my favorite food in the whole world! The crust is so nice and thick, I'm fully satisfied after two slices."

3–3½ cups unbleached or all-purpose flour

1 package (¼ ounce) rapid-rise yeast (2¼ teaspoons)

¾ teaspoon salt

1 cup very warm water (120°F)

2 tablespoons vegetable oil

1 cup pizza sauce

1 cup (4 ounces) shredded low-fat mozzarella cheese

1 can (20 ounces) pineapple chunks, drained

¼ teaspoon garlic powder

Preheat the oven to 400°F. Coat a 12" pizza pan with nonstick spray.

In a large bowl, combine 2 cups flour, yeast, and salt. Stir in water and oil. Add 1 cup flour, or enough to make soft dough.

Turn dough out onto a floured surface and knead 10 minutes, or until smooth and elastic, adding more flour, if necessary. Let dough rest 10 minutes.

With a floured rolling pin, roll dough into 13" circle. Place dough into the prepared pizza pan. Pinch up edges to form a rim. Spread dough with sauce. Evenly sprinkle on cheese. Spoon pineapple evenly over cheese. Sprinkle with garlic powder. Bake 20 to 30 minutes, or until crust is golden brown.

Makes 8 slices

Per 2 slices: *551 calories, 23 g protein, 95 g carbohydrates, 10 g fat, 0 mg cholesterol, 954 mg sodium, 3 g fiber*

Diet Exchanges: *0 milk, 0 vegetable, 1 fruit, 4 bread, 2 meat, 0 fat*

Splurge Meal

1 serving Jodie's Pineapple Pizza

2 cups spinach salad with low-fat ranch dressing

1 cup low-fat frozen yogurt

941 calories

Broccoli-Stuffed Shells

591 Calories

—Anna Burt, Johnston, R.I.

"Add a salad, and this Italian meal delivers your Five-a-Day of vegetables. For a more sophisticated taste, I sometimes use broccoli rabe (a leafier, more bitter kind of broccoli). You could also use a combination of spinach and regular broccoli."

16 jumbo pasta shells

 2 tablespoons extra-virgin olive oil

 1 pound mushrooms, thinly sliced

 1 red onion, chopped

 3 garlic cloves, minced

½ cup red wine or chicken broth

 1 large head broccoli, chopped into florets

 2 teaspoons dried Italian seasoning

1½ cups (12 ounces) reduced-fat ricotta cheese

½ cup (2 ounces) grated Romano cheese

1½ cups tomato sauce

Cook shells according to package directions. Drain.

Preheat the oven to 350°F.

Warm oil in a large skillet over medium heat. Add mushrooms, onion, and garlic. Cook 5 minutes, or until mushrooms are tender but not limp. Add wine or broth, broccoli, and Italian seasoning. Simmer 15 minutes, or until broccoli is tender and liquid is absorbed. Remove from heat and stir in ricotta and Romano.

Stuff shells with broccoli mixture. Spread a thin layer of sauce over bottom of a 13" × 9" baking dish. Arrange shells in dish and top with remaining sauce. Bake 15 minutes, or until heated through.

Makes 4 servings

Per serving: *591 calories, 27 g protein, 90 g carbohydrates, 13 g fat, 16 mg cholesterol, 741 mg sodium, 8 g fiber*

Diet Exchanges: *0 milk, 4 vegetable, 0 fruit, 4 bread, 1½ meat, 1 fat*

Splurge Meal

1 serving Broccoli-Stuffed Shells

1 slice whole-wheat Italian bread toasted and drizzled with 1 teaspoon olive oil

1 cup baked radicchio with low-fat Caesar dressing

1 pear

1 ounce blue cheese

901 calories

Veggie Cassoulet

—Wanda Lea O'Keefe, Philadelphia, Miss.

342 Calories

" At 30 years old, Pat, my 6-foot-tall, 170-pound husband, had sky-high cholesterol. And I was diagnosed with fibrocystic breasts. That's when I learned to cut the fat out of our diet. Now, 6 years later, Pat's cholesterol is at acceptable levels, my condition has improved, and our two sons are pictures of health. This recipe helped get us where we are today. *"*

⅔ cup dried great Northern or navy beans

4½ cups water

2 large onions, chopped

3 garlic cloves, minced

2 leeks, white part only, thinly sliced

4 frozen vegetable-and-grain breakfast links, thawed and sliced

1 jar (7 ounces) roasted red peppers, drained and chopped

2 large carrots, thinly sliced

1 teaspoon salt

½ teaspoon ground black pepper

½ cup dry-pack sun-dried tomatoes

½ teaspoon dried rosemary, crushed

½ cup fresh whole-wheat bread crumbs

Rinse beans and discard any stones or shriveled beans.

In a medium saucepan, combine beans and 3 cups water. Let soak overnight. Drain. Return beans to the pan. Add onions, garlic, and remaining 1½ cups water. Heat to boiling over high heat. Reduce heat to low, cover, and simmer 1 hour. Remove from heat. Stir in leeks, breakfast links, roasted peppers, carrots, salt, and black pepper.

While beans are cooking, soak tomatoes in hot water 10 minutes, or until soft. Drain, reserving soaking liquid. Chop tomatoes.

Preheat the oven to 325°F. Coat a 2-quart baking dish with nonstick spray.

Stir tomatoes and soaking liquid into bean mixture. Spoon into the prepared baking dish. Sprinkle with rosemary. Top with bread crumbs. Bake 1 hour, or until carrots are tender and bread crumbs are golden brown.

Makes 4 servings

Per serving: *342 calories, 17 g protein, 57 g carbohydrates, 5 g fat, 0 mg cholesterol, 887 mg sodium, 5 g fiber*

Diet Exchanges: *0 milk, 2 vegetable, 0 fruit, 2½ bread, 1 meat, 0 fat*

Black-Eyed Pea Stew

317 Calories

—Kim Swearington, Reno, Nev.

"This aromatic dish is packed with flavor, and it's a great source of fiber. Cooking with dried beans is really pretty simple. Just start the beans soaking before you go to bed the night before. Or use the quick-soak method: Place rinsed beans in a large saucepan with enough water to cover and heat to boiling. Cook 2 minutes; remove from the heat, cover, and let stand 1 hour."

1 package (16 ounces) dried black-eyed peas

2 tablespoons olive oil

2 onions, cut into ½" pieces

1 green bell pepper, cut into ½" pieces

8 garlic cloves, minced

2 large potatoes, peeled and cut into ½" cubes

2 cans (14½ ounces each) stewed tomatoes

1 tablespoon dried oregano

1 tablespoon dried thyme

3 bay leaves

¼ teaspoon crushed red-pepper flakes

½ cup chicken stock (optional)

Wash peas and discard any stones or shriveled peas. Place peas in a large saucepan with enough water to cover. Cover and soak 12 hours or overnight. Drain.

In a large saucepan, combine peas and fresh water to cover. Heat to boiling over high heat. Reduce heat to low and simmer 25 to 30 minutes, or until tender. Set aside.

Warm oil in a large saucepan over medium heat. Add onions and bell pepper. Cook 5 minutes, or until tender. Add garlic and cook 1 minute. Stir in potatoes, tomatoes (with juice), oregano, thyme, bay leaves, red-pepper flakes, and peas with about one-fourth of the cooking liquid. Heat to boiling. Reduce heat to low and simmer 90 minutes. If mixture becomes dry, add stock. Remove and discard bay leaves before serving.

Makes 4 servings

Per serving: *317 calories, 8 g protein, 57 g carbohydrates, 8 g fat, 0 mg cholesterol, 275 mg sodium, 12 g fiber*

Diet Exchanges: *0 milk, 3 vegetable, 0 fruit, 2 bread, 0 meat, 1½ fat*

Braised Tofu

—Rowena Low, Boston

" Tofu is a high-quality, low-fat, inexpensive protein source. And it's heart-healthy. In this dish, I use spices and seasonings to intensify tofu's mild flavor. To complement its soft texture, I serve the tofu over brown rice, which has a nutty chewiness. "

2 whole star anise

3 whole cloves

2 cardamom pods

2 cinnamon sticks

1 tablespoon toasted sesame oil

5 slices fresh ginger

2 tablespoons oyster sauce

3 tablespoons low-sodium tamari or soy sauce

1 pound extra-firm tofu, drained and cubed

¾ cup water

2 tablespoons rice vinegar

¼ cup packed brown sugar

⅛ teaspoon crushed red-pepper flakes

2 tablespoons chopped fresh cilantro

2 tablespoons chopped peanuts or sesame seeds (optional)

Heat a large skillet over medium heat until hot. Add anise, cloves, cardamom, and cinnamon. Cook 1 minute, or until fragrant, shaking the pan often. Add oil, ginger, oyster sauce, tamari or soy sauce, and tofu. Cook 2 minutes. Add water, vinegar, brown sugar, and red-pepper flakes. Heat to boiling.

Reduce heat to low, cover, and simmer, turning tofu occasionally, 30 minutes, or until sauce is thickened. Carefully lift out tofu.

With a slotted spoon, remove and discard anise, cloves, cardamom, and cinnamon. Stir in 1 tablespoon cilantro. Spoon sauce over tofu. Sprinkle with remaining 1 tablespoon cilantro and peanuts or sesame seeds, if using.

Makes 4 servings

Per serving: *185 calories, 12 g protein, 16 g carbohydrates, 8 g fat, 0 mg cholesterol, 631 mg sodium, 0 g fiber*

Diet Exchanges: *0 milk, 0 vegetable, 0 fruit, 1 bread, 1½ meat, 0 fat*

Green Mountain at Fox Run

At Green Mountain at Fox Run in Ludlow, Vermont, weight loss is a matter of balance. "Eating healthfully doesn't have to be restrictive," says nutrition director Marsha Hudnall. "People can eat high-fat, high-calorie foods within a balanced diet and still achieve and maintain healthy weights." Another principle at Green Mountain is simplicity. How can only three ingredients add up to a delicious meal? Try it and find out.

EGGPLANT PARMESAN

167 Calories

1 eggplant, peeled and sliced ⅛" thick

1½ cups low-sodium tomato sauce

1⅔ cups (6⅔ ounces) shredded reduced-fat mozzarella cheese

Preheat the broiler.

Place eggplant on a baking sheet and broil 5 minutes on each side to remove moisture. Spoon some tomato sauce into a 9" × 9" baking dish. Top with a layer of eggplant, some cheese, and more sauce. Repeat until all ingredients are used, ending with cheese. Cover with foil and bake 2 hours, or until eggplant is tender. Let stand 10 minutes before serving.

Makes 4 servings

Per serving: *167 calories, 18 g protein, 24 g carbohydrates, 0.5 g fat, 0 mg cholesterol, 363 mg sodium, 1 g fiber*

Diet Exchanges: *0 milk, 3 vegetable, 0 fruit, 0 bread, 1 meat, 0 fat*

Slimming Meal

1 serving Eggplant Parmesan

½ cup rotini pasta with ½ teaspoon olive oil and 1 tablespoon Parmesan cheese

1 cup tossed greens with jarred marinated artichokes

1 poached pear

427 calories

Unstuffed Cabbage

231 Calories

—Tahmina Muradova, Colleyville, Tex.

" All the lovely flavors of stuffed cabbage, but without the difficult and time-consuming steps. "

1 tablespoon olive oil

1 onion, chopped

1 carrot, chopped

1 green bell pepper, cut into 1" pieces

4 garlic cloves, minced

1 small head napa cabbage, cut into 1" pieces

1 tomato, cut into 1" pieces

1 potato, chopped

1/2 cup spicy vegetable juice

1 bay leaf

1 teaspoon salt

1 cup rice

1/2 cup chopped parsley

Warm oil in a large saucepan over medium heat. Add onion, carrot, pepper, and garlic. Cook 10 minutes, or until vegetables are tender. Add cabbage, tomato, potato, vegetable juice, bay leaf, and salt. Heat to boiling. Reduce heat to low and simmer 20 minutes, or until cabbage is tender and liquid is reduced. Remove and discard bay leaf before serving.

Meanwhile, cook rice according to package directions. Serve rice topped with cabbage. Sprinkle with parsley.

Makes 4 servings

Per serving: *231 calories, 5 g protein, 45 g carbohydrates, 4 g fat, 0 mg cholesterol, 671 mg sodium, 2 g fiber*

Diet Exchanges: *0 milk, 2 vegetable, 0 fruit, 2 bread, 0 meat, 1 fat*

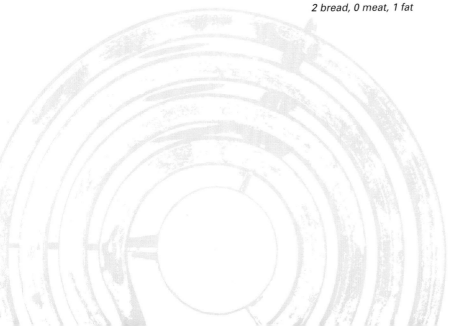

Mediterranean Stuffed Eggplant

259 Calories

—Janie Clark, Eureka Springs, Ark.

"Incorporating whole grains, nuts, and seeds into my diet is increasingly important to me."

¾ cup brown rice

1¼ cups vegetable or chicken broth

2 small eggplants, halved lengthwise

¼ cup dry-pack sun-dried tomatoes

2 teaspoons olive oil

1 onion, chopped

1 garlic clove, minced

¼ cup sliced black olives

¼ cup chopped scallions

¼ cup chopped fresh oregano or 2 tablespoons dried

½ cup (2½ ounces) crumbled feta cheese

3 tablespoons lemon juice

½ teaspoon salt

⅛ teaspoon ground black pepper

In a medium saucepan, combine rice and broth. Heat to boiling over high heat. Reduce heat to low, cover, and simmer 40 to 45 minutes, or until rice is tender.

Preheat the oven to 350°F. Lightly coat a baking sheet with nonstick spray.

Cut out flesh from eggplants. Cube flesh and place in a colander. Lightly salt cubes and set the colander in the sink to drain 15 minutes. Rinse and place in a large bowl.

Place eggplant shells, cut side down, on the prepared baking sheet. Sprinkle 1 tablespoon water all over shells. Bake 10 minutes. Cool.

Soak tomatoes in hot water 10 minutes, or until soft. Drain, chop, and add to cubes.

Warm oil in a large skillet over medium heat. Add onion and garlic. Cook 10 minutes, or until vegetables are tender. Add to eggplant cubes with olives, scallions, oregano, rice, ¼ cup cheese, lemon juice, salt, and pepper. Mix well. Use to stuff each eggplant shell. Top with remaining ¼ cup cheese.

Place stuffed shells on the prepared baking sheet. Bake 25 to 30 minutes, or until hot and cheese is lightly browned.

Makes 4 servings

Per serving: *259 calories, 8 g protein, 42 g carbohydrates, 8 g fat, 12 mg cholesterol, 925 mg sodium, 2 g fiber*

Diet Exchanges: *0 milk, 1 vegetable, 0 fruit, 2 bread, 0 meat, 1 fat*

Slimming Meal

1 serving Mediterranean Stuffed Eggplant

½ cup orecchiette pasta with ½ teaspoon olive oil and chopped fresh basil

6 chilled asparagus spears with grated orange peel and tarragon

1 Chocolate Chunk Cookie (page 292)

396 calories

Simply Sides

Mediterranean Zucchini 228

Mushroom Sauce 228

Twice-Baked Potatoes 229

Orange Sweet Potatoes 230

Sweet Potato Mash 232

Sherried Squash Bake 233

Mark's Potatoes and Tomatoes
   Vinaigrette .235

Herbed Rice 236

Portobello Brown Rice 237

Black Beans and Rice 238

Almond-Mushroom Rice Casserole 239

Broccoli-Cheese Spoon Bread 240

Chicken Stuffing Casserole 242

Easy Yeast Rolls 244

Multigrain Bread 245

Mediterranean Zucchini

168 Calories

—Marie J. Brubaker, Tacoma, Wash.

"The microwave oven makes this side dish in minutes. Perfect for pasta or rice."

1 zucchini, cut into ½" pieces
2 cans (16 ounces each) Italian-style stewed tomatoes
1 can (16 ounces) red kidney beans, rinsed and drained
½ teaspoon ground black pepper

In a large microwaveable bowl, combine zucchini, tomatoes (with juice), beans, and pepper. Microwave on high power 5 to 7 minutes, stirring once, or until zucchini is crisp-tender.

Makes 4 servings

Per serving: *168 calories, 8 g protein, 32 g carbohydrates, 0 g fat, 0 mg cholesterol, 826 mg sodium, 8 g fiber*

Diet Exchanges: *0 milk, 3 vegetable, 0 fruit, 1 bread, 0 meat, 0 fat*

Mushroom Sauce

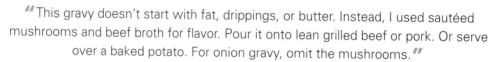
10 Calories

—Dixie Lunderville, Merrillan, Wis.

"This gravy doesn't start with fat, drippings, or butter. Instead, I used sautéed mushrooms and beef broth for flavor. Pour it onto lean grilled beef or pork. Or serve over a baked potato. For onion gravy, omit the mushrooms."

1½ ounces mushrooms, finely chopped
½ cup finely chopped onion
2 tablespoons cornstarch
1 can (14½ ounces) reduced-sodium beef broth or chicken broth
2 tablespoons chopped parsley
1 tablespoon dry sherry (optional)

Coat a medium saucepan with nonstick spray and warm over medium heat. Add mushrooms and onion. Cook, stirring often, 10 minutes, or until tender.

In a small bowl, combine cornstarch and ¼ cup broth. Stir until smooth. Add to mushrooms along with parsley, sherry (if using), and remaining broth. Heat to boiling over high heat, stirring constantly. Reduce heat to low and cook, stirring occasionally, 1 minute.

Makes 2 cups

Per 2 tablespoons: *10 calories, 1 g protein, 2 g carbohydrates, 0 g fat, 0 mg cholesterol, 8 mg sodium, 0 g fiber*

Diet Exchanges: *0 milk, ½ vegetable, 0 fruit, 0 bread, 0 meat, 0 fat*

FROM THE PROS

Green Mountain at Fox Run

Food can be very personal. For many people, it signals a particular memory or the comforts of better times. The folks at the Green Mountain weight-management community at Fox Run in Ludlow, Vermont, understand this principle. That's why they feature calming comfort foods like these savory spuds.

TWICE-BAKED POTATOES

297 Calories

4 **small baking potatoes, scrubbed and patted dry**

3 **tablespoons fat-free milk**

½ **cup (4 ounces) 1% cottage cheese**

1½ **teaspoons finely chopped onion**

1½ **teaspoons chopped chives**

¼ **teaspoon paprika**

¼ **teaspoon garlic powder**

½ **cup (2 ounces) grated Swiss cheese**

Preheat the oven to 350°F.

Prick potatoes with a fork and bake on the oven rack for 45 minutes, or until tender. Let cool. Cut off top lengthwise and scoop out filling, leaving a ¼" shell. Place filling in a medium bowl or in a food processor. Add milk, cottage cheese, onion, chives, paprika, and garlic powder. Mash with a fork or pulse until combined. Spoon back into potato skins. Sprinkle each with 2 tablespoons cheese. Bake 20 minutes, or until heated through and cheese melts.

Makes 4

Per potato: *297 calories, 12 g protein, 53 g carbohydrates, 4 g fat, 14 mg cholesterol, 139 mg sodium, 0 g fiber*

Diet Exchanges: *0 milk, 0 vegetable, 0 fruit, 3 bread, 1 meat, 0 fat*

(Photograph on page 189)

Orange Sweet Potatoes

185 Calories

—Cheryl Olson, San Diego

"These make a great alternative to traditional sweet potatoes for the holidays. When topped with fresh cilantro, they pair well with grilled fish."

1 tablespoon butter

3 large sweet potatoes or yams

1 cup orange juice

1 teaspoon grated orange peel

¾ teaspoon salt

½ teaspoon grated nutmeg

¼ teaspoon ground black pepper

¼ cup packed brown sugar

Preheat the oven to 375°F. Coat a 9" × 9" baking dish with nonstick spray.

Brown butter in a small skillet over medium heat, swirling the skillet, until butter turns a nutty color. Remove from heat and set aside.

Peel sweet potatoes or yams, cut in half lengthwise, and then into ½"-thick slices. Place in the prepared baking dish. Pour orange juice over sweet potatoes or yams. Sprinkle with orange peel, salt, nutmeg, and pepper. Top with brown sugar and browned butter. Cover and bake 40 to 45 minutes, or until sweet potatoes or yams are crisp-tender. Uncover and cook 12 to 15 minutes, or until juices are almost absorbed.

Makes 4 servings

Per serving: *185 calories, 2 g protein, 39 g carbohydrates, 3 g fat, 8 mg cholesterol, 442 mg sodium, 3 g fiber*

Diet Exchanges: *0 milk, 0 vegetable, ½ fruit, 1½ bread, 0 meat, ½ fat*

The Spa at Doral

Visit any spa, and you're bound to see sweet potatoes on the menu. It's not that nutritionists think the white ones are unhealthy, but sweet potatoes offer so much more flavor and nutrients per bite. The guests at the Spa at Doral in Miami love this creamy alternative to traditional mashed potatoes.

SWEET POTATO MASH

353 Calories

2½ **pounds sweet potatoes**

2 **tablespoons honey**

2 **teaspoons butter or margarine**

¼ **cup fat-free evaporated milk**

½ **teaspoon salt**

Preheat the oven to 350°F.

Prick sweet potatoes with a fork and bake on the oven rack 1 hour, or until tender. Remove from the oven and set aside 15 minutes, or until cool enough to handle. Cut potatoes in half and scoop the flesh into a large bowl. Stir in honey, butter or margarine, milk, and salt, mashing potatoes as you stir.

Makes 4 servings

Per serving: *353 calories, 6 g protein, 79 g carbohydrates, 2 g fat, 6 mg cholesterol, 333 mg sodium, 9 g fiber*

Diet Exchanges: *0 milk, 0 vegetable, 0 fruit, 4 bread, 0 meat, 1 fat*

Sherried Squash Bake

97 Calories

—Daria Zawistowski, Hopatcong, N.J.

"This comforting casserole makes a satisfying accompaniment to roast poultry. Any hard-skinned winter squash can be used, such as butternut, buttercup, acorn, or hubbard."

2 **pounds butternut squash, peeled, seeded, and cut into cubes**

½ **cup fat-free milk**

2 **tablespoons unbleached or all-purpose flour**

1 **egg**

2 **tablespoons cream sherry or apple juice**

⅓ **cup packed brown sugar**

½ **teaspoon salt**

¼ **teaspoon ground white or black pepper**

⅛ **teaspoon ground cinnamon**

In a covered saucepan, heat 1" of lightly salted water to boiling. Place squash in a steamer basket and insert into the saucepan. Cover and simmer 7 minutes, or until very tender.

Preheat the oven to 325°F. Coat a 9" × 9" baking dish with nonstick spray.

In a large bowl with a mixer at medium speed, beat squash, milk, flour, egg, sherry or apple juice, brown sugar, salt, and pepper. Spoon mixture into the prepared baking dish. Sprinkle with cinnamon. Bake 30 minutes, or until a wooden pick inserted in the center comes out clean.

Makes 8 servings

Per serving: *97 calories, 3 g protein, 20 g carbohydrates, 1 g fat, 27 mg cholesterol, 155 mg sodium, 0 g fiber*

Diet Exchanges: *0 milk, 0 vegetable, 0 fruit, 1 bread, 0 meat, 0 fat*

It Worked for Me!

Mark Ballard

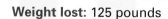

Weight lost: 125 pounds

Time kept it off: 3½ years

Weight-loss strategies: Walking, Healthrider, vegetarian diet, keeping a food and exercise log

Weight-maintenance strategies: Has a 5-pound gain/loss window, weighs in twice a month, uses clothing fit as a guide, exercises daily

From 300 pounds and housebound to 175 pounds and a TV show, Mark Ballard knows that losing weight and keeping it off takes a daily commitment.

"My first diet was in high school. But it wasn't until I turned 30 that I made a commitment to lose the weight and keep it off. By then, my weight wasn't the only thing that was unhealthfully high. My blood pressure began to soar as well. Ever since I could remember, my parents took blood pressure medication. I had friends whose families had never taken these drugs, and I wanted to be like them.

"My track record with diets wasn't very good, so this time I turned to exercise. I decided to start a walking program. On my first day out, I made it only two blocks. I was so hot and tired, I wanted to give up then and there. But instead, I kept going. Every day,

I'd set little goals: 'Tomorrow, I'll see if I can make it to that brown house and back.' Within 6 months, I was walking for an hour-and-a-half without stopping. Eventually, I picked up the pace and after a year-and-a-half, I even ran a 10-K race just to prove to myself that I could do it.

"Once I started exercising, I started losing weight, which spurred me to change my eating habits, too. I didn't think I could give up sweets entirely, but I could do without fried foods and fatty meats. I didn't give up everything. If I wanted a piece of cake, I'd have it. But I kept tabs on myself. Everything I ate I recorded on a calendar. That kept me honest about just how many pieces of cake I'd had lately. The pounds kept coming off.

"Now, I take part in life like I never have.

I go out with my kids to the gym or to water parks. I go to parties. I have so much more energy. My career as an artist and designer is booming. I'm getting more clients, and I'm hosting a local TV show on art. That's a lot more fun than hanging around the kitchen sneaking doughnuts.

"I've found that the motivation has to come from inside you. When you're losing weight, people comment and reinforce the loss. It gives you a little kick each time you drop a few pounds. But when you're just maintaining your weight, the comments stop. To stay motivated, I think back on what it took to get me to where I am today. I know by now that it's easier to keep the weight off than to have to go through taking it all off again." ■

Mark's
Potatoes and Tomatoes Vinaigrette

238 Calories

"This makes a great side dish for grilled fish. Sometimes I have it as a light supper or lunch by itself. It keeps in the fridge for 3 to 4 days."

- 3 potatoes, cut into 1" cubes
- 3 tablespoons olive oil
- ¼ cup white wine vinegar
- 1 tablespoon chopped fresh basil or 1 teaspoon dried
- 1 tablespoon chopped fresh oregano or 1 teaspoon dried
- 1 teaspoon garlic powder
- 2 tomatoes, finely chopped
- 1 green bell pepper, cut into ½" strips
- 1 red bell pepper, cut into ½" strips
- 1 small sweet onion, sliced

Place potatoes in a large saucepan. Cover with water and heat to boiling over high heat. Reduce heat to low, cover, and simmer 10 minutes, or until potatoes are tender. Drain and cool.

In a large bowl, combine oil, vinegar, basil, oregano, and garlic powder. Add tomatoes, bell peppers, onion, and potatoes. Toss to coat. Cover and marinate 2 hours at room temperature.

Makes 4 servings

Per serving: *238 calories, 3 g protein, 30 g carbohydrates, 11 g fat, 0 mg cholesterol, 15 mg sodium, 4 g fiber*

Diet Exchanges: *0 milk, 1 vegetable, 0 fruit, 2 bread, 0 meat, 1 fat*

Herbed Rice

141 Calories

—Scott Mingus, Allentown, Pa.

"I don't like to cook complicated dishes. This one is easy and tasty, and it goes with just about anything."

1 teaspoon olive oil
1 small onion, finely chopped
1 small garlic clove, minced
1 cup long-grain white rice
1 teaspoon dried Italian seasoning
¼ teaspoon ground black pepper
1 bay leaf
2 cups vegetable broth
1 teaspoon butter

Warm oil in a medium saucepan over medium heat. Add onion and garlic. Cook 5 minutes, or until soft. Add rice. Cook 1 minute to coat with oil. Add Italian seasoning, pepper, bay leaf, and broth. Heat to boiling. Reduce heat to low, cover, and simmer 20 minutes, or until rice is tender and liquid is absorbed. Remove and discard bay leaf. Stir in butter until distributed. Fluff with a fork before serving.

Makes 4 servings

Per serving: *141 calories, 3 g protein, 26 g carbohydrates, 3 g fat, 3 mg cholesterol, 514 mg sodium, 1 g fiber*

Diet Exchanges: *0 milk, 0 vegetable, 0 fruit, 1¼ bread, 0 meat, 0 fat*

(Photograph on page 196)

Portobello Brown Rice

226 Calories

—Ellen Burr, Truro, Mass.

*"*Meaty, earthy portobello mushrooms are a great complement to the nutty flavor of brown rice.*"*

½ **cup brown rice**
1 **tablespoon vegetable oil**
6 **ounces portobello mushrooms, sliced**
1 **small onion, chopped**
2 **garlic cloves, minced**
½ **teaspoon lemon-pepper seasoning**
¼ **teaspoon ground turmeric**
¼ **teaspoon dried thyme**
¼ **cup dried cranberries**
¼ **cup shelled pistachios, chopped**
¼ **cup chopped parsley**

Cook rice according to package directions.

Meanwhile, warm oil in a large nonstick skillet over medium-high heat. Add mushrooms, onion, garlic, lemon-pepper seasoning, and turmeric. Cook 5 minutes, or until onion is tender. Stir in thyme, cranberries, pistachios, parsley, and rice. Reduce heat to low and cook 5 minutes, or until heated through.

Makes 4 servings

Per serving: *226 calories, 6 g protein, 33 g carbohydrates, 8 g fat, 0 mg cholesterol, 53 mg sodium, 4 g fiber*

Diet Exchanges: *0 milk, 1 vegetable, 0 fruit, 2 bread, 0 meat, 1 fat*

Black Beans and Rice

188 Calories

—Connie Gregg, Davenport, Iowa

"Some nights, my daughter and I make a big green salad and make a dinner out of this dish. It also complements Mexican main dishes like burritos and enchiladas."

1 cup white rice

1 can (16 ounces) black beans, rinsed and drained

1 can (4 ounces) chopped green chile peppers, drained

1 cup salsa

½ cup (2 ounces) shredded reduced-fat Monterey Jack cheese (optional)

Cook rice according to package directions.
   Preheat the oven to 350°F.
   Add beans, peppers, and salsa to cooked rice. Place over low heat and cook, stirring frequently, 5 minutes, or until heated through. Spoon into a serving dish. Sprinkle with cheese, if using.
   Bake 10 minutes, or until cheese melts.

Makes 4 servings

Per serving: *188 calories, 7 g protein, 42 g carbohydrates, 0 g fat, 0 mg cholesterol, 946 mg sodium, 8 g fiber*

Diet Exchanges: *0 milk, 0 vegetable, 0 fruit, 2 bread, 0 meat, 0 fat*

FROM THE PROS

Green Mountain at Fox Run

Marsha Hudnall, the owner and resident dietitian at this Ludlow, Vermont–based spa, is a firm believer that healthy weight comes from a healthy relationship with food. At Green Mountain, that means serving great-tasting meals that fill your body and soul.

ALMOND-MUSHROOM RICE CASSEROLE

356 Calories

12 ounces sliced mushrooms

2 tablespoons chopped onion

½ cup slivered almonds

1 teaspoon dried basil

½ teaspoon dried oregano

1¼ teaspoons dried thyme

3 cups cooked brown rice

1 cup (8 ounces) 1% cottage cheese

½ cup reduced-sodium vegetable or chicken broth

1 teaspoon reduced-sodium soy sauce

1 cup (4 ounces) shredded Swiss cheese

Preheat the oven to 350°F.

Coat a large nonstick skillet with nonstick spray and warm over medium heat. Add mushrooms, onion, almonds, basil, oregano, and thyme. Cook 8 minutes, or until mushrooms give up their liquid. Remove from heat and spoon into a large bowl. Stir in rice, cottage cheese, broth, and soy sauce. Spoon into a 9" × 9" baking dish and top with cheese.

Cover and bake 10 minutes, or until cheese is melted.

Makes 4 servings

Per serving: *356 calories, 20 g protein, 43 g carbohydrates, 12 g fat, 8 mg cholesterol, 338 mg sodium, 5 g fiber*

Diet Exchanges: *0 milk, 0 vegetable, 0 fruit, 3 bread, 1¼ meat, 0 fat*

Broccoli-Cheese Spoon Bread

169 Calories

—Julie DeMatteo, Clementon, N.J.

"I believe that healthful eating habits should be taught to our children at an early age. One way is to serve vegetables in a kid-friendly style. My two sons love this lower-fat version of spoon bread."

1 can (7 ounces) fat-free evaporated milk

½ cup yellow cornmeal

½ teaspoon sugar

¼ teaspoon ground white or black pepper

½ cup (2 ounces) shredded reduced-fat extra-sharp Cheddar cheese

2 large eggs

2 large egg whites

1½ cups (12 ounces) frozen chopped broccoli, thawed and drained

¼ cup chopped roasted red peppers

¼ teaspoon salt

Preheat the oven to 375°F. Coat a 1-quart baking dish with nonstick spray.

In a medium saucepan over medium heat, gently stir evaporated milk. Gradually add cornmeal and cook, stirring constantly, 2 to 3 minutes, or until thickened. Remove from heat and stir in sugar, white or black pepper, and 6 tablespoons cheese. Stir until cheese melts.

Place eggs in a small bowl. Add ¼ cup of milk mixture, stirring constantly. Stir egg mixture back into milk mixture.

In a medium bowl, beat egg whites until stiff. Fold into milk mixture. Fold in broccoli, roasted peppers, and salt. Pour into the prepared baking dish. Bake 45 to 50 minutes, or until set. Sprinkle with remaining 2 tablespoons cheese.

Makes 4 servings

Per serving: *169 calories, 15 g protein, 15 g carbohydrates, 6 g fat, 118 mg cholesterol, 337 mg sodium, 3 g fiber*

Diet Exchanges: *½ milk, 2 vegetable, 0 fruit, 0 bread, 1 meat, 0 fat*

Chicken Stuffing Casserole

164 Calories

—Pamela Wheeler, Bernalillo, N.Mex.

"Cooking a turkey or chicken stuffing in a baking dish speeds up the time needed to roast the bird. And it's healthier from a food-safety point of view because leftovers are stored separately."

1 package (8 ounces) poultry-flavored stuffing

1 ounce (1/8 cup) dried mushrooms (shiitake or porcini)

1/4 cup dry-pack sun-dried tomatoes

1 tablespoon olive oil

1 small onion, chopped

1 celery rib, chopped

1 2/3 cups hot vegetable or chicken broth

1/4 cup raisins

2 tablespoons chopped parsley

1/2 teaspoon dried rosemary, crumbled

1/4 teaspoon ground black pepper

Place stuffing in a 2-quart baking dish.

Soak mushrooms and tomatoes in hot water for 12 minutes, or until soft. Drain and chop. Stir into stuffing.

Preheat the oven to 450°F.

Warm oil in a medium skillet over medium heat. Add onion and celery. Cook 5 minutes, or until soft. Add to stuffing along with broth, raisins, parsley, rosemary, and pepper. Mix well. Cover and bake 30 minutes, or until heated through.

Makes 8 servings

Per serving: *164 calories, 5 g protein, 31 g carbohydrates, 3 g fat, 15 mg cholesterol, 736 mg sodium, 1 g fiber*

Diet Exchanges: *0 milk, 1 vegetable, 0 fruit, 1 1/2 bread, 0 meat, 1/2 fat*

EASY WAYS TO EAT MORE VEGETABLES AND FRUITS

You've heard the recommendation about eating more produce. The trick is adding in the vegetables and fruits when they're not the main attraction. That way, you'll focus on the main dish but still get the benefits of eating these good-for-you foods. Another benefit is that you'll be full before you overeat. The fiber in vegetables and fruits is very filling and helps keep digestion moving smoothly.

Five servings a day is considered the absolute minimum. And it's not as difficult as you think. First, most servings are a tiny 1/2 cup. So, if you normally start your day with a cup of orange juice, you've knocked off two servings right there. A sandwich made with lots of tomatoes and lettuce is another. A mid-afternoon fruit snack and a serving of vegetables at dinner, and you've nailed it. Not so bad. Here are some more ideas.

- Toss broccoli florets, bell pepper strips, grated carrots, shredded spinach, peas, or sun-dried tomatoes into the cooking water before draining your pasta. These veggies will cook in minutes and add flavor, texture, and color (not to mention nutrients) to your meal.

- Keep a bag of fresh baby carrots in your handbag, briefcase, or desk drawer. Munch on those whenever you feel the need to nibble.

- Add spinach, broccoli, or bell peppers to your pizza and tomatoes or sprouts to your sandwiches.

- Start your next restaurant meal with a salad. (See page 269 for the best salad add-ins.)

- End your next meal with sorbet, fruit crisp, marinated fruit, or another fruit-based dessert.

- Use the last of the warm coals from your barbecue to grill fruits for dessert. When grilled, the natural sugars in fruit caramelize, creating a rich flavor. Try sliced pineapple, bananas (in their skins), apple chunks skewered with pears, and whole peaches. They're delicious served with low-fat vanilla frozen yogurt and sprinkled with grated nutmeg or ground cinnamon.

- Choose fruit juice or vegetable juice instead of carbonated soft drinks. (With that choice, you'll also save about 125 calories, on average.)

- Eat the orange wedges that come with your Chinese meal. Or eat the fruit or vegetable garnishes that come with just about any restaurant meal.

Easy Yeast Rolls

95 Calories

—Teri West, Louisville

"These yeasty treats fill the house with the kind of aroma that says you've been cooking all day. The truth? They take only minutes!"

¾ cup warm water (105°–115°F)
1 tablespoon rapid-rise yeast
2 tablespoons honey
2½ cups reduced-fat biscuit mix
¼–½ cup unbleached or all-purpose flour

In a large bowl, mix water, yeast, and honey. Stir in biscuit mix. Turn dough out onto a lightly floured surface. Knead 10 minutes, or until dough is slightly sticky, working in ¼ cup flour or more as necessary.

Coat a baking sheet with nonstick spray. Shape dough into 16 small rolls. Arrange rolls on the prepared baking sheet. Cover with a clean kitchen towel and let rise in a warm place 45 to 60 minutes, or until doubled in size.

Preheat the oven to 400°F. Bake 13 minutes, or until golden.

Makes 16

Per roll: *95 calories, 2 g protein, 18 g carbohydrates, 1 g fat, 0 mg cholesterol, 235 mg sodium, 0 g fiber*

Diet Exchanges: *0 milk, 0 vegetable, 0 fruit, 1 bread, 0 meat, 0 fat*

Multigrain Bread

101 Calories

—Laurie Nagy, New Westminster, British Columbia

"Here's one-stop shopping for fiber and minerals. Wheat berries, flaxseed, and 7-grain cereal are available in large supermarkets and most health food stores. To make this bread in your bread machine, follow the manufacturer's directions and place the ingredients in the machine in the order recommended by the manufacturer."

¼ **cup wheat berries**
1 **package (¼ ounce) active dry yeast**
¼ **teaspoon + 2 tablespoons sugar**
1½ **cups warm water (105°–115°F)**
1½ **cups whole-wheat flour**
1 **cup unbleached or all-purpose flour**
¼ **cup 7-grain cereal, finely ground**
¼ **cup ground flaxseed**
1 **teaspoon salt**
2 **tablespoons vegetable oil**

In a small saucepan over high heat, heat 1 cup water to boiling. Stir in wheat berries. Cover and reduce heat to low. Simmer 1 hour. Drain and let cool.

In a small bowl, combine yeast, ¼ teaspoon sugar, and ½ cup water. Let stand 5 to 10 minutes, or until yeast foams.

In a large bowl, combine whole-wheat flour, unbleached or all-purpose flour, cereal, flaxseed, salt, and remaining 2 tablespoons sugar. Stir in oil, yeast mixture, wheat berries, and remaining 1 cup water. Stir until a soft dough forms and leaves the side of the bowl.

Turn dough out onto a lightly floured surface and knead 10 minutes, or until smooth and elastic. Shape dough into a ball. Place in a large bowl coated with nonstick spray, turning dough to coat the top with oil. Cover with a clean kitchen towel and let rise in a warm place 2 hours, or until doubled in size.

Coat a 9" × 5" loaf pan with nonstick spray. Punch down dough. Shape dough into an oblong loaf and place in pan. Cover with the towel and let rise in a warm place 1 hour, or until almost doubled in size.

Preheat the oven to 375°F. Bake bread 30 to 35 minutes, or until loaf sounds hollow when tapped lightly. Remove from pan and cool on a rack.

Makes 1 loaf (18 slices)

Per slice: *101 calories, 3 g protein, 17 g carbohydrates, 3 g fat, 0 mg cholesterol, 122 mg sodium, 2 g fiber*

Diet Exchanges: *0 milk, 0 vegetable, 0 fruit, 1 bread, 0 meat, ½ fat*

TIP: I usually grind the cereal and flax in the food processor or a coffee mill.

(Photograph on page 95)

Slimming Salads and Dressings

Sweet and Creamy Spinach Salad 248

Hail Caesar Salad 249

Persian Cucumber Salad 250

Broccoli Slaw Waldorf Salad 251

Asian Slaw 252

Grilled Summer Salad 253

Tahini Dressing 254

Rancho la Puerta Basil
    Yogurt Dressing 254

Creamy Ranch Dressing 255

Blue Cheese Dressing 255

Roasted Garlic Lemon Dressing 255

Romaine Salad with
    Sherry Vinaigrette 256

Wonderful Tuna Salad 258

Crab Salad 260

Tuscan Tuna Salad 261

Sesame Chicken Salad 262

Warm Pepper and Pork Salad 264

Teriyaki Turkey Salad 266

Chicken Oriental Salad 267

Pork Salad with Black-Eyed
    Pea Dressing 268

Black Bean and Corn Salad 270

Lentil-Rice Salad 272

Beans, Beans, Beans Salad 273

Old-Fashioned Potato Salad 274

Tabbouleh Salad 275

Sweet and Creamy Spinach Salad

62 Calories

—Helen Gelb, Tobyhanna, Pa.

"This sour cream–based dressing is good on any greens, but I especially like it on fresh spinach with crumbled bacon. The kids love it, too, so it's a good way to get them to eat their greens without a fuss."

½ cup (4 ounces) reduced-fat sour cream
1 tablespoon milk
2 tablespoons sugar
1 tablespoon red wine vinegar
½ teaspoon salt
¼ teaspoon ground black pepper
1 package (10 ounces) fresh spinach, torn
1 head romaine lettuce, torn
2 celery ribs, thinly sliced
1 small red onion, thinly sliced
⅓ cup crumbled cooked bacon (4 slices)

In a small bowl, mix sour cream, milk, sugar, vinegar, salt, and pepper.

In a large bowl, combine spinach, lettuce, celery, onion, and bacon. Add dressing and toss to coat.

Makes 8 servings

Per serving: *62 calories, 4 g protein, 9 g carbohydrates, 2 g fat, 3 mg cholesterol, 231 mg sodium, 3 g fiber*

Diet Exchanges: *0 milk, 2 vegetable, 0 fruit, 0 bread, 0 meat, ½ fat*

Hail Caesar Salad

—Susan Nichols, Stockton, Calif.

"My husband and I both like to cook and eat. We try to come up with recipes that are low-fat and healthy. Here's one of our successes. We added and subtracted ingredients until it met our standards for taste and health."

2 tablespoons extra-virgin olive oil

2 tablespoons chicken broth

1 tablespoon fat-free plain yogurt

½ teaspoon lemon juice

½ teaspoon Worcestershire sauce

½-1 teaspoon anchovy paste

1 garlic clove, minced

¼ teaspoon ground black pepper

⅛ teaspoon hot-pepper sauce

1 head romaine lettuce, torn

3 tablespoons (¾ ounce) grated Parmesan cheese

½ cup plain croutons

In a large bowl, mix oil, broth, yogurt, lemon juice, Worcestershire sauce, anchovy paste, garlic, black pepper, and hot-pepper sauce. Add lettuce, cheese, and croutons. Toss to coat.

Makes 4 servings

Per serving: *125 calories, 5 g protein, 7 g carbohydrates, 9 g fat, 4 mg cholesterol, 208 mg sodium, 2 g fiber*

Diet Exchanges: *0 milk, 2 vegetable, 0 fruit, 3 bread, 0 meat, 1½ fat*

125 Calories

Deirdra Price, Ph.D.

Author and weight-loss expert Deirdra Price, Ph.D., of San Diego, has a simple eating philosophy: Weight control is a matter of enjoying, not being afraid of, food. We couldn't agree more. Here's a satisfying salad that's not fattening or frightening.

PERSIAN CUCUMBER SALAD

59 Calories

1 cucumber, peeled and cubed
2 plum tomatoes, seeded and finely chopped
¼ cup chopped red onion
¼ cup chopped parsley
2 tablespoons lemon juice
1 tablespoon extra-virgin olive oil
⅛ teaspoon salt
⅛ teaspoon ground black pepper

In a medium bowl, combine cucumber, tomatoes, onion, and parsley.

In a small bowl or measuring cup, mix lemon juice, oil, salt, and pepper. Pour over salad and toss to mix. Let marinate 30 minutes to allow flavors to develop.

Makes 4 servings

Per serving: 59 calories, 1 g protein, 7 g carbohydrates, 4 g fat, 0 mg cholesterol, 76 mg sodium, 1 g fiber

Diet Exchanges: 0 milk, 2 vegetable, 0 fruit, 0 bread, 0 meat, ½ fat

Broccoli Slaw Waldorf Salad

350 Calories

—Roxanne Weirick, Salem, Oreg.

"This slaw makes a good side dish for a summer barbecue. Or serve it with warm whole-wheat rolls for a light supper. It's filling and very satisfying."

- 3 cups (8 ounces) broccoli slaw
- 1 cup finely chopped cooked chicken breast
- 1 large red or green apple, cored and chopped
- ½ cup raisins
- ½ cup green or red seedless grapes
- ½ cup chopped walnuts
- ¼ cup sunflower seeds (optional)
- ½ cup reduced-fat mayonnaise
- 2 tablespoons fat-free milk
- 1 teaspoon honey
- 1 teaspoon lemon juice
- ¼ teaspoon salt
- ⅛ teaspoon celery seed

In a large bowl, combine broccoli slaw, chicken, apple, raisins, grapes, walnuts, and sunflower seeds, if using.

In a small bowl, mix mayonnaise, milk, honey, lemon juice, salt, and celery seed. Pour over broccoli mixture and toss until blended. Chill until ready to serve.

Makes 4 servings

Per serving: *350 calories, 16 g protein, 33 g carbohydrates, 19 g fat, 40 mg cholesterol, 215 mg sodium, 4 g fiber*

Diet Exchanges: *0 milk, 1 vegetable, 2 fruit, 0 bread, 2 meat, 1 fat*

Asian Slaw

76 Calories

—Paige Morehouse, Sonora, Calif.

*"When I feel like grilling fish or burgers, I serve this on the side.
In the cooler months, I add 2 cups of cooked rice and 8 ounces of shredded
cooked chicken to make a complete meal."*

1 cup (3 ounces) broccoli slaw
½ cup shredded carrots
½ cup chopped celery
1½ ounces mushrooms, sliced
¼ cup sliced red bell pepper
¼ cup seasoned rice vinegar
1 tablespoon canola oil
1 teaspoon sesame oil
2–3 drops hot-pepper sauce
1 tablespoon chopped dry roasted peanuts
1 tablespoon chopped fresh cilantro

In a large bowl, combine broccoli slaw, carrots, celery, mushrooms, and bell pepper.

In a small bowl or measuring cup, mix vinegar, canola oil, sesame oil, and hot-pepper sauce. Pour over salad. Garnish with peanuts and cilantro.

Makes 4 servings

Per serving: *76 calories, 2 g protein, 5 g carbohydrates, 6 g fat, 0 mg cholesterol, 36 mg sodium, 2 g fiber*

Diet Exchanges: *0 milk, 2 vegetable, 0 fruit, 0 bread, 0 meat, ½ fat*

(Photograph on page 128)

Grilled Summer Salad

132 Calories

—Darlene Fairfax, Gaithersburg, Md.

" This very low fat salad can be made ahead and served at room temperature. Remember it when you're grilling chicken or fish or even to dress up weeknight burgers. "

DRESSING

- ⅓ cup apricot preserves
- ⅓ cup balsamic vinegar
- 1 garlic clove, minced
- 1 teaspoon chopped fresh rosemary or ½ teaspoon dried
- ¼ teaspoon salt

SALAD

- 1 small eggplant, quartered lengthwise
- 1 large sweet onion, sliced ½" thick
- 1 large zucchini, sliced ½" thick
- 1 large red, yellow, or orange bell pepper, cut into strips
- 4 cups assorted salad greens (red leaf, Boston, arugula, watercress)

To make the dressing:

In a small saucepan, combine preserves, vinegar, garlic, rosemary, and salt. Heat to boiling over medium heat, stirring frequently. Remove from heat.

To make the salad:

Preheat the grill or broiler. Coat the grill rack or broiler pan with nonstick spray.

Grill eggplant, onion, zucchini, and pepper over medium-high heat or broil 4" from the heat 8 to 10 minutes, or until tender. Turn vegetables occasionally and brush with dressing.

Arrange greens on a serving platter and top with grilled vegetables. Pour any remaining dressing over vegetables.

Makes 4 servings

Per serving: *132 calories, 6 g protein, 29 g carbohydrates, 1 g fat, 0 mg cholesterol, 500 mg sodium, 5 g fiber*

Diet Exchanges: *0 milk, 4 vegetable, 0 fruit, ½ bread, 0 meat, 0 fat*

DRESSINGS TO LIVE BY

Aplate of greens is a good thing. Just be smart about what goes on top. The number one source of fat in the average American woman's diet is salad dressing. Hard to believe, but it's true. Here are some satisfying, but not sabo-taging, salad dressings. If you have a small jar with a tight-fitting lid, you can shake up these dressings and store them in the fridge for a few days.

Each recipe makes enough to coat about 6 cups of greens, or 4 servings.

TAHINI DRESSING

2 tablespoons extra-virgin olive oil
1 tablespoon tahini (sesame paste)
1 tablespoon umeboshi plum vinegar (see tip)
1 tablespoon cider vinegar
1 teaspoon Dijon mustard
¼ teaspoon salt
⅛ teaspoon ground black pepper

In a jar or small bowl, mix oil, tahini, plum vinegar, cider vinegar, mustard, salt, and pepper.

Per serving: *89 calories, 1 g protein, 1 g carbohydrates, 9 g fat, 0 mg cholesterol, 165 mg sodium, 0 g fiber*

Diet Exchanges: *0 milk, 0 vegetable, 0 fruit, 0 bread, 0 meat, 2 fat*

TIP: *Umeboshi plum vinegar is a tart, salty Japanese vinegar available in Asian groceries and health food stores.*

RANCHO LA PUERTA BASIL YOGURT DRESSING

¼ cup fat-free plain yogurt
1 shallot, finely chopped
1 scallion, chopped
1 garlic clove, minced
2 tablespoons red wine vinegar
2 tablespoons balsamic vinegar
2 tablespoons water
1 tablespoon chopped fresh basil
½ teaspoon ground black pepper
½ teaspoon chopped fresh thyme
¼ teaspoon chopped fresh cilantro

In a jar or small bowl, mix yogurt, shallot, scallion, garlic, red wine vinegar, balsamic vinegar, water, basil, pepper, thyme, and cilantro.

Per serving: *12 calories, 1 g protein, 2 g carbohydrates, 0 g fat, 0 mg cholesterol, 12 mg sodium, 0 g fiber*

Diet Exchanges: *0 milk, ½ vegetable, 0 fruit, 0 bread, 0 meat, 0 fat*

CREAMY RANCH DRESSING

2 tablespoons 1% cottage cheese

2 teaspoons grated Parmesan cheese

1½ teaspoons low-fat buttermilk

1 teaspoon lemon juice

1 teaspoon water

1 shallot, finely chopped

1 garlic clove, minced

½ teaspoon chopped fresh basil

½ teaspoon chopped fresh oregano

   Pinch of ground black pepper

In a jar or small bowl, mix cottage cheese, Parmesan, buttermilk, lemon juice, water, shallot, garlic, basil, oregano, and pepper.

Per serving: *14 calories, 2 g protein, 1 g carbohydrates, 0 g fat, 1 mg cholesterol, 51 mg sodium, 0 g fiber*

Diet Exchanges: *0 milk, 0 vegetable, 0 fruit, 0 bread, 0 meat, ½ fat*

BLUE CHEESE DRESSING

¼ cup (1 ounce) crumbled blue cheese

2 tablespoons extra-virgin olive oil

2 tablespoons brewed strong black tea

1 tablespoon red wine vinegar

1 shallot, finely chopped

1 teaspoon Dijon mustard

¼ teaspoon Worcestershire sauce

¼ teaspoon salt

   Pinch of ground black pepper

In a jar or small bowl, mix blue cheese, oil, tea, vinegar, shallot, mustard, Worcestershire sauce, salt, and pepper.

Per serving: *88 calories, 2 g protein, 1 g carbohydrates, 9 g fat, 5 mg cholesterol, 267 mg sodium, 0 g fiber*

Diet Exchanges: *0 milk, 0 vegetable, 0 fruit, 0 bread, 0 meat, 2 fat*

ROASTED GARLIC LEMON DRESSING

1 whole head garlic

3 tablespoons lemon juice

1 tablespoon oil

1 tablespoon water

⅛ teaspoon salt

2 tablespoons chopped parsley

Preheat the oven to 400°F.

   Wrap garlic in foil and bake on the oven rack 45 minutes, or until soft. Cool slightly. Squeeze garlic from its skins into a blender or food processor. Add lemon juice, oil, water, and salt. Blend or process until smooth. Stir in parsley.

Per serving: *56 calories, 1 g protein, 6 g carbohydrates, 3 g fat, 0 mg cholesterol, 69 mg sodium, 0 g fiber*

Diet Exchanges: *0 milk, 0 vegetable, 0 fruit, 0 bread, 0 meat, 1 fat*

Romaine Salad with Sherry Vinaigrette

108 Calories

—M. Baldwin, Palo Alto, Calif.

"The nutty flavor of sherry vinegar pairs well with walnuts and blue cheese."

2 tablespoons extra-virgin olive oil
3 tablespoons sherry vinegar
1 tablespoon fat-free mayonnaise
1 tablespoon lemon juice
1 teaspoon sugar
¼ teaspoon salt
¼ teaspoon ground white or black pepper
1 head romaine lettuce, torn
1 red bell pepper, chopped
½ cup toasted walnuts, chopped
¼ cup (1 ounce) crumbled blue cheese

In a small bowl, mix oil, vinegar, mayonnaise, lemon juice, sugar, salt, and white or black pepper.

In a large bowl, combine lettuce, bell pepper, walnuts, and cheese. Add dressing and toss to coat.

Makes 8 servings

Per serving: *108 calories, 4 g protein, 4 g carbohydrates, 9 g fat, 3 mg cholesterol, 154 mg sodium, 2 g fiber*

Diet Exchanges: *0 milk, 1 vegetable, 0 fruit, 0 bread, 0 meat, 2 fat*

Wonderful Tuna Salad 187 Calories

—Doretha Coval, Whitmore Lake, Mich.

"This salad makes a fantastic grilled sandwich with crusty bread. When the weather's cool, I grill the sandwich in a skillet with a little nonstick spray. Don't let the pineapple throw you; it's delicious."

1 can (12 ounces) water-packed solid white tuna, drained

1/3 cup (3 ounces) fat-free plain yogurt

1 can (4 ounces) crushed pineapple, drained

1 celery rib, finely chopped

1/4 cup sweet pickle relish

1/4 cup chopped pecans

1 teaspoon yellow mustard

1/8 teaspoon ground cinnamon

In a medium bowl, mix tuna, yogurt, pineapple, celery, relish, pecans, mustard, and cinnamon.

Makes 4 servings

Per serving: *187 calories, 24 g protein, 11 g carbohydrates, 6 g fat, 26 mg cholesterol, 433 mg sodium, 1 g fiber*

Diet Exchanges: *1/2 milk, 0 vegetable, 1 fruit, 0 bread, 1 meat, 0 fat*

Crab Salad

201 Calories

—Suzanne Exler, Los Angeles

"I especially enjoy this in the summer with a fresh baguette and some greens."

1¼ cups (10 ounces) low-fat plain yogurt

¼ cup reduced-fat mayonnaise

⅓ cup chopped fresh dill

1 tablespoon chopped fresh tarragon or 1 teaspoon dried

2 teaspoons Dijon mustard

¼ teaspoon salt

1 pound lump or imitation crabmeat, chopped

2 cucumbers, seeded and chopped

4 scallions, chopped

In a large bowl, mix yogurt, mayonnaise, dill, tarragon, mustard, and salt. Stir in crabmeat, cucumbers, and scallions. Cover and refrigerate at least 3 hours to blend flavors.

Makes 4 servings

Per serving: *201 calories, 24 g protein, 11 g carbohydrates, 6 g fat, 102 mg cholesterol, 544 mg sodium, 0 g fiber*

Diet Exchanges: *1 milk, 0 vegetable, 0 fruit, 0 bread, 2 meat, 0 fat*

Tuscan Tuna Salad

192 Calories

—Kristen O'Brien, Shelburne, Vt.

"This isn't your ordinary tuna salad. A light and flavorful vinaigrette and white beans turn the old sandwich filling into a satisfying meal. If there's no bread in the house, I serve it on a bed of greens."

2 tablespoons lemon juice

2 tablespoons whole-grain mustard

1 tablespoon olive oil

1 tablespoon balsamic or red wine vinegar

1 garlic clove, minced

¼ teaspoon salt

¼ teaspoon ground black pepper

1 can (16 ounces) white beans, rinsed and drained

1 can (6 ounces) water-packed solid white tuna, drained

3 tablespoons chopped fresh basil

Tomato wedges (optional)

In a large bowl, mix lemon juice, mustard, oil, vinegar, garlic, salt, and pepper. Add beans, tuna, and basil. Toss to mix. Serve with tomato wedges, if using.

Makes 4 servings

Per serving: 192 calories, 19 g protein, 23 g carbohydrates, 6 g fat, 18 mg cholesterol, 801 mg sodium, 7 g fiber

Diet Exchanges: 0 milk, 0 vegetable, 0 fruit, 1½ bread, 1 meat, 0 fat

Sesame Chicken Salad

257 Calories

—Cherie Groves, Newnan, Ga.

"You don't have to bread and deep-fry chicken to make it crunchy and crisp. This recipe uses sesame seeds for crunch and oven heat for cooking. Teriyaki sauce keeps the chicken moist and flavorful."

1 pound boneless, skinless chicken breasts, cut into thin strips

3 tablespoons teriyaki sauce

¼ cup sesame seeds

1 package (16 ounces) coleslaw mix

1 can (5 ounces) Oriental fried noodles

½ cup fat-free honey Dijon salad dressing

Place chicken in a shallow bowl. Toss with teriyaki sauce and let sit 10 minutes.

Preheat the oven to 350°F.

Place sesame seeds on waxed paper. Roll chicken in sesame seeds to coat. Arrange on a baking sheet and bake, turning once, 10 to 12 minutes, or until chicken is no longer pink.

Divide coleslaw among 4 plates. Top each with chicken and noodles. Drizzle with dressing.

Makes 4 servings

Per serving: *257 calories, 22 g protein, 26 g carbohydrates, 8 g fat, 51 mg cholesterol, 772 mg sodium, 4 g fiber*

Diet Exchanges: *0 milk, 1 vegetable, 0 fruit, 1 bread, 2 meat, 0 fat*

Warm Pepper and Pork Salad

—Karen Gazaway, Acworth, Ga.

"When I'm in a real hurry, I use leftover pork or chicken and jarred roasted peppers instead of starting with fresh. I just warm them in the microwave. A sprinkle of sunflower seeds on top is nice, too."

182 Calories

- 3 red, green, and/or yellow bell peppers, seeded and quartered
- ½ pound lean pork tenderloin
- 2 teaspoons olive oil
- ½ onion, thinly sliced
- ¼ head red cabbage, thinly sliced
- 2 celery ribs, thinly sliced
- ½ teaspoon salt
- ⅛ teaspoon ground black pepper
- ¼ cup reduced-fat balsamic vinaigrette dressing
- ¼ cup (1 ounce) shredded reduced-fat Muenster or mozzarella cheese

Preheat the broiler. Place bell peppers on a broiler pan and cook 4" from the heat, turning occasionally, until skin is bubbly and browned all over. Transfer to a paper bag, seal, and set aside 5 minutes, or until cool enough to handle. Remove and discard skin, ribs, and seeds. Cut peppers into strips.

Place pork on the broiler pan and cook 12 to 15 minutes, turning once, or until a thermometer inserted in center reaches 155°F and juices run clear. Let stand 10 minutes. Cut into thin slices.

Warm oil in a medium skillet over medium heat. Add onion, cabbage, celery, salt, and black pepper. Cook, stirring frequently, 10 minutes, or until tender.

Divide cabbage mixture among 4 plates. Arrange peppers and pork on top. Drizzle each with dressing and sprinkle with 1 tablespoon cheese.

Makes 4 servings

Per serving: *182 calories, 16 g protein, 19 g carbohydrates, 5 g fat, 35 mg cholesterol, 581 mg sodium, 4 g fiber*

Diet Exchanges: *0 milk, 3 vegetable, 0 fruit, 0 bread, 1½ meat, 0 fat*

Teriyaki Turkey Salad

272 Calories

—Paul Serkin, Brooklyn, N.Y.

"Depending on the weather, I grill or broil the turkey for this versatile dish. It can be served warm or cold over greens or pasta."

¼ cup packed brown sugar

¼ cup reduced-sodium soy sauce

2 tablespoons lemon juice

1 tablespoon vegetable oil

1 tablespoon sesame oil

1 garlic clove, minced

¼ teaspoon ground ginger

1 pound boneless, skinless turkey breast, cut into 1" cubes

2½ ounces (2 cups) mixed salad greens (red leaf, Boston, arugula, watercress)

¼ cup toasted cashews

In a large resealable plastic bag, combine brown sugar, soy sauce, lemon juice, vegetable oil, sesame oil, garlic, and ginger. Add turkey. Seal and refrigerate at least 20 minutes or up to 3 hours, stirring occasionally.

Coat the grill rack or broiler pan with nonstick spray. Preheat the grill or broiler. Thread meat onto 4 metal skewers. Grill over medium-hot coals or broil 4" from heat 15 minutes, turning occasionally, or until center of meat is no longer pink and juices run clear.

Divide greens among 4 plates. Top each with a skewer. Garnish each with 1 tablespoon cashews.

Makes 4 servings

Per serving: *272 calories, 22 g protein, 17 g carbohydrates, 13 g fat, 44 mg cholesterol, 651 mg sodium, 1 g fiber*

Diet Exchanges: *0 milk, 0 vegetable, 0 fruit, 1 bread, 3 meat, 0 fat*

Chicken Oriental Salad

314 Calories

—Toni Whielty, Carson City, Nev.

"I make this Asian-flavored dish for lunch and light suppers. So far,
I've lost 30 pounds, and I swear this recipe helped."

2 envelopes (3 ounces each) low-fat chicken ramen soup mix

2 cups cubed cooked chicken breast

1 head cabbage, thinly sliced (6 cups)

1 celery rib, thinly sliced

1 red onion, thinly sliced

3 tablespoons seasoned rice vinegar

1 tablespoon canola oil

1 teaspoon sugar (optional)

Set ramen seasoning package aside. Place noodles in a large bowl. Add hot water to cover and soak 10 minutes, or until soft. Drain. Add chicken, cabbage, celery, and onion.

In a small bowl, combine ramen seasoning package, vinegar, oil, and sugar, if using. Pour over salad. Cover and chill 1 hour to allow flavors to blend.

Makes 4 servings

Per serving: *314 calories, 27 g protein, 35 g carbohydrates, 7 g fat, 59 mg cholesterol, 803 mg sodium, 4 g fiber*

Diet Exchanges: *0 milk, 2 vegetable, 0 fruit, ½ bread, 3 meat, 0 fat*

Pork Salad with Black-Eyed Pea Dressing

209 Calories

—Nancy Rossi Brownell, Fishkill, N.Y.

"A little freshly ground black pepper and some hot crusty bread, and this meal is complete. Use a mix of greens like Bibb, escarole, radicchio, mâche, and romaine for more texture, flavor, and color."

1 can (14½ ounces) reduced-sodium chicken broth

¼ cup dry sherry or apple juice

1 tablespoon chopped fresh tarragon or 1 teaspoon dried

2 garlic cloves, minced

½ teaspoon paprika

¼ teaspoon ground sage

¼ teaspoon ground cumin

1 large sweet onion, thinly sliced

2 boneless center-cut pork loin chops, trimmed of visible fat (about 2 to 3 ounces each)

1 can (16 ounces) black-eyed peas, rinsed and drained

1 tablespoon Dijon mustard

10 ounces (8 cups) mixed salad greens (red leaf, Boston, arugula, watercress)

In a medium skillet over medium-high heat, combine ½ cup broth, sherry or apple juice, tarragon, garlic, paprika, sage, cumin, and onion. Heat to boiling and add pork. Reduce heat to low, cover, and simmer, turning meat once, 5 minutes, or until a thermometer inserted in center of pork registers 155°F and juices run clear. Remove pork to a plate and set aside. Stir in remaining broth, black-eyed peas, and mustard. Increase heat to medium-high and heat to boiling. Cook, uncovered, 10 minutes, or until mixture is reduced by half.

Thinly slice pork on the diagonal. Divide greens among 4 large plates. Arrange pork on top. Drizzle with dressing.

Makes 4 servings

Per serving: *209 calories, 17 g protein, 22 g carbohydrates, 6 g fat, 20 mg cholesterol, 676 mg sodium, 5 g fiber*

Diet Exchanges: *0 milk, 2 vegetable, 0 fruit, 1 bread, 1 meat, 0 fat*

BEST SALAD ADD-INS

Salad bars have become the food equivalent of the Internet: too many choices! Here's a hint for navigating your way down the line: the shinier the item, the more fattening it is. How can we be so sure? Because shiny equals oil, as in salad dressing. A thick coating of oil also ensures that ingredients, which have to withstand long hours of display, don't dry out. So go easy on the glossy choices.

Here are the healthiest items on display, plus a few crunchy treats that won't boost calories too much. They're listed from highest to lowest according to calories.

Food	Calories
2 tablespoons sesame seeds	110
2 tablespoons chickpeas	91
2 pickled beets	65
2 tablespoons raisins	54
2 tablespoons bacon bits	48
5 pieces baby corn	43
2 tablespoons chopped hard-cooked eggs	40
2 tablespoons chow mein noodles	30
2 tablespoons kidney beans	28
1 cup sliced fennel	27
5 olives	25
2 tablespoons croutons	23
5 baby carrots	19
5 cherry tomatoes	18
1 cup shredded cabbage	17

Food	Calories
1/4 cup red onions	15
1/4 cup shredded carrots	12
1/4 cup chopped bell peppers	10
1 cup radicchio	9
1 cup romaine lettuce	8
1/4 cup mung bean sprouts	8
1/4 cup alfalfa sprouts	7
1 cup Belgian endive	7
1 cup iceberg lettuce	7
1 cup spinach	7
1/4 cup sliced mushrooms	6
1 cup arugula	5
2 tablespoons chopped scallions	4
1 cup watercress	4
5 cucumber slices	3
2 tablespoons chopped celery	2

Black Bean and Corn Salad

183 Calories

—Robin Kenwood, New York City

"If you like high-flavor food, try this salad. It serves 4 as a main-dish salad or 6 as a side dish. It keeps in the refrigerator for a couple of days."

1 can (15 ounces) black beans, rinsed and drained

2 cups fresh or thawed frozen corn

2 jalapeño chile peppers, seeded and finely chopped (wear plastic gloves when handling)

2 plum tomatoes, seeded and chopped

1/2 cup finely chopped red onion

2 garlic cloves, minced

1/4 cup chopped fresh cilantro

2 tablespoons lime juice

1 tablespoon olive oil

2 teaspoons Southwest-style seasoning mix

1/4 teaspoon salt

In a large bowl, combine beans, corn, peppers, tomatoes, onion, garlic, and cilantro.

In a small bowl or measuring cup, mix lime juice, oil, seasoning mix, and salt. Pour over salad. Cover and refrigerate 1 hour to allow flavors to develop.

Makes 4 servings

Per serving: 183 calories, 8 g protein, 37 g carbohydrates, 4 g fat, 0 mg cholesterol, 768 mg sodium, 8 g fiber

Diet Exchanges: 0 milk, 1 vegetable, 0 fruit, 2 bread, 0 meat, 1/2 fat

Lentil-Rice Salad

412 Calories

—Frances Taylor, Ottawa, Ontario

"I like the fennel in this salad, but another flavor can be used, such as ground coriander or cumin. Sometimes I serve it without the onion and dressing for a nutritious hot rice dish."

½ cup dry brown lentils

1 tablespoon curry powder

2 cups cooked basmati rice

½ cup finely chopped Spanish onion

½ cup pine nuts

½ cup raisins or currants

1 teaspoon fennel seeds, crushed (see tip)

2 tablespoons extra-virgin olive oil

1 tablespoon white wine vinegar

½ teaspoon mustard powder

½ teaspoon salt

Place lentils in a large saucepan. Cover with water and add curry powder. Heat to boiling over high heat. Reduce heat to low, cover, and simmer 20 minutes. Drain and set aside to cool. Add rice, onion, nuts, raisins or currants, and fennel seeds.

In a small bowl or measuring cup, mix oil, vinegar, mustard powder, and salt. Pour over salad and toss to mix.

Makes 4 servings

Per serving: *412 calories, 15 g protein, 56 g carbohydrates, 18 g fat, 0 mg cholesterol, 276 mg sodium, 2 g fiber*

Diet Exchanges: *0 milk, 0 vegetable, 0 fruit, 3 bread, 0 meat, 4 fat*

TIP: To crush fennel seeds, use a mortar and pestle. Or place the seeds between sheets of waxed paper and crush with a rolling pin or the bottom of a small heavy saucepan.

Beans, Beans, Beans Salad

226 Calories

—Navarre Bautista, Monterey, Calif.

" I took a classic three-bean salad and updated it. It's still a winner. Use your favorite bean combo, like kidney beans, green beans, wax beans, chickpeas, or black beans. "

3 cans (16 ounces each) beans (kidney, wax, green, or black), rinsed and drained

1 green bell pepper, cut into thin strips

1 small red onion, thinly sliced

1 jar (7 ounces) roasted red peppers, drained and cut into strips

⅓ cup balsamic vinegar

¼ cup olive oil

1 teaspoon salt

1 teaspoon dried Italian seasoning

½ teaspoon mustard powder

¼ teaspoon ground black pepper

In a large bowl, combine beans, bell pepper, onion, roasted peppers, vinegar, oil, salt, Italian seasoning, mustard powder, and black pepper. Toss to mix. Cover and refrigerate 2 hours or overnight.

Makes 8 servings

Per serving: *226 calories, 8 g protein, 36 g carbohydrates, 8 g fat, 0 mg cholesterol, 789 mg sodium, 8 g fiber*

Diet Exchanges: *0 milk, 0 vegetable, 0 fruit, 2 bread, 0 meat, 1 fat*

Dean Ornish, M.D.

In his research at the Preventive Medicine Research Institute in Sausalito, California, Dean Ornish, M.D., demonstrated that heart disease can be reversed without drugs or surgery. One of the best "side effects" of his plan is weight loss. Dr. Ornish's approach includes exercise, stress control, and a mostly vegetarian diet. But that doesn't mean crunching on "hippie" food. This delicious salad is about as mainstream, yet lean, as you can get.

OLD-FASHIONED POTATO SALAD

212 Calories

3 **eggs**
3 **pounds red-skinned potatoes**
3 **celery ribs, finely chopped**
1 **small red onion, finely chopped**
¾ **cup fat-free mayonnaise**
¼ **cup cider vinegar**
3 **tablespoons sweet pickle relish**
1 **tablespoon chopped parsley**
1½ **teaspoons salt**
¼ **teaspoon ground black pepper**

Place whole eggs in a small saucepan. Cover with hot water and heat to boiling over high heat. Reduce heat to low, cover, and simmer 12 minutes. Drain and cool in cold water. Remove and discard egg shells. Cut eggs in half. Remove and discard yolks. Chop whites.

Heat 2" water to boiling in a large saucepan. Put potatoes in a steamer basket and place in the saucepan. Cover and steam 30 to 35 minutes, or until fork-tender. Remove from heat and set aside to cool. When cool enough to handle, peel and cut into small cubes.

In a large bowl, combine celery, onion, mayonnaise, vinegar, relish, parsley, salt, pepper, potatoes, and egg whites.

Makes 8 servings

Per serving: *212 calories, 6 g protein, 44 g carbohydrates, 2 g fat, 80 mg cholesterol, 775 mg sodium, 3 g fiber*

Diet Exchanges: *0 milk, 0 vegetable, 0 fruit, 2 bread, ½ meat, 0 fat*

Tabbouleh Salad

122 Calories

—Katia Nessif, Arcadia, Calif.

" I serve this traditional Lebanese salad on lettuce or grape leaves, stuffed inside pita bread, or as a dip with pita chips for scooping. "

2 cups chopped parsley
½ cup chopped fresh mint
½ cup chopped scallions
½ cup lemon juice
3 tablespoons extra-virgin olive oil
½ teaspoon salt
¼ teaspoon allspice
⅔ cup fine-grain bulgur
2 tomatoes, seeded and chopped

In a large bowl, combine parsley, mint, scallions, lemon juice, oil, salt, and allspice.

Place bulgur in another large bowl. Cover with boiling water. Cover and let stand 4 minutes, or until bulgur is just tender. Drain.

Stir bulgur into parsley mixture. Cover and refrigerate 2 hours or overnight. Stir in tomatoes just before serving.

Makes 8 servings

Per serving: *122 calories, 3 g protein, 17 g carbohydrates, 5 g fat, 0 mg cholesterol, 146 mg sodium, 3 g fiber*

Diet Exchanges: *0 milk, 0 vegetable, 0 fruit, 1 bread, 0 meat, 1 fat*

Sweet Treats

Peanut Butter Cake with
   Chocolate Frosting 278

Chocolate-Raspberry Avalanche Cake . . .280

Yummy Pineapple Cake 282

Carrot Cake with Cream
   Cheese Frosting 284

Pumpkin Cake .285

Banana Chocolate Chip Bread 286

The Duchess's Chocolate
   Mousse Tartlets 289

Double Chocolate Chip
   Fudge Brownies 290

Chocolate Chunk Cookies 292

Chocolate-Pecan Meringues 294

John's Gingerbread 296

Hamantaschen .297

Tapioca Pudding 298

Quick Rice Pudding 299

Pumpkin-Ginger Rice Pudding 300

Corn Crepes with Strawberry Sauce 301

Black Cherry Baked Apples 302

Baked Apple with Papaya Sauce 304

Cranberry-Apple Crisp 305

Wonton Fruit Cups 306

Guiltless Banana Split 307

Roasted Fruit Wraps with
   Dipping Sauce 308

Pistachio-Pineapple Yogurt Pie 310

Tiramisu 313

Potluck Trifle 314

Peanut Butter Cake with Chocolate Frosting

—Don Mauer, Raleigh, N.C.

"When my friend Peter had a birthday, I created a peanut butter cake using reduced-fat peanut butter. I frosted it with a rich, smooth chocolate frosting. It had only 3 grams of fat per serving, and Peter said it was his best birthday cake ever."

CAKE

- ⅔ cup unsweetened applesauce
- 2 cups sifted cake flour
- 3 teaspoons baking powder
- ½ cup reduced-fat or natural peanut butter
- 1 cup packed brown sugar
- 1 teaspoon vanilla extract
- 2 large eggs
- 1 large egg white
- ¾ cup fat-free milk

FROSTING

- 2⅔ cups sifted confectioners' sugar
- 6 tablespoons low-fat margarine or butter
- ½ cup Dutch-process or regular cocoa powder
- 1 teaspoon vanilla extract
- 3 teaspoons fat-free milk

To make the cake:

Place a strainer over a deep bowl. Spoon applesauce into the strainer and set aside to drain 15 minutes (you should have about ⅓ cup drained applesauce). Discard the liquid.

Preheat the oven to 350°F. Coat a 13" × 9" baking dish with nonstick spray.

In a medium bowl, combine flour and baking powder.

In a large bowl, with an electric mixer, beat peanut butter 2 minutes. Add drained applesauce and beat 2 minutes. Beat in brown sugar 3 minutes, or until creamy. Beat in vanilla extract. Beat in eggs, one at a time. Beat in egg white. Beat in milk. Add flour mixture and mix on low until moistened.

Pour batter into the prepared baking dish and bake 20 to 25 minutes, or until center of cake springs back when pressed. Cool completely in the dish on a rack.

To make the frosting:

In a food processor or large bowl, combine half of confectioners' sugar, the margarine or butter, cocoa, and vanilla extract. Process or beat until confectioners' sugar dissolves. Add remaining confectioners' sugar and 2 teaspoons milk. Process or beat just until smooth. If frosting is too thick, add remaining 1 teaspoon milk.

Spread frosting on cooled cake.

Makes 24 servings

Per serving: *160 calories, 3 g protein, 31 g carbohydrates, 3 g fat, 18 mg cholesterol, 133 mg sodium, 1 g fiber*

Diet Exchanges: *0 milk, 0 vegetable, 0 fruit, 1½ bread, 0 meat, 1 fat*

160 Calories

Chocolate-Raspberry Avalanche Cake

206 Calories

—Lisa Keys, Middlebury, Conn.

" This cake is easier than it looks (and sounds!). It's all done in a square baking dish and ends up like a chocolate brownie cake served with chocolate sauce and raspberry cream. Yum! "

1¾ cups cake flour
1 cup sugar
½ cup unsweetened cocoa powder
1 teaspoon baking powder
½ teaspoon baking soda
¼ teaspoon salt
1½ cups (12 ounces) low-fat plain yogurt
2 tablespoons canola oil
1 teaspoon vanilla extract
3 egg whites
1¼ cups fresh raspberries
2 tablespoons honey
2 tablespoons hot water
¼ cup raspberry preserves

Preheat the oven to 350°F. Coat a 9" × 9" baking dish with nonstick spray.

In a large bowl, combine flour, ½ cup sugar, ¼ cup cocoa, baking powder, baking soda, and salt.

In a medium bowl, combine 1 cup yogurt, oil, and vanilla extract.

In a small bowl, beat egg whites until soft peaks form. Gradually beat in remaining ½ cup sugar until stiff peaks form. Stir yogurt

mixture into flour mixture just until moistened. Fold in egg whites.

Pour into the prepared baking dish. Sprinkle evenly with 1 cup raspberries. Bake 40 minutes, or until a wooden pick inserted in center comes out clean. Cool in the pan on a rack 10 minutes. Remove from the pan and cool completely. Cut into 12 squares.

In another small bowl, mix honey, water, and remaining ¼ cup cocoa.

In another medium bowl, mix remaining ½ cup yogurt and preserves. Serve each square with a dollop of raspberry cream and a drizzle of chocolate sauce.

Makes 12 servings

Per serving: *206 calories, 4 g protein, 41 g carbohydrates, 3 g fat, 2 mg cholesterol, 171 mg sodium, 1 g fiber*

Diet Exchanges: *0 milk, 0 vegetable, ½ fruit, 2 bread, 0 meat, ½ fat*

Yummy Pineapple Cake

277 Calories

—Judy Temple, Wellsburg, W.Va.

"This recipe turns a box of cake mix into a sunny-tasting pineapple treat. It's the perfect dessert for potlucks."

1 package (18 ounces) yellow cake mix

¾ cup liquid egg substitute or 3 eggs

1 cup water

1 can (20 ounces) unsweetened crushed pineapple

1 package (8 ounces) fat-free cream cheese

2 cups fat-free milk

1 package (1 ounce) sugar-free vanilla-flavored pudding and pie filling

⅛ teaspoon ground cinnamon

⅛ teaspoon ground nutmeg

1 cup reduced-fat whipped topping

1 can (15½ ounces) mandarin oranges, drained (optional)

Preheat the oven to 325°F or according to cake mix package directions. Coat a 13" × 9" baking dish with nonstick spray.

Prepare cake mix according to package directions using egg substitute or eggs and water. Pour into the prepared baking dish. Bake according to package directions.

Remove from the oven and cool in the pan on a rack. Poke holes all over cake with the handle of a small wooden spoon. Pour pineapple (with juice) over cake.

In a large bowl, with an electric mixer, beat cream cheese until smooth. Add milk, pudding mix, cinnamon, and nutmeg. Beat 3 minutes. Pour over pineapple. Top with whipped topping. Decorate with oranges, if using. Cover and refrigerate at least 4 hours.

Makes 12 servings

Per serving: *277 calories, 8 g protein, 46 g carbohydrates, 6 g fat, 3 mg cholesterol, 543 mg sodium, 0 g fiber*

Diet Exchanges: *0 milk, 0 vegetable, 0 fruit, 3 bread, 0 meat, 1 fat*

FROM THE PROS

Dean Ornish, M.D.

Despite it's healthy-sounding name, carrot cake is one of the most fattening dessert choices you can make. It's typically prepared with loads of oil. Luckily, in the hands of healthy-heart guru Dean Ornish, of the Preventive Medicine Research Institute in Sausalito, California, this cake becomes as good for you as it is tasty. Look for carrot puree in the baby food section of your supermarket.

CARROT CAKE WITH CREAM CHEESE FROSTING

164 Calories

2 cups shredded carrots (about 2 large)
¾ cup sugar
1 can (4 ounces) crushed pineapple
1 jar (4 ounces) carrot puree
4 egg whites or ½ cup liquid egg substitute
2 teaspoons vanilla extract
½ teaspoon salt
1¼ cups cake flour
1¼ cups oat bran
2 teaspoons baking soda
1½ teaspoons ground cinnamon
1 package (8 ounces) fat-free cream cheese, softened

Preheat the oven to 425°F. Coat a 9" round cake pan with nonstick spray.

In a large bowl, mix carrots, ½ cup sugar, pineapple (with juice), carrot puree, egg whites or egg substitute, vanilla extract, and salt.

In another large bowl, combine flour, oat bran, baking soda, and cinnamon. Fold in carrot mixture just until combined.

Pour into the prepared pan and bake 30 minutes, or until lightly browned and firm to the touch. Cool in the pan on a rack 10 minutes. Remove from the pan.

In a medium bowl, with an electric mixer, beat cream cheese and remaining ¼ cup sugar. Spread evenly over cake.

Makes 12 servings

Per serving: *164 calories, 7 g protein, 27 g carbohydrates, 1 g fat, 0 mg cholesterol, 361 mg sodium, 2 g fiber*

Diet Exchanges: *0 milk, 1 vegetable, 1 fruit, 1 bread, 0 meat, 0 fat*

Pumpkin Cake

188 Calories

—Elizabeth A. Snyder, Belcamp, Md.

"In the fall months, this is my favorite snacking cake. Wrap each serving individually and store in the freezer for a ready take-along treat."

1 can (29 ounces) pumpkin puree

1½ cups fat-free milk

¾ cup fat-free dry milk

6 egg whites

¾ cup sugar

1½ teaspoons ground cinnamon

1½ teaspoons ground allspice

1 package (9 ounces) yellow cake mix

⅓ cup packed brown sugar

¼ cup butter

¾ cup chopped walnuts (optional)

Preheat the oven to 350°F. Coat a 13" × 9" baking dish with nonstick spray.

In a large bowl, using an electric mixer, beat pumpkin, milk, and dry milk until smooth. Beat in egg whites, sugar, cinnamon, and allspice. Pour into the prepared baking dish.

In a medium bowl, combine cake mix and brown sugar. Using a fork or pastry blender, cut in butter until crumbly. Sprinkle evenly over pumpkin mixture. Sprinkle with walnuts, if using.

Cover with foil and bake 45 minutes. Remove foil and bake 15 to 20 minutes, or until golden brown and a wooden pick inserted in center comes out clean. Cool completely in the pan before cutting.

Makes 16 servings

Per serving: *188 calories, 5 g protein, 33 g carbohydrates, 5 g fat, 9 mg cholesterol, 188 mg sodium, 2 g fiber*

Diet Exchanges: *0 milk, 0 vegetable, 0 fruit, 2 bread, 0 meat, 1 fat*

Banana Chocolate Chip Bread

239 Calories

—Linda Ann Archie, Raymond, N.H.

"Bananas with cinnamon and chocolate with cinnamon are two of my favorite flavor combinations. In this recipe, all three flavors are combined into one sweet treat.**"**

1½ cups unbleached or all-purpose flour
1½ teaspoons baking powder
½ teaspoon baking soda
½ teaspoon salt
½ teaspoon ground cinnamon
½ cup sugar
2 egg whites or ¼ cup liquid egg substitute
½ cup fat-free vanilla yogurt
2 tablespoons butter, melted
3 large ripe bananas
½ cup mini semisweet chocolate morsels

Preheat the oven to 350°F. Coat an 8" × 4" loaf pan with nonstick spray.

In a medium bowl, combine flour, baking powder, baking soda, salt, and cinnamon.

In a large bowl, with an electric mixer, beat sugar and egg whites or egg substitute until light and fluffy. Blend in yogurt and butter. Mash bananas with a fork and stir into yogurt mixture. Stir in flour mixture. Fold in chocolate chips. Pour into the prepared pan.

Bake 50 to 55 minutes, or until a wooden pick inserted in center comes out clean.

Remove from the oven. Cool 10 minutes in the pan on a rack. Remove from the pan and cool completely.

Makes 1 loaf (10 slices)

Per slice: *239 calories, 5 g protein, 42 g carbohydrates, 6 g fat, 8 mg cholesterol, 284 mg sodium, 1 g fiber*

Diet Exchanges: *0 milk, 0 vegetable, 1 fruit, 1½ bread, 0 meat, 1 fat*

It Worked for Me!

Sarah, the Duchess of York

VITAL STATS

Weight lost: 70 pounds

Time kept it off: 2 years

Weight-loss strategies:
Exercising, good diet planning, support from other dieters

Weight-maintenance strategies: Healthy eating plan, regular exercise, continued vigilance, helping others achieve success

Her weight was out of control, and so was her life. But now, the Duchess of York is strong, centered, and lean.

They once called her the Duchess of Pork. But today, Fergie is fighting back. "While I can laugh at all the names, at the time, I felt humiliated, alone, and defeated," she says. "I felt as if I were on a downward spiral spinning faster and faster. Yet, I have learned that rock bottom can be a powerful place from where to restart one's life. There's no place to go but up."

Sarah is now Weight Watchers' spokesperson. She qualified by losing weight along with other dieters on the plan. And she credits them with being part of her support network. "In the past years, I have learned a tremendous amount about eating the right foods, exercising, and banishing bad habits. I have learned these lessons from women who have refused to become victims: my old friends, my new friends at Weight Watchers, and health and fitness experts I have met on my travels. Happily, I can call on these people when I need them most."

With her new commitment to herself and her weight, Sarah finds that her taste preferences are healthier now, too. "I have a new list of favorite foods because my tastes and habits have changed. Now, instead of simply giving in to my penchant for sausage rolls and mayonnaise, I seek out food that is good for my body."

Sarah no longer sees food as the enemy. "Now, I use food as a way to control my life. I recognize that fresh, wholesome foods will keep me steady and energized. I still enjoy my ham sandwiches, but now I know that I can have a little and still maintain control.

"I work every single day at staying healthy and trim. It certainly is one of the greatest challenges I have ever encountered. But now that I am a mother—a mother who wants to set a good example for her daughters—I know that living a healthy, happy life is a priority." ■

The Duchess's Chocolate Mousse Tartlets

100 Calories

One of the reasons so many women love Fergie is because she seems like one of us. Her passion for chocolate confirms that suspicion. Here's one way to enjoy the temptation royally. Look for mini phyllo shells in the freezer section of your supermarket.

6 tablespoons sugar
1 egg white
⅛ teaspoon cream of tartar
1½ ounces unsweetened chocolate, melted
12 mini phyllo shells, at room temperature

In a small saucepan over medium heat, combine 4 tablespoons sugar with 2 tablespoons water. Cook, swirling the pan periodically, 8 minutes, or until syrup boils and registers 240°F on a candy thermometer.

In a medium bowl, with an electric mixer, beat egg white until frothy. Add cream of tartar and remaining 2 tablespoons sugar. Beat until stiff, glossy peaks form. Gradually beat in syrup, mixing until the bowl is no longer hot. With a rubber spatula, fold in chocolate.

Divide the mixture among phyllo shells. Cover with plastic wrap and refrigerate at least 1 hour before serving.

Makes 12 servings

Per serving: *100 calories, 2 g protein, 17 g carbohydrates, 3 g fat, 0 mg cholesterol, 97 mg sodium, 0 g fiber*

Diet Exchanges: *0 milk, 0 vegetable, 0 fruit, 1 bread, 0 meat, ½ fat*

Double Chocolate Chip Fudge Brownies

174 Calories

—Don Mauer, Raleigh, N.C.

"Everyone who tastes these brownies mistakes them for their high-fat cousins."

¾ cup unsweetened applesauce
1 cup unbleached or all-purpose flour
⅔ cup unsweetened cocoa powder
½ teaspoon salt
1 large egg
2 large egg whites
2 cups sugar
1 teaspoon vanilla extract
¼ cup mini semisweet chocolate morsels

Place a strainer over a deep bowl. Spoon applesauce into the strainer and set aside to drain 15 minutes (you should have about ½ cup drained applesauce). Discard the liquid in the bowl.

Preheat the oven to 350°F. Coat a nonstick 11" × 7" baking dish with butter-flavored nonstick spray. Set aside.

In a medium bowl, combine flour, cocoa, and salt.

In a large bowl, beat egg and egg whites until frothy. Add sugar, drained applesauce, and vanilla extract. Stir until sugar dissolves. Add flour mixture and chocolate morsels. Stir just until dry ingredients are moistened.

Pour batter into the prepared baking dish and bake 30 minutes. Cool in the pan on a rack.

Makes 15

Per brownie: *174 calories, 3 g protein, 40 g carbohydrates, 2 g fat, 14 mg cholesterol, 86 mg sodium, 0 g fiber*

Diet Exchanges: *0 milk, 0 vegetable, 0 fruit, 2 bread, 0 meat, ½ fat*

Chocolate Chunk Cookies

77 Calories

—Jayne Tingley, London, Ontario

" These aren't your everyday chocolate chip cookies. Oatmeal keeps these moist and flavorful. If you can find chocolate chunks or pieces, they make for a dramatic cookie (large supermarkets carry them). Traditional chips work just fine, too. "

1 cup unbleached or all-purpose flour

1 cup whole-wheat flour

½ cup quick-cooking oats

1 teaspoon baking soda

½ teaspoon salt

1 cup sugar

½ cup packed brown sugar

⅓ cup butter or margarine

2 egg whites

2 tablespoons 1% milk

1 teaspoon vanilla extract

1 package (6 ounces) semisweet chocolate pieces or morsels

Preheat the oven to 375°F. Coat 2 baking sheets with nonstick spray.

In a large bowl, combine unbleached or all-purpose flour, whole-wheat flour, oats, baking soda, and salt.

In another large bowl, combine sugar, brown sugar, butter or margarine, egg whites, milk, and vanilla extract. Add flour mixture and stir just until moistened. Stir in chocolate pieces.

Drop by rounded teaspoonfuls, 2" apart, on the prepared baking sheets. Bake 10 to 12 minutes, or until lightly browned around the edges. Remove cookies to racks to cool.

Makes 48

Per cookie: *77 calories, 1 g protein, 13 g carbohydrates, 2 g fat, 3 mg cholesterol, 63 mg sodium, 1 g fiber*

Diet Exchanges: *0 milk, 0 vegetable, 0 fruit, ½ bread, 0 meat, ½ fat*

Chocolate-Pecan Meringues

36 Calories

—Jane Imm, Gibsonia, Pa.

"When you need a sweet, crunchy cookie, but almost no fat, try these. If you use a food processor to chop the pecans, be careful not to grind them so fine that they become pecan paste!"

3 egg whites
⅛ teaspoon cream of tartar
⅓ cup sugar
2 tablespoons unsweetened cocoa powder
¼ cup finely ground pecans
¼ cup strawberry or raspberry preserves

Preheat the oven to 250°F. Line a baking sheet with parchment paper or foil.

In a large bowl, beat egg whites until frothy. Add cream of tartar and beat until stiff.

In a small bowl, combine sugar and cocoa. Gradually beat into egg whites. Fold in pecans.

Spoon meringue into 1½" mounds on the prepared baking sheet. Using the back of a spoon, depress the centers and build up the sides of each meringue to form a shallow cup.

Bake 1 hour. Do not open the oven door. Turn off the oven and let meringues cool in the oven. Store in an airtight container. When ready to serve, fill each with preserves.

Makes 16

Per cookie: *36 calories, 1 g protein, 6 g carbohydrates, 1 g fat, 0 mg cholesterol, 15 mg sodium, 0 g fiber*

Diet Exchanges: *0 milk, 0 vegetable, 0 fruit, ½ bread, 0 meat, 0 fat*

(Hamantaschen recipe on page 297)

FROM THE PROS

Dean Ornish, M.D.

Ahh . . . gingerbread. Sweet, spicy, and satisfying, whether it's warm from the oven or at room temperature. All that and calorie-savvy, too! Dean Ornish, M.D., of the Preventive Medicine Research Institute in Sausalito, California, who proved that a healthy diet can reverse heart disease, wows us once again with this delightful quick bread from a friend.

JOHN'S GINGERBREAD

150 Calories

⅔ cup (about 5 ounces) fat-free sour cream

½ cup unsweetened applesauce

⅓ cup liquid egg substitute or 1 extra-large egg

3 tablespoons brown sugar

2 tablespoons molasses

¾ cup whole-wheat flour

¾ cup unbleached or all-purpose flour

4 teaspoons ground ginger

1 teaspoon ground cinnamon

½ teaspoon ground cloves

1 teaspoon baking soda

1 teaspoon baking powder

½ teaspoon salt

Preheat the oven to 350°F. Coat a 9" × 9" or 8" × 8" baking dish with non-stick spray.

In a large bowl, combine sour cream, applesauce, egg substitute or egg, brown sugar, and molasses.

In a medium bowl, combine whole-wheat flour, unbleached or all-purpose flour, ginger, cinnamon, cloves, baking soda, baking powder, and salt. Sift onto a piece of waxed paper. Add to sour cream mixture and stir just until moistened. Do not overmix. Batter may be lumpy.

Spread evenly in the prepared baking dish. Bake 25 minutes, or until gingerbread rises to the top of the pan and a wooden pick inserted in center comes out clean. Cool in the pan on a rack 30 minutes before cutting.

Makes 8 servings

Per serving: *150 calories, 5 g protein, 30 g carbohydrates, 1 g fat, 0 mg cholesterol, 393 mg sodium, 2 g fiber*

Diet Exchanges: *0 milk, 0 vegetable, 0 fruit, 2 bread, 0 meat, 0 fat*

Hamantaschen

67 Calories

—Babette Miles, Miami

"These traditional Jewish cookies are shaped like triangular hats filled with jam. Browning the butter intensifies its flavor, so you don't need as much."

½ cup soft light butter

1 egg

½ cup sugar

1 teaspoon vanilla extract

3 cups unbleached or all-purpose flour

1 teaspoon baking powder

⅛ teaspoon salt

¼ cup apricot or raspberry jam

Preheat the oven to 350°F. Coat a large baking sheet with nonstick spray.

Melt butter in a small saucepan over medium heat until nutty brown, constantly swirling the pan. Set aside.

In a large bowl, with an electric mixer, beat egg and sugar. Gradually beat in butter and vanilla extract.

In a medium bowl, combine flour, baking powder, and salt. Gradually stir into egg mixture. Turn dough onto a lightly floured surface and knead until smooth, adding more flour if necessary. Roll into 36 balls and place on the prepared baking sheet. Press into 1½" circles. Place a scant ½ teaspoon jam in the center of each. Fold 3 sides of dough over filling to form a triangle.

Bake 25 minutes, or until lightly browned.

Makes 36

Per cookie: *67 calories, 1 g protein, 13 g carbohydrates, 1 g fat, 8 mg cholesterol, 31 mg sodium, 0 g fiber*

Diet Exchanges: *0 milk, 0 vegetable, 0 fruit, 1 bread, 0 meat, 0 fat*

(Photograph on page 295)

Tapioca Pudding

—Susan Jones, Midlothian, Va.

*"Cardamom and cinnamon give this pudding a sweet aroma.
An added bonus: It's a great source of calcium."*

4 cups fat-free milk

3 tablespoons quick-cooking tapioca

⅓ cup sugar

1 egg, beaten

1 egg white

¼ teaspoon ground cardamom or coriander

¼ teaspoon ground cinnamon

¼ cup raisins

1 teaspoon vanilla extract

In a 4-quart saucepan, combine milk, tapioca, sugar, egg, egg white, cardamom or coriander, and cinnamon. Heat to boiling over medium heat. Reduce heat to low and simmer, stirring constantly, 5 minutes. Remove from heat and stir in raisins and vanilla extract. Pour into a serving bowl. Refrigerate until cold.

Makes 8 servings

Per serving: *115 calories, 6 g protein, 22 g carbohydrates, 1 g fat, 29 mg cholesterol, 95 mg sodium, 0 g fiber*

Diet Exchanges: *½ milk, 0 vegetable, 0 fruit, 1 bread, 0 meat, 0 fat*

Quick Rice Pudding

119 Calories

—Laura Janese, Niagara Falls, N.Y.

*"*When you're craving something creamy and homey-tasting, here's a fat-free alternative to high-fat splurges.*"*

4 cups fat-free milk

1 cup quick-cooking long-grain white rice

¼ cup raisins

1 package (1 ounce) vanilla-flavored pudding and pie filling

2 egg whites

¼ teaspoon ground cinnamon

⅛ teaspoon ground nutmeg

In a medium saucepan, combine milk, rice, raisins, pudding mix, and egg whites. Heat to boiling over medium-high heat, stirring constantly. Reduce heat to low and simmer 5 minutes.

Remove from heat and cool 5 minutes, stirring twice.

Pour into dessert bowls. Sprinkle with cinnamon and nutmeg. Serve warm.

Makes 8 servings

Per serving: *119 calories, 6 g protein, 23 g carbohydrates, 0 g fat, 2 mg cholesterol, 105 mg sodium, 0 g fiber*

Diet Exchanges: *½ milk, 0 vegetable, 0 fruit, 1 bread, 0 meat, 0 fat*

Pumpkin-Ginger Rice Pudding

209 Calories

—Erica Berman, Toronto, Ontario

"Arborio rice makes a very creamy rice pudding. You can dress this up with dates, raisins, or nuts. I like it topped with fat-free vanilla frozen yogurt."

½ cup sugar

1 vanilla bean, split lengthwise, or 1 teaspoon vanilla extract

1 tablespoon grated fresh ginger

1½ teaspoons pumpkin pie spice

4 cups fat-free milk

1 cup Arborio rice

½ can (8 ounces) pure pumpkin puree

In a large saucepan, combine sugar, vanilla bean (if using), ginger, pumpkin pie spice, and 1 cup milk. (If using vanilla extract, add along with pumpkin puree at the end.) Heat to boiling over medium heat. Reduce heat to low and simmer 5 minutes. Remove and discard vanilla bean, if using. Stir in rice.

Add remaining 3 cups milk, 1 cup at a time, and cook, stirring frequently, 30 minutes, or until rice is tender and most of milk is absorbed but still creamy. Stir in pumpkin puree and vanilla extract, if using. Cook until pudding is thick and heated through. Serve warm.

Makes 8 servings

Per serving: *209 calories, 7 g protein, 44 g carbohydrates, 0 g fat, 2 mg cholesterol, 65 mg sodium, 1 g fiber*

Diet Exchanges: *1 milk, 0 vegetable, 0 fruit, 1 bread, 0 meat, 0 fat*

Rancho la Puerta

At Rancho la Puerta health and fitness spa, located outside San Diego in Tecate, Baja California, Mexico, chef Bill Wavrin is a popular guy. He has a friendly personality and a winning way with desserts. This one is among his most requested treats.

CORN CREPES WITH STRAWBERRY SAUCE

131 Calories

1 cup whole wheat flour

⅓ cup cornmeal

¼ teaspoon ground cinnamon

¼ teaspoon ground cardamom

¼ teaspoon ground nutmeg

4 egg whites

2 cups fat-free milk

1 tablespoon honey

½ teaspoon vanilla extract

2 cups strawberries, hulled and sliced

½ cup apple juice

3 tablespoons lime juice

In a large bowl, combine flour, cornmeal, cinnamon, cardamom, and nutmeg.

In a medium bowl, beat egg whites until frothy. Add milk, honey, and vanilla extract. Pour into flour mixture until just combined. Do not overmix. Cover and refrigerate at least 30 minutes.

Meanwhile, in a small saucepan over medium-low heat, combine strawberries, apple juice, and lime juice. Simmer 5 minutes, or until berries soften.

Coat a nonstick griddle or skillet with nonstick spray and warm over medium heat. Spoon about 3 tablespoons batter onto the griddle or skillet and cook 1 minute, or until bubbles break on top and underside is golden. Turn and cook a few seconds, or until set. Remove to a plate and keep warm. Repeat with remaining batter. Serve crepes with strawberry sauce.

Makes 8 servings

Per serving: *131 calories, 7 g protein, 26 g carbohydrates, 1 g fat, 1 mg cholesterol, 62 mg sodium, 3 g fiber*

Diet Exchanges: *0 milk, 0 vegetable, 1 fruit, 1 bread, 0 meat, 0 fat*

Black Cherry Baked Apples

132 Calories

—Scott Coleman, Brooklyn, N.Y.

" As simple as it is unusual. 'Nuf said. "

4 baking apples

½ teaspoon cinnamon

¼ cup dried cherries or raisins

¼ cup chopped walnuts

1 cup diet black cherry soda

Preheat the oven to 375°F. Using an apple corer or small knife, remove apple cores from stem ends without cutting all the way through the other end. Place apples in a 9" × 9" baking dish.

Sprinkle cinnamon inside and outside of apples. Spoon cherries or raisins and walnuts into apples. Drizzle a little soda into each apple. Pour remaining soda into the baking dish. Bake 20 minutes, or until tender.

Makes 4 servings

Per serving: *132 calories, 1 g protein, 33 g carbohydrates, 1 g fat, 0 mg cholesterol, 5 mg sodium, 3 g fiber*

Diet Exchanges: *0 milk, 0 vegetable, 2 fruit, 0 bread, 0 meat, 0 fat*

FROM THE PROS

Golden Door

Chef Michel Stroot is a pioneer in spa cuisine. One of his many culinary contributions is being able to make healthy foods like fruits and vegetables as mouthwateringly appealing as the sticky, gooey fattening stuff. Here's a popular example from the Golden Door spa in Escondido, California.

BAKED APPLE WITH PAPAYA SAUCE

201 Calories

4 Golden Delicious apples, cored

4 teaspoons raisins

4 teaspoons honey

½ teaspoon ground cinnamon

½ cup unsweetened apple juice

1 papaya, peeled and seeded

1 teaspoon lime juice

1 teaspoon finely chopped crystallized ginger

4 fresh mint sprigs

Preheat the oven to 350°F. Place apples in a 9" × 9" baking dish. Spoon 1 teaspoon raisins into each apple. Drizzle with honey and sprinkle with cinnamon. Pour apple juice around apples in the dish. Cover loosely with foil and bake 50 to 60 minutes, or until fork-tender. Allow to cool in the dish.

In a blender, combine papaya, lime juice, ginger, and juices from baked apples. Blend until smooth. Place apples on small plates and spoon sauce over each. Garnish with mint.

Makes 4 servings

Per serving: *201 calories, 1 g protein, 51 g carbohydrates, 1 g fat, 0 mg cholesterol, 11 mg sodium, 5 g fiber*

Diet Exchanges: *0 milk, 0 vegetable, 3 fruit, 0 bread, 0 meat, 0 fat*

Cranberry-Apple Crisp

273 Calories

—Mary McMurtrey, Pleasant Grove, Utah

" I like to put a cranberry twist on the basic yummy fruit crisp. Serve this with vanilla frozen yogurt if ice cream isn't in your calorie budget. "

1 can (16 ounces) whole berry cranberry sauce

5 baking apples, peeled and sliced

1 teaspoon ground cinnamon

¼ teaspoon ground nutmeg

2 tablespoons + 1 cup unbleached or all-purpose flour

1 cup packed brown sugar

1 cup quick-cooking oats

¼ teaspoon salt

¼ cup butter or margarine, melted

Preheat the oven to 375°F.

In a large bowl, combine cranberry sauce, apples, cinnamon, nutmeg, and 2 tablespoons flour. Spoon into a 13" × 9" baking dish.

In another large bowl, combine brown sugar, oats, salt, and remaining 1 cup flour. Stir in butter or margarine until well-distributed. Sprinkle evenly over fruit. Bake 35 to 40 minutes, or until hot and bubbly.

Makes 12 servings

Per serving: *273 calories, 4 g protein, 55 g carbohydrates, 5 g fat, 10 mg cholesterol, 97 mg sodium, 4 g fiber*

Diet Exchanges: *0 milk, 0 vegetable, 2 fruit, 1½ bread, 0 meat, 1 fat*

Wonton Fruit Cups

99 Calories

—Susan Burns, Pennington, N.J.

" My husband, who has diabetes, inspires me to create new recipes like this treat, which we both enjoy. If you're in a hurry, replace the wonton wrappers with prepared phyllo shells from the freezer case of your supermarket. (Wonton wrappers are available in the refrigerated produce section of most supermarkets.) "

24 **wonton wrappers**

2 **tablespoons butter or margarine, melted**

1/3 **cup strawberry all-fruit spread**

1 **cup (8 ounces) low-fat lemon yogurt**

1¼ **cups fresh blueberries, blackberries, or raspberries**

Preheat the oven to 350°F.

Using a 12-cup muffin pan or two 6-cup muffin pans, line each cup with a wonton wrapper. Brush wonton wrappers with a little butter. Place a second wrapper diagonally on top of each of the first ones, making sure that the points of the wrappers make sides to the cup. Brush second wrapper with a little butter. Bake 10 minutes, or until golden brown. Cool. Remove from pan.

Spoon about 1 teaspoon of all-fruit spread into each wonton shell.

Place yogurt in a medium bowl. Fold in 1 cup berries. Spoon yogurt mixture evenly into wonton shells. Top with remaining ¼ cup berries.

Makes 12

Per fruit cup: *99 calories, 3 g protein, 17 g carbohydrates, 2 g fat, 8 mg cholesterol, 133 mg sodium, 1 g fiber*

Diet Exchanges: *0 milk, 0 vegetable, 1 fruit, ½ bread, 0 meat, 0 fat*

Guiltless Banana Split

299 Calories

—Lynn Metzker, Charlotte, N.C.

*"Sweet, fruity, and creamy! This has all the best parts of the
real thing without the caloric consequences."*

1 banana, peeled and sliced lengthwise
1 slice fresh pineapple
4 large strawberries, hulled
2 tablespoons chocolate syrup
1 tablespoon low-fat whipped topping

Place banana on a plate. Cut wedges from pineapple slice and arrange on half of banana. Place strawberries, point up, on other half of banana. Drizzle with chocolate syrup and top with whipped topping.

Makes 1 serving

Per serving: *299 calories, 3 g protein, 72 g carbohydrates, 2 g fat, 0 mg cholesterol, 25 mg sodium, 7 g fiber*

Diet Exchanges: *0 milk, 0 vegetable, 3 fruit, 1½ bread, 0 meat, 0 fat*

Roasted Fruit Wraps with Dipping Sauce

—Kurt Wait, Redwood City, Calif.

"As a single dad, I do all the cooking for my son and myself. This is a great way to include fruits in our daily diet. It's like a warm fruit turnover without all the fat or fuss. And it keeps me light on my feet for tennis."

DIPPING SAUCE

- 1 cup low-fat vanilla yogurt
- 2 teaspoons finely chopped crystallized ginger
- 2 tablespoons orange juice

FRUIT WRAPS

- 2 Golden Delicious apples, peeled and sliced
- 2 peaches or 1 mango, peeled and sliced
- 4 slices canned pineapple, halved
- 2 tablespoons orange juice
- 4 teaspoons sugar
- ½ teaspoon pumpkin pie spice
- 4 flour tortillas (8" diameter)

To make the dipping sauce:

In a small bowl, mix yogurt, ginger, and orange juice. Cover and refrigerate.

To make the fruit wraps:

Preheat the oven to 425°F. Coat a large nonstick baking sheet with nonstick spray. Add apples, peaches or mango, pineapple, orange juice, sugar, and pumpkin pie spice. Toss to coat and spread in a single layer. Bake 10 to 15 minutes, or until fruit is tender.

Place one-fourth of warm fruit down the center of each tortilla. Roll up like an envelope and place, seam side down, on a nonstick baking sheet. Bake 8 to 10 minutes, or until crisp and golden. Cut each wrap in half diagonally. Serve with sauce.

Make 4 servings

Per serving: *293 calories, 6 g protein, 61 g carbohydrates, 4 g fat, 4 mg cholesterol, 213 mg sodium, 3 g fiber*

Diet Exchanges: *0 milk, 0 vegetable, 2 fruit, 2 bread, 0 meat, ½ fat*

Pistachio-Pineapple Yogurt Pie

257 Calories

—Alice Booth, Linwood, N.J.

" It looks like grasshopper pie, but this frozen dessert has a taste all its own. The flavors of pineapple and pistachio marry deliciously! "

3 cups low-fat vanilla frozen yogurt, softened

1 can (8 ounces) crushed pineapple, drained

1 package (1 ounce) sugar-free instant pistachio pudding mix

1 chocolate cookie crumb pie crust (9")

¼ cup chocolate syrup

In a large bowl, combine yogurt, pineapple, and pudding mix. Spoon into pie crust. Cover and freeze at least 6 hours, or until firm. Drizzle with chocolate syrup before serving.

Makes 8 servings

Per serving: *257 calories, 5 g protein, 40 g carbohydrates, 9 g fat, 0 mg cholesterol, 387 mg sodium, 1 g fiber*

Diet Exchanges: *½ milk, 0 vegetable, 0 fruit, 2 bread, 0 meat, 1 fat*

GET A GRIP ON CHOCOLATE

What is the one thing that the high priest of low-fat cooking and healthy eating, Dean Ornish, M.D., of the Preventive Medicine Research Institute in Sausalito, California, is never willing to give up? You guessed it: chocolate. He loves to finish his meals with one small, exquisitely rich, mouth-coating, dense, dark piece of chocolate.

And who can blame him? For many people, especially those watching their weight, chocolate calls louder than any other flavor. And most nutritionists say: Give in. When you eat around a food trying to avoid the one thing that you really want, you're apt to eat more calories than if you ate what you wanted in the first place.

That doesn't mean you should grab a huge piece of fudge at the first nudge of a craving. Have a little. Psychologically speaking, some is better than none.

One note of caution: Don't waste your time on fat-free ersatz chocolate candy bars and fake chocolate coatings. They won't give you the satisfaction of real chocolate. Is this the voice of experience? You betcha. Try one of these chocolatey, but saner, choices. They're listed from most calories to least.

Chocolate	Calories
1 cup low-fat hot cocoa	157
2 tablespoons M & M's	125
5 Hershey's Kisses	121
1 cup Cocoa Puffs	120
¼ cup chocolate morsels	100
½ cup fat-free chocolate sorbet	100
3 chocolate wafer cookies	78
2 chocolate graham cracker sheets	60
1 marshmallow dipped in chocolate syrup	50

Tiramisu

313 Calories

—Larry Benson, Los Angeles

"The classic Italian recipe has troppo fat and calories. (That means a lot!) This version may have more calories than diet gelatin, but it's far more satisfying, too."

1 large package (3.4 ounces) instant vanilla-flavored pudding and pie filling

1 teaspoon instant coffee granules

1 cup (8 ounces) reduced-fat ricotta cheese

1 package (8 ounces) reduced-fat cream cheese

½ cup confectioners' sugar

1 teaspoon rum extract

½ cup mini semisweet chocolate morsels

1 package (10 ounces) low-fat pound cake or lady fingers

1 cup brewed strong black coffee

1 tablespoon unsweeteened cocoa
Chocolate curls (optional)

Prepare pudding according to package directions, using 1% milk. Add coffee granules. Cover and refrigerate until well-chilled.

In a medium bowl, combine ricotta, cream cheese, confectioners' sugar, and rum extract. Fold in chocolate morsels and pudding.

Cut pound cake into thin slices or separate lady fingers. Arrange one-fourth of slices in a single layer on the bottom of a large glass bowl. Set remaining cake aside. Drizzle cake in bowl with ¼ cup brewed coffee. Spread one-third of ricotta mixture over cake in bowl. Top with another one-fourth of cake. Drizzle with another ¼ cup coffee. Repeat layering 2 more times, ending with cake. Sprinkle top with cocoa. Garnish with chocolate curls, if using.

Makes 8 servings

Per serving: *313 calories, 6 g protein, 53 g carbohydrates, 10 g fat, 20 mg cholesterol, 522 mg sodium, 0 g fiber*

Diet Exchanges: *0 milk, 0 vegetable, 0 fruit, 3 bread, 0 meat, 2 fat*

Potluck Trifle

275 Calories

—Barbara Pashkoff, Jericho, N.Y.

" This is one of those tastes-even-better-the-next-day kind of recipes, which makes it a winner at potlucks. Plus, it's fat-free. "

1 **large package (3.4 ounces) fat-free instant vanilla pudding mix**

1 **package (10 ounces) fat-free pound cake, cut into ½" slices**

1 **jar (10 ounces) all-fruit raspberry preserves**

¼ **cup dry sherry or orange juice**

3 **ripe bananas, sliced**

Prepare pudding according to package directions, using fat-free milk.

Arrange a single layer of cake in the bottom of a deep glass bowl. Spread with one-third of preserves and sprinkle with a generous tablespoon of sherry or orange juice. Top with one-third of banana slices and one-third of pudding. Continue layering 2 more times, ending with pudding. Cover with plastic wrap and refrigerate a few hours before serving.

Makes 8 servings

Per serving: *275 calories, 2 g protein, 68 g carbohydrates, 0 g fat, 0 mg cholesterol, 196 mg sodium, 1 g fiber*

Diet Exchanges: *0 milk, 0 vegetable, 2 fruit, 2 bread, 0 meat, 0 fat*

Two Weeks to a Slimmer You

Here's where it all comes together: 14 days of menus that really work. We took a wide range of recipes from the book and organized them into a variety of meals that balance flavors, textures, and colors (not to mention calories). You'll find everything from Blueberry-Pecan Pancakes to Grilled Pork Chops. And Chocolate-Raspberry Avalanche Cake, Chocolate Chunk Cookies, and chocolate morsels. These menus prove that losing weight doesn't mean depriving yourself.

Each daily menu includes not three, but five "meals." Morning and afternoon snacks keep you from getting too hungry and overeating at main meals. But you may want to save one of these snacks for later if your appetite alarm rings more loudly in the evening. For other snack ideas, see "50 Low-Calorie Snacks" on page 121.

Beverages aren't included here. That's up to you. Diet sodas, water, tea, coffee, and seltzer or club soda are calorie-free. Regular sodas add about 250 calories. Wine and beer add between 100 and 150 calories per serving.

Notice that the menus are calculated for 1,500; 2,000; or 2,500 calories. To find the calorie level that's right for you, see "How Many Calories Do You Eat Now?" on page 18. Adjust the menus as needed for your calorie intake by omitting an item or adding foods.

Think of these menus as suggestions. And think seasonal. Corn on the cob, baby spinach, strawberries, and melons are short-lived treats that can be substituted for any of the fruit and vegetable ideas that follow—without dramatically altering a day's total calories. When you make freshness a priority, you'll please your senses and your spirit. And that's the kind of soul-satisfying eating that leads to weight-loss success.

Day 1

MENU	CALORIE LEVELS		
	1,500	**2,000**	**2,500**
Breakfast			
Hot Banana-Wheat Cereal (page 72)	1 serving	1 serving	1 serving
Fat-free milk	1 cup	1 cup	1 cup
Orange segments	½ cup	1 cup	1½ cups
Snack			
Peanuts	1 Tbsp	2 Tbsp	2 Tbsp
Lunch			
Creamy Carrot-Potato Soup (page 96)	1 serving	1 serving	2 servings
Pita Pizza (page 109)	1 serving	1 serving	2 servings
Snack			
Low-fat yogurt with	½ cup	1 cup	1 cup
Trail mix	1 Tbsp	2 Tbsp	2 Tbsp
Dinner			
Chicken Fiesta Mexicana (page 127)	1 serving	1 serving	1½ servings
Baked tortilla chips	1 cup	1 cup	1 cup
Brown rice	1 cup	1½ cups	1½ cups
Chocolate-Pecan Meringues (page 294)	1	3	3
TOTAL CALORIES	**1,470**	**1,812**	**2,437**

MENU

	CALORIE LEVELS		
	1,500	**2,000**	**2,500**
Breakfast			
Blueberry-Pecan Pancakes (page 66)	1 serving	1 serving	2 servings
Maple syrup	1 Tbsp	2 Tbsp	3 Tbsp
Orange juice	¾ cup	¾ cup	¾ cup
Snack			
Whole-wheat toast with	1 slice	1 slice	1 slice
Peanut butter	2 tsp	1 Tbsp	1 Tbsp
Lunch			
Wonderful Tuna Salad (page 258) with	1 serving	1 serving	2 servings
Lettuce and shredded carrots on	1 cup	2 cups	2 cups
Whole-wheat bread	1 slice	2 slices	2 slices
Chocolate Chunk Cookies (page 292)	1	2	2
Snack			
Miso soup	½ cup	1 cup	2 cups
Whole-wheat crackers	—	4	6
Dinner			
Beef 'n' Macaroni Skillet Supper (page 145)	1 serving	1 serving	1 serving
Steamed broccoli with lemon zest	1 cup	1 cup	1 cup
Whole-wheat Italian bread	1 slice	2 slices	2 slices
Cantaloupe	¼	½	½
TOTAL CALORIES	**1,504**	**2,018**	**2,531**

MENU	CALORIE LEVELS		
	1,500	**2,000**	**2,500**
Breakfast			
Chopra Granola (page 73)	1 serving	1 serving	1 serving
Fat-free milk	1 cup	1 cup	1 cup
Grapefruit juice	¾ cup	¾ cup	¾ cup
Snack			
Fig bar	1	2	2
Fat-free milk	½ cup	1 cup	1 cup
Lunch			
Black Bean and Corn Salad (page 270)	1 serving	1 serving	2 servings
On shredded romaine lettuce	1 cup	2 cups	2 cups
Baked tortilla chips	1 cup	2 cups	2 cups
Salsa	1 Tbsp	1 Tbsp	1 Tbsp
Snack			
Hard-cooked egg	1	1	1
Stone-ground crackers	2	4	6
Dinner			
Tuscan Bean Soup with Sausage (page 154)	1 serving	1 serving	2 servings
Italian bread dipped in	1 slice	2 slices	2 slices
Olive oil	½ tsp	1 tsp	2 tsp
Chocolate-Raspberry Avalanche Cake (page 280)	1 serving	1 serving	1 serving
TOTAL CALORIES	**1,534**	**1,978**	**2,471**

MENU	CALORIE LEVELS		
	1,500	**2,000**	**2,500**
Breakfast			
Good Morning Muffins (page 64)	1	1	2
Orange juice	¾ cup	¾ cup	¾ cup
Low-fat fruit-flavored yogurt	½ cup	1 cup	1 cup
Snack			
1% cottage cheese	⅓ cup	⅔ cup	1 cup
Rice cake	1	2	2
Lunch			
Quick Chicken Pasta Salad (page 90) on	1 serving	1 serving	1½ servings
1 cup shredded romaine lettuce	1 cup	1 cup	1 cup
Italian bread	1 slice	2 slices	2 slices
Pear	—	1	1
Snack			
Sliced turkey breast	1 slice	2 slices	2 slices
Whole-wheat bread	1 slice	2 slices	2 slices
Dinner			
Crab Cakes (page 166)	1 serving	1 serving	1 serving
Baked tomato halves	1	1	1
Steamed carrots	½ cup	½ cup	½ cup
Honeydew melon	⅛	⅛	⅛
TOTAL CALORIES	**1,504**	**1,591**	**2,508**

MENU	CALORIE LEVELS		
	1,500	**2,000**	**2,500**
Breakfast			
Jumbo Cinnamon-Raisin Muffins (page 68)	1	1	1
Orange juice	¾ cup	¾ cup	¾ cup
Low-fat fruit-flavored yogurt	½ cup	1 cup	1 cup
Snack			
Mini pita stuffed with	1	1	1
Refried beans and	¼ cup	¼ cup	¼ cup
Lettuce	1 leaf	1 leaf	1 leaf
Lunch			
Broccoli Soup (page 94)	1 serving	2 servings	2 servings
Goat cheese and	1 oz	1 oz	2 oz
Sliced small tomato and	1	1	1
Arugula and	¼ cup	¼ cup	¼ cup
Olive oil on	½ tsp	½ tsp	½ tsp
Italian bread	1 slice	1 slice	2 slices
Snack			
Frozen juice bar	1	1	1
Almonds	2 Tbsp	2 Tbsp	2 Tbsp
Dinner			
Grilled Pork Chops (page 196)	1 serving	1 serving	2 servings
Brown rice	½ cup	1 cup	1½ cups
Steamed broccoli rabe with lemon and garlic	½ cup	1 cup	1 cup
Chocolate-Raspberry Avalanche Cake (from Day 3, page 280)	1 serving	1 serving	1 serving
TOTAL CALORIES	**1,498**	**1,916**	**2,503**

Day 6

MENU	CALORIE LEVELS		
	1,500	**2,000**	**2,500**
Breakfast			
Bran flakes	1 cup	1 cup	2 cups
Banana	½	1	1
Fat-free milk	½ cup	1 cup	1½ cups
Snack			
Low-fat fruit-flavored yogurt	½ cup	1 cup	1 cup
Fig bar	—	2	3
Lunch			
Canyon Ranch Burger (page 100)	1	1	1
Shredded carrots and fresh dill tossed with	½ cup	1 cup	1 cup
Olive oil	1 tsp	2 tsp	2 tsp
Watermelon chunks	1 cup	2 cups	2 cups
Snack			
Graham crackers (2" squares) with	6	6	6
Peanut butter	2 tsp	2 tsp	2 tsp
Dinner			
Vegetable Lasagna (page 210)	1 serving	1 serving	2 servings
Italian bread	1 slice	1 slice	2 slices
Green beans with	½ cup	1 cup	1 cup
Sliced almonds	1 Tbsp	1 Tbsp	2 Tbsp
Tiramisu (page 313)	1 serving	1 serving	1 serving
TOTAL CALORIES	**1,551**	**2,033**	**2,581**

MENU	CALORIE LEVELS		
	1,500	**2,000**	**2,500**
Breakfast			
Scrambled eggs	1	2	2
Whole-wheat toast	1 slice	2 slices	2 slices
Canadian bacon	1 slice	2 slices	2 slices
Orange juice	¾ cup	¾ cup	¾ cup
Snack			
Fat-free milk	½ cup	1 cup	1 cup
Goldfish crackers	25	50	50
Lunch			
Sweet Potato and Leek Soup (page 101)	1 serving	1 serving	2 servings
Tabbouleh Salad (page 275)	1 serving	1 serving	2 servings
Apple	1	1	1
Snack			
Cheese stick	1	2	2
Stone-ground whole-wheat crackers	3	4	6
Dinner			
Unfried Crunchy Chicken (page 128)	1 serving	1 serving	1½ servings
Brown rice with mint and tomato	½ cup	1 cup	1½ cups
Steamed green beans	½ cup	1 cup	1 cup
The Duchess's Chocolate Mousse Tartlets (page 289)	1 serving	1 serving	1 serving
TOTAL CALORIES	**1,492**	**1,998**	**2,508**

Day 8

MENU	CALORIE LEVELS		
	1,500	**2,000**	**2,500**
Breakfast			
Peanut Butter and Banana Shake (page 122)	1 serving	1 serving	1 serving
Snack			
Sliced strawberries	1 cup	1 cup	1 cup
1% cottage cheese	⅓ cup	1 cup	1 cup
Lunch			
Sliced avocado	⅛	¼	¼
Easy Huevos Rancheros (page 54)	1 serving	1 serving	2 servings
Salsa	1 Tbsp	1 Tbsp	1 Tbsp
Orange segments	1 cup	1 cup	1 cup
Snack			
Peanuts	1 Tbsp	2 Tbsp	3 Tbsp
Semisweet chocolate morsels	2 Tbsp	2 Tbsp	2 Tbsp
Dinner			
Lamb Chops with Herbed Apricot Sauce (page 157)	1 serving	1 serving	2 servings
Couscous	½ cup	1 cup	1 cup
Steamed green peas with mint	½ cup	1 cup	1 cup
Blueberries with	1 cup	1 cup	1 cup
Low-fat vanilla yogurt	½ cup	1 cup	1 cup
TOTAL CALORIES	**1,520**	**2,022**	**2,530**

MENU	CALORIE LEVELS		
	1,500	**2,000**	**2,500**
Breakfast			
Orange-Raisin Tea Bread (page 77)	1 slice	2 slices	2 slices
Low-fat vanilla yogurt	1/2 cup	1 cup	1 cup
Banana	1/2	1	1
Snack			
Sesame bread stick	2	2	2
Peanut butter	1 1/2 tsp	1 Tbsp	1 Tbsp
Lunch			
Tomato-Crab Bake (page 110)	1 serving	1 serving	1 serving
Cooked canned Mexican-style corn	1/2 cup	1/2 cup	1 cup
Italian bread	—	1 slice	2 slices
Pear	1	1	1
Snack			
Low-fat granola	2 Tbsp	2 Tbsp	1/4 cup
Low-fat fruit-flavored yogurt	1/2 cup	1 cup	1 cup
Dinner			
Roast chicken	4 oz	4 oz	6 oz
Chicken Stuffing Casserole (page 242)	1 serving	1 serving	2 servings
Steamed broccoli with orange zest	1/2 cup	1 cup	1 cup
Roasted butternut squash with rosemary	1/2 cup	1 cup	1 cup
John's Gingerbread (page 296)	1 serving	1 serving	1 serving
TOTAL CALORIES	**1,520**	**2,049**	**2,541**

Day 10

MENU	CALORIE LEVELS		
	1,500	**2,000**	**2,500**
Breakfast			
Lemon Scones (page 70)	1	1	2
Low-fat fruit-flavored yogurt	½ cup	1 cup	1 cup
Snack			
Apple	½	1	1
Reduced-fat Cheddar cheese	¾ oz	1½ oz	1½ oz
Lunch			
Tuscan Tuna Salad (page 261)	1 serving	1 serving	2 servings
Sliced small tomato with basil	1	1	1
Stone-ground whole-wheat crackers	3	6	6
Snack			
Baked tortilla chips	5	10	10
Smoked turkey breast	1 slice	2 slices	2 slices
Low-fat milk	¾ cup	¾ cup	1 cup
Dinner			
Red Chile Steak Burritos (page 150)	1 serving	1 serving	1 serving
Brown rice	½ cup	1 cup	1 cup
Steamed zucchini and yellow squash with red bell pepper	½ cup	½ cup	1 cup
Hamantaschen (page 297)	1	1	3
TOTAL CALORIES	**1,519**	**2,005**	**2,499**

Day 11

MENU	CALORIE LEVELS		
	1,500	**2,000**	**2,500**
Breakfast			
Oatmeal	1 cup	1 cup	1 cup
Fat-free milk	½ cup	1 cup	1 cup
Grapefruit juice	½ cup	1 cup	1 cup
Snack			
Raisins	½ cup	½ cup	½ cup
Peanuts	1½ tsp	1½ tsp	1 Tbsp
Lunch			
Black beans	½ cup	1 cup	1 cup
With fat-free Italian dressing	1 Tbsp	1 Tbsp	2 Tbsp
Spinach Squares (page 105)	½ cup	1 cup	1 cup
Baked tortilla chips	½ cup	½ cup	1 cup
Snack			
Cantaloupe	¼ melon	¼ melon	½ melon
1% cottage cheese	⅓ cup	⅔ cup	⅔ cup
Dinner			
Salmon Teriyaki (page 165)	1 serving	1 serving	1½ servings
Brown rice	—	1 cup	1 cup
Sautéed Chinese cabbage with sprouts	½ cup	½ cup	½ cup
Steamed long or green beans	½ cup	½ cup	½ cup
Yummy Pineapple Cake (page 282)	1 serving	1 serving	1 serving
TOTAL CALORIES	**1,505**	**1,980**	**2,476**

Day 12

MENU	CALORIE LEVELS		
	1,500	**2,000**	**2,500**
Breakfast			
Buttermilk Fruit Smoothie (page 120)	1 serving	1 serving	1½ servings
Snack			
Miso soup	½ cup	1 cup	1 cup
Sesame bread sticks	1	2	2
Lunch			
Sandwich on whole-wheat bread with	2 slices	2 slices	4 slices
Herbed Cheese Spread (page 115) and	2 servings	2 servings	3 servings
Alfalfa sprouts	¼ cup	¼ cup	½ cup
Snack			
Fat-free milk	½ cup	1 cup	1 cup
Graham crackers (2" squares)	3	6	6
Dinner			
Lentil-Sausage Stew (page 200)	1 serving	1 serving	1 serving
Romaine lettuce with	1 cup	1 cup	1 cup
Low-calorie vinaigrette	1 Tbsp	1 Tbsp	1 Tbsp
Whole-wheat Italian bread	1 slice	2 slices	2 slices
Low-fat vanilla frozen yogurt with	½ cup	1 cup	1½ cups
Chocolate syrup	1 Tbsp	2 Tbsp	2 Tbsp
TOTAL CALORIES	**1,500**	**1,986**	**2,521**

Day 13

MENU	CALORIE LEVELS		
	1,500	**2,000**	**2,500**
Breakfast			
Scrambled eggs	1	2	2
Roasted Home Fries (page 57)	1 serving	1 serving	1 serving
Canadian bacon	1 slice	2 slices	2 slices
Whole wheat toast	1 slice	2 slices	2 slices
Snack			
Frozen juice bar	—	1	1
Fat-free milk	1 cup	1 cup	1 cup
Graham crackers (2" squares)	3	6	6
Lunch			
Tofu Burger (page 86)	1 serving	1 serving	2 servings
Carrot, cut into sticks	1	2	1
Snack			
Air-popped popcorn with	3 cups	3 cups	3 cups
Parmesan cheese	1 Tbsp	1 Tbsp	1 Tbsp
Dinner			
Lemon Red Snapper with Jalapeños (page 201)	1 serving	1 serving	2 servings
Baked sweet potato	1	1	1
Steamed green beans with	½ cup	1 cup	1 cup
Pine nuts	1 Tbsp	2 Tbsp	2 Tbsp
Pear	1	1	1
TOTAL CALORIES	**1,523**	**2,023**	**2,497**

Day 14

MENU	CALORIE LEVELS		
	1,500	**2,000**	**2,500**
Breakfast			
Easy Ham and Cheese "Soufflé" (page 58)	1 serving	1 serving	1 serving
Cantaloupe	¼ melon	¼ melon	¼ melon
Snack			
Stone-ground whole-wheat crackers	2	4	6
Peanut butter	1½ tsp	1 Tbsp	1 Tbsp
Lunch			
Chicken Oriental Salad (page 267)	1 serving	1½ servings	2 servings
Rice cake	1	1	2
Mandarin orange sections	1 cup	1 cup	1 cup
Snack			
Whole-wheat toast	1 slice	1 slice	2 slices
Sliced turkey breast	1 slice	2 slices	3 slices
Dinner			
Shrimp Risotto (page 205)	1 serving	1½ servings	2 servings
Steamed broccoli with lemon and garlic	½ cup	1 cup	1 cup
Pistachio-Pineapple Yogurt Pie (page 310)	1 serving	1 serving	1 serving
TOTAL CALORIES	**1,524**	**1,997**	**2,511**

Credits

Photography

Interior photographs by Mitch Mandel/ Rodale Images, except photos on pages 76, 164, and 188 © by Lisa Koenig, and "After" photos on the following pages:

Page 2: Alan Wychuck/Liaison Agency

Page 24: Paul T. Chan

Page 29: Layne Kennedy

Page 37: Tim Sloan/*The Washington Post*

Page 41: Will Yurman/Liaison Agency

Page 49: Phil Matt/Liaison Agency

Page 92: © Lemay Design and Photography

Page 108: © Alan Levenson/Corbis

Page 112: © Jimmy Williams

Page 134: Bruce Kluckhohn/Liaison Agency

Page 168: Joe Radice/Press Enterprise

Page 190: 1996 © Capital Cities/ABC, Inc.

Page 214: © Robert Neumann

Page 234: © Don Chambers/Pelosi & Chambers

Page 288: Gordon Munro/Courtesy of Weight Watchers International

Photography Props

We would like to thank the following companies that generously donated props for the photography in this book.

Emile Henry
(available in department or cookware stores; visit their Web site at www.emilehenry.com)

- Portobellos and Goat Cheese (page 107): baking dish
- Taco Bake (page 149): baking dish and bowls
- Confetti Meat Loaf (page 193): baking dish
- El Dorado Casserole (page 195): baking dish

- Seafood Chowder (page 203): baking dish
- Vegetable Lasagna (page 211): baking dish

Mesa International
(available in department stores)

- Vegetable Quesadillas (page 85): pitcher
- Salmon Chowder (page 99): salad plate
- Mediterranean Pasta (page 163): bowl
- White Chicken Chili (page 187): bowl
- Seafood Chowder (page 203): soup bowl
- Yummy Pineapple Cake (page 283): swirl pattern mug

Pfaltzgraff
(available in department stores or by visiting www.pfaltzgraff.com)

- Blueberry Brunch Cake (page 75): large bowl
- Hot Black Bean Dip (page 117): bowl
- Unfried Crunchy Chicken (page 128): plate
- Fettuccine with Pot-Lickin' Chicken Sauce (page 156): flatware
- Veggie Cassoulet (page 219): baking dish and plates

Wedgwood
(available in department or china stores or by visiting www.wedgwood.co.uk)

- Breakfast in a Cup (page 61): small plate
- Lemon Scones (page 71): small plate
- Tomato-Crab Bake (page 111): small plate
- Tomatoes and Zucchini with Meatballs (page 147): soup plate
- Warm Pepper and Pork Salad (page 265): white plate, salt and pepper shakers
- Chocolate-Raspberry Avalanche Cake (page 281): plate, pitcher, and bowl
- Hamantaschen and Chocolate-Pecan Meringues (page 295): plates, cups, and saucers

Recipes

The recipes for Chopra Granola (page 73) and Tofu Burgers (page 86) are from *Perfect Weight* by Deepak Chopra, M.D. Copyright © 1994 by Deepak Chopra, M.D. Reprinted by permission of Harmony Books, a division of Random House, Inc.

The recipes for Canyon Ranch Burgers (page 100) and Salmon Teriyaki (page 165) are adapted from *Canyon Ranch Cooking—Bringing the Spa Home* by Jeanne Jones. Copyright © 1998 by Jeanne Jones. Reprinted by permission of HarperCollins Publishers, Inc.

The recipes for Salsa Mexicana (page 119) and Corn Crepes with Strawberry Sauce (page 301) are from *Rancho la Puerta Cookbook* by Bill Wavrin. Copyright © 1998 by Golden Door. Used by permission of Broadway Books, a division of Random House, Inc.

The recipes for Lamb Chops with Herbed Apricot Sauce (page 157) and Chinese Chicken in a Bag (page 184) are adapted from *Healthy Cooking for People Who Don't Have Time to Cook* by Jeanne Jones. Copyright © 1997 by Jeanne Jones. Reprinted by permission of Rodale Inc.

The recipes for Linguine Montecatini (page 160) and Sweet Potato Mash (page 232) are from Jackie Abreu, chef, the Spa at Doral, Miami.

The recipe for Flounder Dijon (page 171) is from *7 Steps to Wellness: Control Your Weight, Control Your Life!!* by Howard J. Rankin, Ph.D. Reprinted by permission of Howard J. Rankin, Ph.D., Step-Wise Press.

The recipe for Joan's Jewel of the Nile Chicken Kabobs (page 191) is from *Healthy Cooking* by Joan Lunden. Copyright © 1996 by New Life Entertainment, Inc. By permission of Little, Brown and Company (Inc.).

The recipes for Eggplant Parmesan (page 222), Twice-Baked Potatoes (page 229), and Almond-Mushroom Rice Casserole (page 239) are from Marsha Hudnall, M.S., R.D., nutrition director at Green Mountain at Fox Run, a women's center for healthy living without dieting, located in Ludlow, Vermont.

The recipe for Persian Cucumber Salad (page 250) is from *Healing the Hungry Self: The Diet-Free Solution to Lifelong Weight Management* by Deirdra Price, Ph.D. Reprinted by permission of Plume Publishing.

The recipes for Creamy Ranch Dressing (page 255) and Baked Apple with Papaya Sauce (page 304) are adapted from *The Golden Door Cookbook* by Michel Stroot. Copyright © 1997 by Golden Door. Used by permission of Broadway Books, a division of Random House, Inc.

The recipes for Old-Fashioned Potato Salad (page 274), Carrot Cake with Cream Cheese Frosting (page 284), and John's Gingerbread (page 296) are adapted from *Everyday Cooking with Dr. Dean Ornish* by Dean Ornish, M.D. Copyright © 1996 by Dean Ornish, M.D. Reprinted by permission of HarperCollins Publishers, Inc.

The recipes for Peanut Butter Cake with Chocolate Frosting (page 278) and Double Chocolate Chip Fudge Brownies (page 290) are adapted from *A Guy's Guide to Great Eating: Big-Flavored, Fat-Reduced Recipes for Men Who Love to Eat* by Don Mauer. Copyright © 1999 by Don Mauer & Associates, Inc. Reprinted by permission of Houghton Mifflin Company. All rights reserved.

The recipe for The Duchess's Chocolate Mousse Tartlets (page 289) is reprinted with the permission of Simon & Schuster, Inc., from *Dining with the Duchess* by the Duchess of York and Weight Watchers International, Inc. Copyright © 1998 by the Duchess of York and Weight Watchers International, Inc.

Index

<u>Underscored</u> page references indicate boxed text. **Boldface** references indicate photographs.

A

Almonds
    Almond-Mushroom Rice Casserole, <u>239</u>
    Chopra Granola, <u>73</u>
    Good Morning Muffins, 64
    Orange-Almond Chicken, 136, **137**
Angel hair pasta
    Angel Hair Pasta with Clam Pesto, 164, **164**
    Mediterranean Pasta, 162, **163**
Apples
    Baked Apple with Papaya Sauce, <u>304</u>
    Black Cherry Baked Apples, 302, **303**
    Broccoli Slaw Waldorf Salad, 251
    Cranberry-Apple Crisp, 305
    Good Morning Muffins, 64
    Quick Breakfast Crisp, 65
    Roasted Fruit Wraps with Dipping Sauce, 308, **309**
Apricots, dried
    Lamb Chops with Herbed Apricot Sauce, <u>157</u>
Arborio rice
    Chicken and Rice Italiano, 126
    Pumpkin-Ginger Rice Pudding, 300
    Shrimp Risotto, 205
Artichokes
    Greek Island Chicken, 130, **131**
    Quick Black Bean and Artichoke Dip, 118
Asian-style dishes
    Asian Slaw, **128**, 252
    Asian Veggie Wraps, 208
    Braised Tofu, 221
    Brown Rice Vegetable Stir-Fry, 176
    Chicken Oriental Salad, 267
    Chinese Chicken in a Bag, <u>184</u>
    Debra's Vegetable-Shrimp Stir-Fry, 93
    Marlene's Chicken and Vegetable Stir-Fry, 135
    Orange-Almond Chicken, 136, **137**
    Salmon Teriyaki, <u>165</u>
    Sesame Chicken Salad, 262, **263**
    Sesame Sauce, <u>141</u>
    Teriyaki Turkey Salad, 266
Asparagus
    Debra's Vegetable-Shrimp Stir-Fry, 93

B

Bacon
    Sweet and Creamy Spinach Salad, 248
Bagels
    Egg Salad on a Bagel, <u>63</u>
Baked goods, low-fat, <u>42–43</u>, 48, 50
Bananas
    Banana Chocolate Chip Bread, 286, **287**
    Buttermilk Fruit Smoothie, 120
    Guiltless Banana Split, 307
    Hot Banana-Wheat Cereal, 72
    Peanut Butter and Banana Shake, 122
    Potluck Trifle, 314, **315**
    Purple Power Shake, 123
Basil
    Angel Hair Pasta with Clam Pesto, 164, **164**
    Norma's Grilled Garlicky Salmon, 169
    Rancho la Puerta Basil Yogurt Dressing, <u>254</u>
    Roasted Vegetable Wraps, 80, **81**
    Shrimp in Tomato Sauce over Pasta, 206, **207**
    Tuscan Tuna Salad, 261
Beans, dried, 40
    Baked Black Beans with Orzo, 87
    Beans, Beans, Beans Salad, 273
    Black Bean and Corn Burritos, 178

Beans, dried (continued)
  Black Bean and Corn Salad, 270, **271**
  Black Beans and Rice, 238
  Black-Eyed Pea Stew, 220
  Easy Huevos Rancheros, 54, **55**
  Ensalada Mexicana Vegetariana, 179, **179**
  Feta Farfalle Salad, 91, **91**
  Garbanzo-Sausage Soup, 197
  Green Salad Roll-Up, 82, **83**
  Hot Black Bean Dip, 116, **117**
  Lentil-Rice Salad, 272
  Lentil-Sausage Stew, 200
  Mediterranean Zucchini, 228
  Meximix, 213
  Pollo Loco, 188, **188**
  Pork Salad with Black-Eyed Pea Dressing,
    268
  Quick Black Bean and Artichoke Dip, 118
  Quick Black Bean Enchiladas, 177
  Quick Chicken Pasta Salad, 90
  Santa Fe Sauce, <u>141</u>
  Spicy Pork and Beans Stew, 198, **199**
  Taco Bake, 148, **149**
  Tuscan Bean Soup with Sausage, 154, **155**
  Tuscan Tuna Salad, 261
  Vegetable Quesadillas, 84, **85**
  Veggie Cassoulet, 218, **219**
  White Chicken Chili, 186, **187**
Beans, green
  Beans, Beans, Beans Salad, 273
  Garden Vegetable Soup, 97
Bean sprouts
  Green Salad Roll-Up, 82, **83**
Beef, fat in, <u>39</u>, <u>44</u>
Beef recipes
  Beef 'n' Macaroni Skillet Supper, 145
  Canyon Ranch Burgers, <u>100</u>
  Confetti Meat Loaf, 192, **193**
  El Dorado Casserole, 194, **195**
  Red Chile Steak Burritos, 150, **151**
  Roast Sirloin Steak, 189, **189**

  Taco Bake, 148, **149**
  Tomatoes and Zucchini with Meatballs,
    146, **147**
Beets
  Garden Vegetable Soup, 97
Bell peppers
  Asian Slaw, **128**, 252
  Beans, Beans, Beans Salad, 273
  Black-Eyed Pea Stew, 220
  Chicken Fajitas, 142, **143**
  Confetti Meat Loaf, 192, **193**
  Debra's Vegetable-Shrimp Stir-Fry, 93
  Dinah's Shredded Chicken Spread, 113
  Ensalada Mexicana Vegetariana, 179, **179**
  Fettuccine with Pot-Lickin' Chicken Sauce,
    156, **156**
  Grilled Summer Salad, 253
  Joan's Jewel of the Nile Chicken Kabobs, 191
  Lentil-Sausage Stew, 200
  Mark's Potatoes and Tomatoes Vinaigrette,
    235
  Meximix, 213
  Pepperonata Sauce, <u>140–41</u>
  Roasted Home Fries, 57, **61**
  Roasted Vegetable Wraps, 80, **81**
  Romaine Salad with Sherry Vinaigrette, 256,
    257
  Shrimp Creole, 174, **175**
  Spicy Pork and Beans Stew, 198, **199**
  Spinach Squares, 105
  Unstuffed Cabbage, 223
  Veggie Cassoulet, 218, **219**
  Very Vegetable Soup, 209
  Warm Pepper and Pork Salad, 264, **265**
Berries. See specific berries
Beverages, <u>47</u>
  Buttermilk Fruit Smoothie, 120
  Go-Go Gazpacho, <u>63</u>
  Peanut Butter and Banana Shake, 122
  Purple Power Shake, 123
  Smooth Sailing, <u>63</u>

Black beans
    Baked Black Beans with Orzo, 87
    Beans, Beans, Beans Salad, 273
    Black Bean and Corn Burritos, 178
    Black Bean and Corn Salad, 270, **271**
    Black Beans and Rice, 238
    Hot Black Bean Dip, 116, **117**
    Quick Black Bean and Artichoke Dip, 118
    Quick Black Bean Enchiladas, 177
    Santa Fe Sauce, <u>141</u>
    Spicy Pork and Beans Stew, 198, **199**
Blackberries
    Wonton Fruit Cups, 306, **306**
Black-eyed peas
    Black-Eyed Pea Stew, 220
    Pork Salad with Black-Eyed Pea Dressing,
        268
Blood cholesterol levels, 7
Blueberries
    Blueberry Brunch Cake, 74, **75**
    Blueberry-Pecan Pancakes, 66, **67**
    Purple Power Shake, 123
    Wonton Fruit Cups, 306, **306**
Blue cheese
    Blue Cheese Dressing, <u>255</u>
    Romaine Salad with Sherry Vinaigrette, 256,
        257
Body image, 23
Body Mass Index (BMI)
    calculating, <u>8–9</u>
    and diseases, 7
    statistics on, <u>4–5</u>
Bow-tie pasta. *See* Farfalle pasta
Bran. *See* Oat bran
Bread. *See also* Muffins; Tortillas
    Banana Chocolate Chip Bread, 286, **287**
    Easy Yeast Rolls, 244, **244**
    John's Gingerbread, <u>296</u>
    Lemon Scones, 70, **71**
    Multigrain Bread, **95**, 245
    Orange-Raisin Tea Bread, 77

Bread, pita
    Pita Pizza, 109
Bread group, in food pyramid
    importance of, 21
    selecting from, 34
    serving sizes, 16
Breakfast, importance of, 21, <u>63</u>
Breakfast and brunch dishes
    Banana Chocolate Chip Bread, 286, **287**
    Beyond PB & J, <u>63</u>
    Blueberry Brunch Cake, 74, **75**
    Blueberry-Pecan Pancakes, 66, **67**
    Breakfast in a Cup, 60, **61**
    Chocolate Chip Coffee Cake, 76, **76**
    Chopra Granola, <u>73</u>
    Easy Ham and Cheese "Soufflé," 58, **59**
    Easy Huevos Rancheros, 54, **55**
    Egg Salad on a Bagel, <u>63</u>
    Fat-Free Skillet Home Fries, 57
    Go-Go Gazpacho, <u>63</u>
    Go-gurt, <u>63</u>
    Good Morning Muffins, 64
    Hot Banana-Wheat Cereal, 72
    Jumbo Cinnamon-Raisin Muffins, 68, **69**
    Lemon Scones, 70, **71**
    Meatless Mexican Chorizo, **55**, 56
    More Than a Muffin, <u>63</u>
    Orange-Raisin Tea Bread, 77
    Peanut Butter and Banana Shake, 122
    Pizza Pick-Me-Up, <u>63</u>
    Quick Breakfast Crisp, 65
    Roasted Home Fries, 57, **61**
    Salmon Sandwich, <u>63</u>
    Savory Hash-Browned Potatoes, 62
    Smooth Sailing, <u>63</u>
    Tomato-Crab Bake, 110, **111**
    Waffle Sandwich, <u>63</u>
Broccoli
    Asian Slaw, **128**, 252
    Asian Veggie Wraps, 208
    Broccoli-Cheddar Soup, 94

Broccoli *(continued)*
  Broccoli-Cheese Spoon Bread, 240, **241**
  Broccoli Slaw Waldorf Salad, 251
  Broccoli Soup, 94, **95**
  Broccoli-Stuffed Shells, 216, **217**
  Vegetable Lasagna, 210, **211**
Brownies
  Double Chocolate Chip Fudge Brownies,
    290, **291**
Bulgur, 50
  Ensalada Mexicana Vegetariana,
    179, **179**
  Tabbouleh Salad, 275
Burgers
  Canyon Ranch Burgers, <u>100</u>
  Tofu Burgers, <u>86</u>
Burritos
  Black Bean and Corn Burritos, 178
  Red Chile Steak Burritos, 150, **151**
Butter, for cooking, 51, <u>86</u>
Buttermilk
  Buttermilk Fruit Smoothie, 120
  Creamy Ranch Dressing, <u>255</u>
  Salmon Chowder, 98, **99**
Butternut squash
  Sherried Squash Bake, 233

C

Cabbage
  Asian Veggie Wraps, 208
  Chicken Oriental Salad, 267
  Debra's Vegetable-Shrimp Stir-Fry, 93
  Garden Vegetable Soup, 97
  Sesame Chicken Salad, 262, **263**
  Tuscan Bean Soup with Sausage, 154, **155**
  Unstuffed Cabbage, 223
  Very Vegetable Soup, 209
  Warm Pepper and Pork Salad, 264, **265**
Caesar salad
  Hail Caesar Salad, 249
Cake flour, 50

Cakes
  Blueberry Brunch Cake, 74, **75**
  Carrot Cake with Cream Cheese Frosting, <u>284</u>
  Chocolate Chip Coffee Cake, 76, **76**
  Chocolate-Raspberry Avalanche Cake, 280, **281**
  John's Gingerbread, <u>296</u>
  Peanut Butter Cake with Chocolate Frosting,
    278, **279**
  Pumpkin Cake, 285
  Yummy Pineapple Cake, 282, **283**
Calories
  burned during exercise, <u>27</u>
  in chocolate, <u>312</u>
  keeping track of, 11, <u>18–19</u>, 21
  low-calorie food substitutions, <u>42–43</u>
  in one pound of fat, 10
  in reduced-fat foods, <u>22</u>
  in selected foods, <u>39</u>, <u>204</u>
Cannellini beans. *See* White beans
Canyon Ranch Health Resorts, <u>100</u>, <u>157</u>, <u>165</u>, <u>184</u>
Carbohydrate snacks, <u>121</u>
Carolina Wellness Retreat, <u>171</u>
Carrots
  Asian Slaw, **128**, 252
  Asian Veggie Wraps, 208
  Brown Rice Vegetable Stir-Fry, 176
  Carrot Cake with Cream Cheese Frosting, <u>284</u>
  Creamy Carrot-Potato Soup, 96
  Flounder Dijon, <u>171</u>
  Garbanzo-Sausage Soup, 197
  Garden Vegetable Soup, 97
  Good Morning Muffins, 64
  Roasted Vegetable Wraps, 80, **81**
  Slow-Cooked Pork Stew, 152, **153**
  Tofu Burgers, <u>86</u>
  Unstuffed Cabbage, 223
  Veggie Cassoulet, 218, **219**
  Very Vegetable Soup, 209
Cashews
  cashew milk, making, 77
  Teriyaki Turkey Salad, 266

Casseroles, 43
   Almond-Mushroom Rice Casserole, 239
   Broccoli-Cheese Spoon Bread, 240, **241**
   Broccoli-Stuffed Shells, 216, **217**
   Chicken Stuffing Casserole, 242
   Confetti Enchiladas, 144
   Easy Ham and Cheese "Soufflé," 58, **59**
   El Dorado Casserole, 194, **195**
   Meximix, 213
   Quick Black Bean Enchiladas, 177
   Sherried Squash Bake, 233
   Spinach Lasagna, 212
   Taco Bake, 148, **149**
   Vegetable Lasagna, 210, **211**
   Veggie Cassoulet, 218, **219**
Catfish
   Baked Catfish with Dill Sauce, 170
Celery
   Asian Slaw, **128**, 252
   Brown Rice Vegetable Stir-Fry, 176
   Garden Vegetable Soup, 97
   Old-Fashioned Potato Salad, 274
Cereal
   Chopra Granola, 73
   Hot Banana-Wheat Cereal, 72
Cheddar cheese, 39
   Baked Black Beans with Orzo, 87
   Beef 'n' Macaroni Skillet Supper, 145
   Breakfast in a Cup, 60, **61**
   Broccoli-Cheddar Soup, 94
   Broccoli-Cheese Spoon Bread, 240, **241**
   Chicken Fajitas, 142, **143**
   Chicken Fiesta Mexicana, 127
   Confetti Enchiladas, 144
   Easy Ham and Cheese "Soufflé," 58, **59**
   El Dorado Casserole, 194, **195**
   Ensalada Mexicana Vegetariana, 179, **179**
   Herbed Cheese Spread, 115
   Hot Black Bean Dip, 116, **117**
   Meximix, 213
   Quick Black Bean Enchiladas, 177

   Taco Bake, 148, **149**
   Vegetable Quesadillas, 84, **85**
   White Chicken Chili, 186, **187**
Cheese. *See also specific cheeses*
   low-fat, 48
   selecting, 45
   serving sizes for, 17
Cherries, dried
   Black Cherry Baked Apples, 302, **303**
Chicken
   fat in, 39, 44
   simple sauces for, 140–41
Chicken recipes
   Big-Flavor Chicken, 129
   Broccoli Slaw Waldorf Salad, 251
   Chicken and Rice Italiano, 126
   Chicken Fajitas, 142, **143**
   Chicken Fettuccine, 182, **183**
   Chicken Fiesta Mexicana, 127
   Chicken Oriental Salad, 267
   Chicken Therese, 133
   Chinese Chicken in a Bag, 184
   Confetti Enchiladas, 144
   Dinah's Shredded Chicken Spread, 113
   Fettuccine with Pot-Lickin' Chicken Sauce,
      156, **156**
   Greek Island Chicken, 130, **131**
   Joan's Jewel of the Nile Chicken Kabobs,
      191
   Mango Chicken, 132
   Marlene's Chicken and Vegetable
      Stir-Fry, 135
   Orange-Almond Chicken, 136, **137**
   Pollo Loco, 188, **188**
   Quick Chicken Pasta Salad, 90
   Secret Chicken, 185
   Sesame Chicken Salad, 262, **263**
   Skillet Chicken with Tomatoes, 138
   Slow-Cooker Lemon Chicken, 139
   Unfried Crunchy Chicken, 128, **128**
   White Chicken Chili, 186, **187**

Chickpeas
    Beans, Beans, Beans Salad, 273
    Garbanzo-Sausage Soup, 197
    Green Salad Roll-Up, 82, **83**
Chile peppers
    green
        Baked Black Beans with Orzo, 87
        Black Bean and Corn Burritos, 178
        Black Beans and Rice, 238
        Confetti Enchiladas, 144
        El Dorado Casserole, 194, **195**
        Red Chile Steak Burritos, 150, **151**
        Spicy Dipper Rolls, 104
        Taco Bake, 148, **149**
    jalapeño
        Black Bean and Corn Burritos, 178
        Black Bean and Corn Salad, 270, **271**
        Lemon Red Snapper with Jalapeños, 201
        Pollo Loco, 188, **188**
        Quick Black Bean and Artichoke Dip, 118
        Quick Black Bean Enchiladas, 177
        Spicy Pork and Beans Stew, 198, **199**
    Salsa Mexicana, <u>119</u>
Chili
    Pollo Loco, 188, **188**
    White Chicken Chili, 186, **187**
Chocolate
    calories in, <u>312</u>
    glaze, making, 76
    low-fat substitutes for, 50
Chocolate recipes
    Banana Chocolate Chip Bread, 286, **287**
    Chocolate Chip Coffee Cake, 76, **76**
    Chocolate Chunk Cookies, 292, **293**
    Chocolate-Pecan Meringues, 294, **295**
    Chocolate-Raspberry Avalanche Cake,
        280, **281**
    Double Chocolate Chip Fudge Brownies,
        290, **291**
    The Duchess's Chocolate Mousse Tartlets, 289
    Guiltless Banana Split, 307

    Peanut Butter Cake with Chocolate Frosting,
        278, **279**
    Pistachio-Pineapple Yogurt Pie, 310, **311**
    Tiramisu, 313
Chopra, Deepak, <u>73</u>, <u>86</u>
Chowders
    Salmon Chowder, 98, **99**
    Seafood Chowder, 202, **203**
Cilantro
    Black Bean and Corn Burritos, 178
    Black Bean and Corn Salad, 270, **271**
    Salsa Mexicana, <u>119</u>
    Santa Fe Sauce, <u>141</u>
Cinnamon
    Jumbo Cinnamon-Raisin Muffins, 68, **69**
Clams
    Angel Hair Pasta with Clam Pesto, 164,
        164
    Seafood Chowder, 202, **203**
Cocoa powder, 50
Coconut
    Chopra Granola, <u>73</u>
    Good Morning Muffins, 64
Coffee cake
    Blueberry Brunch Cake, 74, **75**
    Chocolate Chip Coffee Cake, 76, **76**
Coleslaw. *See* Slaws
Cookies
    Chocolate Chunk Cookies, 292, **293**
    Chocolate-Pecan Meringues, 294, **295**
    Hamantaschen, **295**, 297
Cooking techniques, low-fat, 50–51
Cookware, 38, 40
Corn
    Black Bean and Corn Burritos, 178
    Black Bean and Corn Salad, 270, **271**
    Confetti Enchiladas, 144
    Garbanzo-Sausage Soup, 197
Cottage cheese
    Almond-Mushroom Rice Casserole, <u>239</u>
    Creamy Ranch Dressing, <u>255</u>

Quick Black Bean Enchiladas, 177
Twice-Baked Potatoes, <u>229</u>
Crabmeat
Crab Cakes, 166, **167**
Crab Salad, 260
Tomato-Crab Bake, 110, **111**
Cracked wheat
Hot Banana-Wheat Cereal, 72
Cranberries, dried
Chopra Granola, <u>73</u>
Portobello Brown Rice, 237
Cranberry sauce
Cranberry-Apple Crisp, 305
Cravings, food, 23
Cream cheese
Carrot Cake with Cream Cheese Frosting, <u>284</u>
Dinah's Shredded Chicken Spread, 113
El Dorado Casserole, 194, **195**
Roasted Garlic Spread, 114
Salmon Sandwich, <u>63</u>
Spicy Dipper Rolls, 104
Spinach Squares, 105
Tiramisu, 313
Yummy Pineapple Cake, 282, **283**
Crepes
Corn Crepes with Strawberry Sauce, <u>301</u>
Crisps
Cranberry-Apple Crisp, 305
Quick Breakfast Crisp, 65
Crock-Pots, alternatives to, 152, 186
Cucumbers
Crab Salad, 260
Ensalada Mexicana Vegetariana, 179, **179**
Go-Go Gazpacho, <u>63</u>
Persian Cucumber Salad, <u>250</u>
Currants
Chopra Granola, <u>73</u>
Lentil-Rice Salad, 272
Curry powder
Joan's Jewel of the Nile Chicken Kabobs, 191
Lentil-Rice Salad, 272

D

Dairy products, selecting, 16, 36
Dates
Good Morning Muffins, 64
Desserts
Baked Apple with Papaya Sauce, <u>304</u>
Banana Chocolate Chip Bread, 286, **287**
Black Cherry Baked Apples, 302, **303**
Carrot Cake with Cream Cheese Frosting, <u>284</u>
Chocolate Chunk Cookies, 292, **293**
Chocolate-Pecan Meringues, 294, **295**
Chocolate-Raspberry Avalanche Cake, 280, **281**
Corn Crepes with Strawberry Sauce, <u>301</u>
Cranberry-Apple Crisp, 305
Double Chocolate Chip Fudge Brownies, 290, **291**
The Duchess's Chocolate Mousse Tartlets, 289
Guiltless Banana Split, 307
Hamantaschen, **295**, 297
John's Gingerbread, <u>296</u>
Peanut Butter Cake with Chocolate Frosting, 278, **279**
Pistachio-Pineapple Yogurt Pie, 310, **311**
Potluck Trifle, 314, **315**
Pumpkin Cake, 285
Pumpkin-Ginger Rice Pudding, 300
Quick Breakfast Crisp, 65
Quick Rice Pudding, 299
Roasted Fruit Wraps with Dipping Sauce, 308, **309**
Tapioca Pudding, 298
Tiramisu, 313
Wonton Fruit Cups, 306, **306**
Yummy Pineapple Cake, 282, **283**
Dietary Exchange System, 16, 20
Diet plan menus, 316–30
Diets. *See also* Weight loss
effect on metabolism, 3
ending, 28

Diets *(continued)*
  fad diets, 21
  rapid weight-loss diets, 10–11
Dill
  Baked Catfish with Dill Sauce, 170
  Crab Salad, 260
Dining out, healthy options for, 46–47, 88–89
Dinners. *See* Main dishes
Dips
  Baked Black Beans with Orzo, 87
  Hot Black Bean Dip, 116, **117**
  Quick Black Bean and Artichoke Dip, 118
  Roasted Garlic Spread, 114
  Salsa Mexicana, 119
Diseases, obesity and, 4–5, 7

E

Eggplant
  Eggplant Parmesan, 222
  Grilled Summer Salad, 253
  Mediterranean Stuffed Eggplant, 224, **225**
Eggs
  Breakfast in a Cup, 60, **61**
  Broccoli-Cheese Spoon Bread, 240, **241**
  Easy Ham and Cheese "Soufflé," 58, **59**
  Easy Huevos Rancheros, 54, **55**
  Egg Salad on a Bagel, 63
  Old-Fashioned Potato Salad, 274
  Spinach Squares, 105
Egg yolks, 48
Enchiladas
  Confetti Enchiladas, 144
  Quick Black Bean Enchiladas, 177
Exercise, 25–26, 27, 28, 30

F

Fajitas
  Chicken Fajitas, 142, **143**
Farfalle pasta
  Feta Farfalle Salad, 91, **91**
  Quick Chicken Pasta Salad, 90

Fat-and-calorie-count books, 11
Fats
  calories in, 10, 21, 30, 204
  in chicken, 39, 44
  in fried foods, 88
  in ground beef, 39, 44
  in pork, 39
  reduced-fat foods, 21, 22
  in salad dressings, 254
  in salmon, 39
  serving sizes for, 17, 20
Fennel seeds, crushing, 272
Feta cheese
  Feta Farfalle Salad, 91, **91**
  Greek Island Chicken, 130, **131**
  Mediterranean Pasta, 162, **163**
  Mediterranean Stuffed Eggplant,
    224, **225**
Fettuccine
  Chicken Fettuccine, 182, **183**
  Fettuccine with Pot-Lickin' Chicken Sauce,
    156, **156**
  Mushroom and Tofu Fettuccine, 161
Fiber, 21, 32, 45, 204, 243
Fish
  calorie-saving swaps, 46
  protein, fats, and calories in, 39
  serving sizes for, 17
Fish recipes. *See also* Shellfish
  Baked Catfish with Dill Sauce, 170
  Flounder Dijon, 171
  Lemon Red Snapper with Jalapeños, 201
  Norma's Grilled Garlicky Salmon, 169
  Salmon Chowder, 98, **99**
  Salmon Sandwich, 63
  Salmon Teriyaki, 165
  Salmon with Lemon-Caper Cream Sauce, 172,
    173
  Seafood Chowder, 202, **203**
  Tuscan Tuna Salad, 261
  Wonderful Tuna Salad, 258, **259**

Flax seeds
    Chopra Granola, <u>73</u>
    Multigrain Bread, **95**, 245
Flounder
    Flounder Dijon, <u>171</u>
Food Guide Pyramid, 11, 16
Food labels, <u>32</u>, <u>33</u>
Food processors, 38
Fruits. *See also specific fruits*
    eating more, 30, <u>243</u>
    selecting, 36
    serving sizes for, 16

G

Garbanzo beans. *See* Chickpeas
Garlic, roasting, 50–51
Garlic recipes
    Angel Hair Pasta with Clam Pesto, 164, **164**
    Black-Eyed Pea Stew, 220
    Broccoli-Stuffed Shells, 216, **217**
    Brown Rice Vegetable Stir-Fry, 176
    Chicken Fettuccine, 182, **183**
    Debra's Vegetable-Shrimp Stir-Fry, 93
    Easy Rigatoni, 159
    Feta Farfalle Salad, 91, **91**
    Fettuccine with Pot-Lickin' Chicken Sauce,
        156, **156**
    Greek Island Chicken, 130, **131**
    Grilled Pork Chops, 196, **196**
    Hail Caesar Salad, 249
    Herbed Rice, **196**, 236
    Lentil-Sausage Stew, 200
    Linguine Montecatini, <u>160</u>
    Marlene's Chicken and Vegetable
        Stir-Fry, 135
    Mushroom and Tofu Fettuccine, 161
    Norma's Grilled Garlicky Salmon, 169
    Pollo Loco, 188, **188**
    Portobello Brown Rice, 237
    Red Chile Steak Burritos, 150, **151**
    Roasted Garlic Lemon Dressing, <u>255</u>

    Roasted Garlic Spread, 114
    Salmon Teriyaki, <u>165</u>
    Salmon with Lemon-Caper Cream Sauce,
        172, **173**
    Salsa Mexicana, <u>119</u>
    Sesame Sauce, <u>141</u>
    Shrimp Creole, 174, **175**
    Shrimp in Tomato Sauce over Pasta, 206, **207**
    Slow-Cooked Pork Stew, 152, **153**
    Spicy Pork and Beans Stew, 198, **199**
    Spicy Spaghetti Marinara, 158
    Unfried Crunchy Chicken, 128, **128**
    Unstuffed Cabbage, 223
    Veggie Cassoulet, 218, **219**
    Very Vegetable Soup, 209
    White Chicken Chili, 186, **187**
Gazpacho
    Go-Go Gazpacho, <u>63</u>
Ghee, <u>73</u>, <u>86</u>
Ginger
    Baked Apple with Papaya Sauce, <u>304</u>
    Braised Tofu, 221
    Chinese Chicken in a Bag, <u>184</u>
    Debra's Vegetable-Shrimp Stir-Fry, 93
    John's Gingerbread, <u>296</u>
    Pumpkin-Ginger Rice Pudding, 300
    Roasted Fruit Wraps with Dipping Sauce,
        308, **309**
    Salmon Teriyaki, <u>165</u>
    Sesame Sauce, <u>141</u>
Goat cheese
    Lemon Goat Cheese Sauce, <u>140</u>
    Portobellos and Goat Cheese, 106, **107**
Golden Door, <u>304</u>
Grains. *See also specific grains*
    fiber in, 21, 45
Granola
    Chopra Granola, <u>73</u>
Grapes
    Broccoli Slaw Waldorf Salad, 251
Gravy strainers, 38

Green beans
  Beans, Beans, Beans Salad, 273
  Garden Vegetable Soup, 97
Green chile peppers. *See* Chile peppers, green
Green Mountain at Fox Run, 23, <u>222</u>, <u>229</u>, <u>239</u>
Grilling, 51

H

Ham
  Easy Ham and Cheese "Soufflé," 58, **59**
  Pepperonata Sauce, <u>140–41</u>
Herbs, 45
High blood pressure, 7
Hunger mechanism, 20–21, 30

I

Italian restaurants, <u>89</u>

J

Jalapeño chile peppers. *See* Chile peppers, jalapeño
Jones, Jeanne, <u>157</u>, <u>184</u>

K

Kabobs
  Joan's Jewel of the Nile Chicken Kabobs, 191
Kidney beans
  Beans, Beans, Beans Salad, 273
  Feta Farfalle Salad, 91, **91**
  Mediterranean Zucchini, 228
  Meximix, 213
  Spicy Pork and Beans Stew, 198, **199**
Kitchen equipment, 38, 40
Kitchen pantry items, 40, 44–45
Kitchen tools, 38, 40
Knives, 38

L

Lamb
  Lamb Chops with Herbed Apricot Sauce, <u>157</u>

Lasagna
  Meximix, 213
  Spinach Lasagna, 212
  Vegetable Lasagna, 210, **211**
Leeks
  Brown Rice Vegetable Stir-Fry, 176
  Garbanzo-Sausage Soup, 197
  Sweet Potato and Leek Soup, 101
  Veggie Cassoulet, 218, **219**
Legumes. *See also* Beans, dried
  serving size for, 17
Lemons
  Lemon Goat Cheese Sauce, <u>140</u>
  Lemon Scones, 70, **71**
  Roasted Garlic Lemon Dressing, <u>255</u>
  Salmon with Lemon-Caper Cream Sauce, 172, **173**
  Secret Chicken, <u>185</u>
  Tabbouleh Salad, 275
Lentils
  Lentil-Rice Salad, 272
  Lentil-Sausage Stew, 200
Lettuce
  Canyon Ranch Burgers, <u>100</u>
  Ensalada Mexicana Vegetariana, 179, **179**
  Green Salad Roll-Up, 82, **83**
  Grilled Summer Salad, 253
  Hail Caesar Salad, 249
  Pork Salad with Black-Eyed Pea Dressing, 268
  Romaine Salad with Sherry Vinaigrette, 256, **257**
  Sweet and Creamy Spinach Salad, 248
  Teriyaki Turkey Salad, 266
Linguine
  Linguine Montecatini, <u>160</u>
Lunch dishes
  Baked Black Beans with Orzo, 87
  Black Bean and Corn Salad, 270, **271**
  Broccoli-Cheddar Soup, 94
  Broccoli Slaw Waldorf Salad, 251

Broccoli Soup, 94, **95**

Canyon Ranch Burgers, <u>100</u>

Chicken Oriental Salad, 267

Crab Salad, 260

Creamy Carrot-Potato Soup, 96

Debra's Vegetable-Shrimp Stir-Fry, 93

Dinah's Shredded Chicken Spread, 113

Easy Ham and Cheese "Soufflé," 58, **59**

Easy Huevos Rancheros, 54, **55**

Egg Salad on a Bagel, <u>63</u>

Feta Farfalle Salad, 91, **91**

Garden Vegetable Soup, 97

Go-Go Gazpacho, <u>63</u>

Green Salad Roll-Up, 82, **83**

Mark's Potatoes and Tomatoes
    Vinaigrette, 235

Peanut Butter and Banana Shake, 122

Pork Salad with Black-Eyed Pea
    Dressing, 268

Portobellos and Goat Cheese, 106, **107**

Quick Chicken Pasta Salad, 90

Roasted Vegetable Wraps, 80, **81**

Salmon Chowder, 98, **99**

Salmon Sandwich, <u>63</u>

Sesame Chicken Salad, 262, **263**

Spinach Squares, 105

Sweet Potato and Leek Soup, 101

Teriyaki Turkey Salad, 266

Tofu Burgers, <u>86</u>

Tomato-Crab Bake, 110, **111**

Tuscan Tuna Salad, 261

Vegetable Quesadillas, 84, **85**

Waffle Sandwich, <u>63</u>

Warm Pepper and Pork Salad, 264, **265**

Wonderful Tuna Salad, 258, **259**

Lunches, in restaurants, <u>88–89</u>

Lunden, Joan, <u>190</u>

m

Macaroni

Beef 'n' Macaroni Skillet Supper, 145

Main dishes

beef

Beef 'n' Macaroni Skillet Supper, 145

Confetti Meat Loaf, 192, **193**

El Dorado Casserole, 194, **195**

Red Chile Steak Burritos, 150, **151**

Roast Sirloin Steak, 189, **189**

Taco Bake, 148, **149**

Tomatoes and Zucchini with Meatballs,
    146, **147**

chicken

Big-Flavor Chicken, 129

Broccoli Slaw Waldorf Salad, 251

Chicken and Rice Italiano, 126

Chicken Fajitas, 142, **143**

Chicken Fettuccine, 182, **183**

Chicken Fiesta Mexicana, 127

Chicken Oriental Salad, 267

Chicken Therese, 133

Chinese Chicken in a Bag, <u>184</u>

Confetti Enchiladas, 144

Fettuccine with Pot-Lickin' Chicken Sauce,
    156, **156**

Greek Island Chicken, 130, **131**

Joan's Jewel of the Nile Chicken Kabobs,
    191

Mango Chicken, 132

Marlene's Chicken and Vegetable
    Stir-Fry, 135

Orange-Almond Chicken, 136, **137**

Pollo Loco, 188, **188**

Secret Chicken, <u>185</u>

Sesame Chicken Salad, 262, **263**

Skillet Chicken with Tomatoes, 138

Slow-Cooker Lemon Chicken, 139

Unfried Crunchy Chicken, 128, **128**

White Chicken Chili, 186, **187**

fish

Baked Catfish with Dill Sauce, 170

Flounder Dijon, <u>171</u>

Lemon Red Snapper with Jalapeños, 201

Main dishes (continued)
  fish (continued)
    Norma's Grilled Garlicky Salmon, 169
    Salmon Teriyaki, 165
    Salmon with Lemon-Caper Cream Sauce, 172, **173**
    Seafood Chowder, 202, **203**
  lamb
    Lamb Chops with Herbed Apricot Sauce, 157
  meatless
    Angel Hair Pasta with Clam Pesto, 164, **164**
    Asian Veggie Wraps, 208
    Black Bean and Corn Burritos, 178
    Black Bean and Corn Salad, 270, **271**
    Black Beans and Rice, 238
    Black-Eyed Pea Stew, 220
    Braised Tofu, 221
    Broccoli-Stuffed Shells, 216, **217**
    Brown Rice Vegetable Stir-Fry, 176
    Easy Rigatoni, 159
    Eggplant Parmesan, 222
    Ensalada Mexicana Vegetariana, 179, **179**
    Jodie's Pineapple Pizza, 215
    Linguine Montecatini, 160
    Mediterranean Pasta, 162, **163**
    Mediterranean Stuffed Eggplant, 224, **225**
    Meximix, 213
    Mushroom and Tofu Fettuccine, 161
    Portobellos and Goat Cheese, 106, **107**
    Quick Black Bean Enchiladas, 177
    Spicy Spaghetti Marinara, 158
    Spinach Lasagna, 212
    Spinach Squares, 105
    Unstuffed Cabbage, 223
    Vegetable Lasagna, 210, **211**
    Veggie Cassoulet, 218, **219**
    Very Vegetable Soup, 209
  pork
    Garbanzo-Sausage Soup, 197
    Grilled Pork Chops, 196, **196**
    Lentil-Sausage Stew, 200
    Pork Salad with Black-Eyed Pea Dressing, 268
    Slow-Cooked Pork Stew, 152, **153**
    Spicy Pork and Beans Stew, 198, **199**
    Warm Pepper and Pork Salad, 264, **265**
  shellfish
    Crab Cakes, 166, **167**
    Debra's Vegetable-Shrimp Stir-Fry, 93
    Seafood Chowder, 202, **203**
    Shrimp Creole, 174, **175**
    Shrimp in Tomato Sauce over Pasta, 206, **207**
    Shrimp Risotto, 205
  turkey
    Confetti Meat Loaf, 192, **193**
    El Dorado Casserole, 194, **195**
    Garbanzo-Sausage Soup, 197
    Lentil-Sausage Stew, 200
    Taco Bake, 148, **149**
    Teriyaki Turkey Salad, 266
    Tomatoes and Zucchini with Meatballs, 146, **147**
    Tuscan Bean Soup with Sausage, 154, **155**
  weekend
    Asian Veggie Wraps, 208
    Black-Eyed Pea Stew, 220
    Braised Tofu, 221
    Broccoli-Stuffed Shells, 216, **217**
    Chicken Fettuccine, 182, **183**
    Chinese Chicken in a Bag, 184
    Confetti Meat Loaf, 192, **193**
    Eggplant Parmesan, 222
    El Dorado Casserole, 194, **195**
    Garbanzo-Sausage Soup, 197
    Grilled Pork Chops, 196, **196**
    Joan's Jewel of the Nile Chicken Kabobs, 191
    Jodie's Pineapple Pizza, 215
    Lemon Red Snapper with Jalapeños, 201
    Lentil-Sausage Stew, 200
    Mediterranean Stuffed Eggplant, 224, **225**

Meximix, 213
Pollo Loco, 188, **188**
Roast Sirloin Steak, 189, **189**
Seafood Chowder, 202, **203**
Secret Chicken, <u>185</u>
Shrimp in Tomato Sauce over Pasta, 206, **207**
Shrimp Risotto, 205
Spicy Pork and Beans Stew, 198, **199**
Spinach Lasagna, 212
Unstuffed Cabbage, 223
Vegetable Lasagna, 210, **211**
Veggie Cassoulet, 218, **219**
Very Vegetable Soup, 209
White Chicken Chili, 186, **187**
weeknight
  Angel Hair Pasta with Clam Pesto, 164, **164**
  Baked Catfish with Dill Sauce, 170
  Beef 'n' Macaroni Skillet Supper, 145
  Big-Flavor Chicken, 129
  Black Bean and Corn Burritos, 178
  Brown Rice Vegetable Stir-Fry, 176
  Chicken and Rice Italiano, 126
  Chicken Fajitas, 142, **143**
  Chicken Fiesta Mexicana, 127
  Chicken Therese, 133
  Confetti Enchiladas, 144
  Crab Cakes, 166, **167**
  Easy Rigatoni, 159
  Ensalada Mexicana Vegetariana, 179, **179**
  Fettuccine with Pot-Lickin' Chicken Sauce, 156, **156**
  Flounder Dijon, <u>171</u>
  Greek Island Chicken, 130, **131**
  Lamb Chops with Herbed Apricot Sauce, <u>157</u>
  Linguine Montecatini, <u>160</u>
  Mango Chicken, 132
  Marlene's Chicken and Vegetable Stir-Fry, 135
  Mediterranean Pasta, 162, **163**
  Mushroom and Tofu Fettuccine, 161
  Norma's Grilled Garlicky Salmon, 169
  Orange-Almond Chicken, 136, **137**
  Quick Black Bean Enchiladas, 177
  Red Chile Steak Burritos, 150, **151**
  Salmon Teriyaki, <u>165</u>
  Salmon with Lemon-Caper Cream Sauce, 172, **173**
  Shrimp Creole, 174, **175**
  Skillet Chicken with Tomatoes, 138
  Slow-Cooked Pork Stew, 152, **153**
  Slow-Cooker Lemon Chicken, 139
  Spicy Spaghetti Marinara, 158
  Taco Bake, 148, **149**
  Tomatoes and Zucchini with Meatballs, 146, **147**
  Tuscan Bean Soup with Sausage, 154, **155**
  Unfried Crunchy Chicken, 128, **128**
Mangos, 132
  Caribbean Salsa, <u>140</u>
  Mango Chicken, 132
  Purple Power Shake, 123
Marinades, 51
Measuring cups and spoons, 38, 40
Meat. *See also* Beef; Beef recipes; Lamb; Pork
  calorie-saving swaps, <u>46</u>
  lean cuts of, 36, 38
  protein, fats, and calories in, <u>39</u>
  serving sizes for, 17
Meatballs
  Tomatoes and Zucchini with Meatballs, 146, **147**
Meat loaf
  Confetti Meat Loaf, 192, **193**
Meat substitutes
  Meatless Mexican Chorizo, **55**, 56
  Meximix, 213
  Veggie Cassoulet, 218, **219**
Menus, for 14 days, 316–30
Meringues
  Chocolate-Pecan Meringues, 294, **295**

Mexican restaurants, 89
Microwave ovens, 38
Mint
    Caribbean Salsa, 140
    Tabbouleh Salad, 275
Monounsaturated fats, 17
Monterey Jack cheese
    Black Beans and Rice, 238
    Chicken Fiesta Mexicana, 127
    Confetti Enchiladas, 144
    El Dorado Casserole, 194, **195**
    Meximix, 213
    Pollo Loco, 188, **188**
Mood foods, 25
Mozzarella cheese
    Eggplant Parmesan, 222
    Jodie's Pineapple Pizza, 215
    Pita Pizza, 109
    Spinach Lasagna, 212
    Tomato-Crab Bake, 110, **111**
    Vegetable Lasagna, 210, **211**
    Warm Pepper and Pork Salad, 264, **265**
Muffins
    Breakfast in a Cup, 60, **61**
    Good Morning Muffins, 64
    Jumbo Cinnamon-Raisin Muffins, 68, **69**
    More Than a Muffin, 63
Mushrooms
    Almond-Mushroom Rice Casserole, 239
    Asian Slaw, **128**, 252
    Asian Veggie Wraps, 208
    Breakfast in a Cup, 60, **61**
    Broccoli-Stuffed Shells, 216, **217**
    Chicken Stuffing Casserole, 242
    Chicken Therese, 133
    Easy Ham and Cheese "Soufflé," 58, **59**
    Mushroom and Tofu Fettuccine, 161
    Mushroom Sauce, 140, 228
    Orange-Almond Chicken, 136, **137**
    Pollo Loco, 188, **188**
    Portobello Brown Rice, 237

    Portobellos and Goat Cheese, 106, **107**
    Roasted Vegetable Wraps, 80, **81**
    Spinach Squares, 105
    Tomato-Crab Bake, 110, **111**
Mustard
    Baked Catfish with Dill Sauce, 170
    Big-Flavor Chicken, 129
    Blue Cheese Dressing, 255
    Chicken Therese, 133
    Crab Salad, 260
    Flounder Dijon, 171
    Pork Salad with Black-Eyed Pea Dressing, 268
    Slow-Cooked Pork Stew, 152, **153**
    Tahini Dressing, 254
    Tuscan Tuna Salad, 261
    Wonderful Tuna Salad, 258, **259**

n

Navy beans. *See* White beans
Nonstick skillets, 38
Noodles
    Beef 'n' Macaroni Skillet Supper, 145
    Chicken Oriental Salad, 267
    Sesame Chicken Salad, 262, **263**
Nuts. *See also specific nuts*
    to toast, 51

o

Oat bran
    Blueberry-Pecan Pancakes, 66, **67**
    Carrot Cake with Cream Cheese
        Frosting, 284
Oats
    Chocolate Chip Coffee Cake, 76, **76**
    Chocolate Chunk Cookies, 292, **293**
    Chopra Granola, 73
    Cranberry-Apple Crisp, 305
    Quick Breakfast Crisp, 65
Obesity, statisics on, 4–5
Oils, cooking, 50
Olive oil, 40

Olives
    Chicken Fettuccine, 182, **183**
    El Dorado Casserole, 194, **195**
    Ensalada Mexicana Vegetariana, 179, **179**
    Feta Farfalle Salad, 91, **91**
    Fettuccine with Pot-Lickin' Chicken Sauce,
        156, **156**
    Greek Island Chicken, 130, **131**
    Mediterranean Pasta, 162, **163**
    Mediterranean Stuffed Eggplant, 224, **225**
    Portobellos and Goat Cheese, 106, **107**
    Tomato-Crab Bake, 110, **111**
Omega-3 fatty acids, 165
Onions
    Beans, Beans, Beans Salad, 273
    Black Bean and Corn Salad, 270, **271**
    Black-Eyed Pea Stew, 220
    Broccoli-Cheddar Soup, 94
    Broccoli Soup, 94, **95**
    Broccoli-Stuffed Shells, 216, **217**
    Canyon Ranch Burgers, 100
    Chicken Fajitas, 142, **143**
    Chicken Fettuccine, 182, **183**
    Chicken Therese, 133
    Confetti Meat Loaf, 192, **193**
    Dinah's Shredded Chicken Spread, 113
    Easy Rigatoni, 159
    El Dorado Casserole, 194, **195**
    Fettuccine with Pot-Lickin' Chicken Sauce,
        156, **156**
    Garden Vegetable Soup, 97
    Greek Island Chicken, 130, **131**
    Grilled Summer Salad, 253
    Herbed Rice, **196**, 236
    Joan's Jewel of the Nile Chicken
        Kabobs, 191
    Lentil-Rice Salad, 272
    Lentil-Sausage Stew, 200
    Mediterranean Pasta, 162, **163**
    Meximix, 213
    Mushroom Sauce, 140, 228

Old-Fashioned Potato Salad, 274
Pepperonata Sauce, 140–41
Pollo Loco, 188, **188**
Portobello Brown Rice, 237
Red Chile Steak Burritos, 150, **151**
Roasted Home Fries, 57, **61**
Salsa Mexicana, 119
Savory Hash-Browned Potatoes, 62
Shrimp Creole, 174, **175**
Slow-Cooked Pork Stew, 152, **153**
Spicy Pork and Beans Stew, 198, **199**
Spicy Spaghetti Marinara, 158
Spinach Squares, 105
Sweet Potato and Leek Soup, 101
Unstuffed Cabbage, 223
Vegetable Quesadillas, 84, **85**
Veggie Cassoulet, 218, **219**
Very Vegetable Soup, 209
White Chicken Chili, 186, **187**
Oranges
    Orange-Almond Chicken, 136, **137**
    Orange-Raisin Tea Bread, 77
    Orange Sweet Potatoes, 230, **231**
    Yummy Pineapple Cake, 282, **283**
Ornish, Dean, 274, 284, 296, 312
Orzo
    Baked Black Beans with Orzo, 87
Oven-frying, 51
Overweight individuals
    family history and, 6
    statistics on, 4–5
Oysters
    Seafood Chowder, 202, **203**

P

Pancakes
    Blueberry-Pecan Pancakes, 66, **67**
Pantry items, 40, 44–45
Papayas
    Baked Apple with Papaya Sauce, 304
    Caribbean Salsa, 140

Parmesan cheese
    Creamy Ranch Dressing, <u>255</u>
    Hail Caesar Salad, 249
    Vegetable Lasagna, 210, **211**
Parsley
    Mushroom and Tofu Fettuccine, 161
    Persian Cucumber Salad, <u>250</u>
    Portobello Brown Rice, 237
    Shrimp in Tomato Sauce over Pasta,
        206, **207**
    Tabbouleh Salad, 275
    Tomato-Crab Bake, 110, **111**
Parsnips
    Slow-Cooked Pork Stew, 152, **153**
Pasta, 21
    Angel Hair Pasta with Clam Pesto, 164, **164**
    Baked Black Beans with Orzo, 87
    Beef 'n' Macaroni Skillet Supper, 145
    Broccoli-Stuffed Shells, 216, **217**
    Chicken Fettuccine, 182, **183**
    Chicken Oriental Salad, 267
    Easy Rigatoni, 159
    Feta Farfalle Salad, 91, **91**
    Fettuccine with Pot-Lickin' Chicken Sauce,
        156, **156**
    Linguine Montecatini, <u>160</u>
    Mediterranean Pasta, 162, **163**
    Mushroom and Tofu Fettuccine, 161
    Quick Chicken Pasta Salad, 90
    Seafood Chowder, 202, **203**
    Shrimp in Tomato Sauce over Pasta,
        206, **207**
    Spicy Spaghetti Marinara, 158
    Spinach Lasagna, 212
    Vegetable Lasagna, 210, **211**
Peaches
    Buttermilk Fruit Smoothie, 120
    Purple Power Shake, 123
    Roasted Fruit Wraps with Dipping Sauce,
        308, **309**
    Smooth Sailing, <u>63</u>

Peanut butter, <u>39</u>
    Beyond PB & J, <u>63</u>
    Peanut Butter and Banana Shake, 122
    Peanut Butter Cake with Chocolate Frosting,
        278, **279**
Pears
    Quick Breakfast Crisp, 65
Peas
    Garden Vegetable Soup, 97
Pecans
    Blueberry-Pecan Pancakes, 66, **67**
    Chocolate-Pecan Meringues, 294, **295**
    Wonderful Tuna Salad, 258, **259**
Peppers. *See* Bell peppers; Chile peppers
Pesto
    Angel Hair Pasta with Clam Pesto, 164, **164**
Pies
    low-fat crusts for, 50
    Pistachio-Pineapple Yogurt Pie, 310, **311**
Pimientos
    Dinah's Shredded Chicken Spread, 113
Pineapple
    Caribbean Salsa, <u>140</u>
    Carrot Cake with Cream Cheese Frosting, <u>284</u>
    Guiltless Banana Split, 307
    Jodie's Pineapple Pizza, 215
    Pistachio-Pineapple Yogurt Pie, 310, **311**
    Roasted Fruit Wraps with Dipping Sauce, 308,
        309
    Wonderful Tuna Salad, 258, **259**
    Yummy Pineapple Cake, 282, **283**
Pine nuts
    Angel Hair Pasta with Clam Pesto, 164, **164**
    Chopra Granola, <u>73</u>
    Lentil-Rice Salad, 272
    Tofu Burgers, <u>86</u>
Pinto beans
    Taco Bake, 148, **149**
Pistachios
    Pistachio-Pineapple Yogurt Pie, 310, **311**
    Portobello Brown Rice, 237

Pitas
    Pita Pizza, 109
Pizza
    Jodie's Pineapple Pizza, 215
    Pita Pizza, 109
    Pizza Pick-Me-Up, 63
Pizza restaurants, 89
Plastic bags, 40
Plastic spray bottles, 40
Polyunsaturated fats, 17
Popcorn poppers, 40
Pork, 39
    Breakfast in a Cup, 60, **61**
    Easy Ham and Cheese "Soufflé," 58, **59**
    Garbanzo-Sausage Soup, 197
    Grilled Pork Chops, 196, **196**
    Lentil-Sausage Stew, 200
    Pepperonata Sauce, 140–41
    Pork Salad with Black-Eyed Pea Dressing, 268
    Slow-Cooked Pork Stew, 152, **153**
    Spicy Pork and Beans Stew, 198, **199**
    Sweet and Creamy Spinach Salad, 248
    Warm Pepper and Pork Salad, 264, **265**
Portion sizes
    calories and, 204
    convenience food, 35
    for food groups, 16–17, 20
    limiting, 30
    restaurant, 35, 88
    take-out food, 35
    visualizing, 21, 162
Portobello mushrooms
    Portobello Brown Rice, 237
    Portobellos and Goat Cheese, 106, **107**
    Roasted Vegetable Wraps, 80, **81**
Potatoes. *See also* Sweet potatoes
    Black-Eyed Pea Stew, 220
    Creamy Carrot-Potato Soup, 96
    Fat-Free Skillet Home Fries, 57
    Garden Vegetable Soup, 97
    Mark's Potatoes and Tomatoes Vinaigrette, 235

Old-Fashioned Potato Salad, 274
    Roasted Home Fries, 57, **61**
    Salmon Chowder, 98, **99**
    Savory Hash-Browned Potatoes, 62
    Slow-Cooked Pork Stew, 152, **153**
    Twice-Baked Potatoes, 229
    Unstuffed Cabbage, 223
Poultry. *See also* Chicken; Chicken
        recipes; Turkey
    calorie-saving swaps, 46
    lean parts of, 38
    serving sizes for, 17
Pound cake
    Potluck Trifle, 314, **315**
    Tiramisu, 313
Price, Deirdra, 23, 250
Protein, sources of, 39
Protein snacks, 121
Puddings
    Potluck Trifle, 314, **315**
    Pumpkin-Ginger Rice Pudding, 300
    Quick Rice Pudding, 299
    Tapioca Pudding, 298
Pumpkin
    Pumpkin Cake, 285
    Pumpkin-Ginger Rice Pudding, 300

Q

Quesadillas
    Vegetable Quesadillas, 84, **85**
Quiz, weight-loss personality, 12–15

R

Raisins
    Baked Apple with Papaya Sauce, 304
    Black Cherry Baked Apples, 302, **303**
    Broccoli Slaw Waldorf Salad, 251
    Chicken Stuffing Casserole, 242
    Good Morning Muffins, 64
    Jumbo Cinnamon-Raisin Muffins, 68, **69**
    Lentil-Rice Salad, 272

Raisins *(continued)*
    Orange-Raisin Tea Bread, 77
    Quick Rice Pudding, 299
    Tapioca Pudding, 298
Rancho la Puerta, 119, 254, 301
Raspberries
    Chocolate-Raspberry Avalanche Cake, 280, **281**
    Potluck Trifle, 314, **315**
    Purple Power Shake, 123
    Wonton Fruit Cups, 306, **306**
Recipes, from pros
    Canyon Ranch Health Resorts, 100, 157, 165, 184
    Carolina Wellness Retreat, 171
    Chopra, Deepak, 73, 86
    Golden Door, 304
    Green Mountain at Fox Run, 222, 229, 239
    Ornish, Dean, 274, 284, 296
    Price, Deirdra, 250
    Rancho la Puerta, 119, 254, 301
    Spa at Doral, 160, 232
Recipes, revising, 42–43, 48, 50–51
Red snapper
    Lemon Red Snapper with Jalapeños, 201
Refried beans
    Easy Huevos Rancheros, 54, **55**
    Ensalada Mexicana Vegetariana, 179, **179**
    Hot Black Bean Dip, 116, **117**
    Vegetable Quesadillas, 84, **85**
Restaurants
    healthy options at, 46–47, 88–89
    portion sizes in, 35
Rice
    Almond-Mushroom Rice Casserole, 239
    Black Beans and Rice, 238
    Brown Rice Vegetable Stir-Fry, 176
    Chicken and Rice Italiano, 126
    Confetti Meat Loaf, 192, **193**
    Herbed Rice, **196**, 236
    Lentil-Rice Salad, 272
    Marlene's Chicken and Vegetable Stir-Fry, 135

    Mediterranean Stuffed Eggplant, 224, **225**
    Portobello Brown Rice, 237
    Pumpkin-Ginger Rice Pudding, 300
    Quick Rice Pudding, 299
    Shrimp Risotto, 205
    Unstuffed Cabbage, 223
Ricotta cheese
    Broccoli-Stuffed Shells, 216, **217**
    El Dorado Casserole, 194, **195**
    More Than a Muffin, 63
    Roasted Vegetable Wraps, 80, **81**
    Spinach Lasagna, 212
    Tiramisu, 313
    Vegetable Lasagna, 210, **211**
Rigatoni
    Easy Rigatoni, 159
Risotto
    Shrimp Risotto, 205
Rolls
    Easy Yeast Rolls, 244
    Spicy Dipper Rolls, 104
Roll-ups
    Green Salad Roll-Up, 82, **83**
Romano cheese
    Broccoli-Stuffed Shells, 216, **217**

S

Salad bars, 204, 269
Salad dressing recipes
    Blue Cheese Dressing, 255
    Creamy Ranch Dressing, 255
    Rancho la Puerta Basil Yogurt Dressing, 254
    Roasted Garlic Lemon Dressing, 255
    Tahini Dressing, 254
Salad dressings, reducing fat in, 43, 50
Salads
    Asian Slaw, **128**, 252
    Beans, Beans, Beans Salad, 273
    Black Bean and Corn Salad, 270, **271**
    Broccoli Slaw Waldorf Salad, 251
    Chicken Oriental Salad, 267

Crab Salad, 260

Dinah's Shredded Chicken Spread, 113

Egg Salad on a Bagel, 63

Ensalada Mexicana Vegetariana, 179, **179**

Feta Farfalle Salad, 91, **91**

Green Salad Roll-Up, 82, **83**

Grilled Summer Salad, 253

Hail Caesar Salad, 249

Lentil-Rice Salad, 272

Mark's Potatoes and Tomatoes Vinaigrette, 235

Old-Fashioned Potato Salad, 274

Persian Cucumber Salad, 250

Pork Salad with Black-Eyed Pea
    Dressing, 268

Quick Chicken Pasta Salad, 90

Romaine Salad with Sherry Vinaigrette,
    256, **257**

Sesame Chicken Salad, 262, **263**

Sweet and Creamy Spinach Salad, 248

Tabbouleh Salad, 275

Teriyaki Turkey Salad, 266

Tuscan Tuna Salad, 261

Warm Pepper and Pork Salad,
    264, **265**

Wonderful Tuna Salad, 258, **259**

Salmon, 39

    Norma's Grilled Garlicky Salmon, 169

    Salmon Chowder, 98, **99**

    Salmon Sandwich, 63

    Salmon Teriyaki, 165

    Salmon with Lemon-Caper Cream Sauce,
        172, **173**

Salsa, as sauce

    Black Bean and Corn Burritos, 178

    Black Beans and Rice, 238

    Chicken Fiesta Mexicana, 127

    Confetti Meat Loaf, 192, **193**

    Hot Black Bean Dip, 116, **117**

    Quick Black Bean Enchiladas, 177

    Spicy Dipper Rolls, 104

    Vegetable Quesadillas, 84, **85**

Salsas

    Caribbean Salsa, 140

    Salsa Mexicana, 119

Sandwiches, 88. See also Sandwich spreads

    Asian Veggie Wraps, 208

    Beyond PB & J, 63

    Canyon Ranch Burgers, 100

    Green Salad Roll-Up, 82, **83**

    Roasted Vegetable Wraps, 80, **81**

    Salmon Sandwich, 63

    Tofu Burgers, 86

    Waffle Sandwich, 63

Sandwich spreads

    Dinah's Shredded Chicken Spread, 113

    Egg Salad on a Bagel, 63

    Salmon Sandwich, 63

    Tuscan Tuna Salad, 261

    Wonderful Tuna Salad, 258, **259**

Sarah, Duchess of York, 288–89

Sauces. See also Salsas

    Lemon Goat Cheese Sauce, 140

    Mushroom Sauce, 140, 228

    Pepperonata Sauce, 140–41

    Santa Fe Sauce, 141

    Sesame Sauce, 141

Sausages

    Breakfast in a Cup, 60, **61**

    Garbanzo-Sausage Soup, 197

    Lentil-Sausage Stew, 200

    Tuscan Bean Soup with Sausage, 154, **155**

Sausages, meatless

    Meatless Mexican Chorizo, **55**, 56

    Veggie Cassoulet, 218, **219**

Scallions

    Asian Veggie Wraps, 208

    Chicken Fettuccine, 182, **183**

    Chinese Chicken in a Bag, 184

    Confetti Enchiladas, 144

    Crab Salad, 260

    Debra's Vegetable-Shrimp Stir-Fry, 93

    Fat-Free Skillet Home Fries, 57

Scallions *(continued)*
Feta Farfalle Salad, 91, **91**
Herbed Cheese Spread, 115
Lemon Red Snapper with Jalapeños, 201
Mango Chicken, 132
Mediterranean Stuffed Eggplant, 224, **225**
Salmon Teriyaki, 165
Shrimp in Tomato Sauce over Pasta, 206, **207**
Spicy Dipper Rolls, 104
Tabbouleh Salad, 275

Scallops
Seafood Chowder, 202, **203**

Scones
Lemon Scones, 70, **71**

Sesame seeds
Chopra Granola, 73
Sesame Chicken Salad, 262, **263**
Sesame Sauce, 141

Shallots
Blue Cheese Dressing, 255
Creamy Ranch Dressing, 255
Orange-Almond Chicken, 136, **137**
Rancho la Puerta Basil Yogurt Dressing, 254

Shellfish
Angel Hair Pasta with Clam Pesto, 164, **164**
Crab Cakes, 166, **167**
Crab Salad, 260
Debra's Vegetable-Shrimp Stir-Fry, 93
Seafood Chowder, 202, **203**
Shrimp Creole, 174, **175**
Shrimp in Tomato Sauce over Pasta,
206, **207**
Shrimp Risotto, 205
Tomato-Crab Bake, 110, **111**

Shell pasta
Broccoli-Stuffed Shells, 216, **217**
Seafood Chowder, 202, **203**

Shrimp
Debra's Vegetable-Shrimp Stir-Fry, 93
Seafood Chowder, 202, **203**
Shrimp Creole, 174, **175**

Shrimp in Tomato Sauce over Pasta, 206, **207**
Shrimp Risotto, 205

Side dishes
Almond-Mushroom Rice Casserole, 239
Asian Slaw, **128**, 252
Beans, Beans, Beans Salad, 273
Black Bean and Corn Salad, 270, **271**
Black Beans and Rice, 238
Broccoli-Cheese Spoon Bread, 240, **241**
Broccoli Slaw Waldorf Salad, 251
Chicken Stuffing Casserole, 242
Easy Yeast Rolls, 244, **244**
Fat-Free Skillet Home Fries, 57
Grilled Summer Salad, 253
Hail Caesar Salad, 249
Herbed Rice, **196**, 236
Lentil-Rice Salad, 272
Mark's Potatoes and Tomatoes Vinaigrette, 235
Mediterranean Zucchini, 228
Multigrain Bread, **95**, 245
Mushroom Sauce, 228
Old-Fashioned Potato Salad, 274
Orange Sweet Potatoes, 230, **231**
Persian Cucumber Salad, 250
Portobello Brown Rice, 237
Roasted Home Fries, 57, **61**
Romaine Salad with Sherry Vinaigrette, 256,
257
Savory Hash-Browned Potatoes, 62
Sherried Squash Bake, 233
Sweet and Creamy Spinach Salad, 248
Sweet Potato Mash, 232
Tabbouleh Salad, 275
Twice-Baked Potatoes, 229

Simmons, Richard, 108

Slaws
Asian Slaw, **128**, 252
Broccoli Slaw Waldorf Salad, 251

Slimming Meals, 87, 93, 94, 96, 129, 138, 139, 166,
171, 174, 178, 196, 201, 209, 222, 224

Slow cookers, alternatives to, 152, 186

Snacks, low-calorie, 46–47, 121
Snacks, nibbles, and mini-meals
  Baked Black Beans with Orzo, 87
  Buttermilk Fruit Smoothie, 120
  Dinah's Shredded Chicken Spread, 113
  Herbed Cheese Spread, 115
  Hot Black Bean Dip, 116, **117**
  Peanut Butter and Banana Shake, 122
  Pita Pizza, 109
  Portobellos and Goat Cheese, 106, **107**
  Purple Power Shake, 123
  Quick Black Bean and Artichoke Dip, 118
  Quick Breakfast Crisp, 65
  Roasted Garlic Spread, 114
  Salsa Mexicana, 119
  Spicy Dipper Rolls, 104
  Spinach Squares, 105
  Tomato-Crab Bake, 110, **111**
Soufflés
  Easy Ham and Cheese "Soufflé," 58, **59**
Soups, 42
  Broccoli-Cheddar Soup, 94
  Broccoli Soup, 94, **95**
  Creamy Carrot-Potato Soup, 96
  Garbanzo-Sausage Soup, 197
  Garden Vegetable Soup, 97
  Go-Go Gazpacho, 63
  Salmon Chowder, 98, **99**
  Seafood Chowder, 202, **203**
  Sweet Potato and Leek Soup, 101
  Tuscan Bean Soup with Sausage, 154, **155**
  Very Vegetable Soup, 209
Southwestern-style dishes
  Black Bean and Corn Burritos, 178
  Black Bean and Corn Salad, 270, **271**
  Black Beans and Rice, 238
  Chicken Fajitas, 142, **143**
  Chicken Fiesta Mexicana, 127
  Confetti Enchiladas, 144
  Easy Huevos Rancheros, 54, **55**
  El Dorado Casserole, 194, **195**

  Ensalada Mexicana Vegetariana, 179, **179**
  Hot Black Bean Dip, 116, **117**
  Meatless Mexican Chorizo, **55**, 56
  Meximix, 213
  Pollo Loco, 188, **188**
  Quick Black Bean and Artichoke Dip, 118
  Quick Black Bean Enchiladas, 177
  Red Chile Steak Burritos, 150, **151**
  Salsa Mexicana, 119
  Santa Fe Sauce, 141
  Spicy Dipper Rolls, 104
  Spicy Pork and Beans Stew, 198, **199**
  Taco Bake, 148, **149**
  Vegetable Quesadillas, 84, **85**
  White Chicken Chili, 186, **187**
Soy sauce
  Asian Veggie Wraps, 208
  Braised Tofu, 221
  Brown Rice Vegetable Stir-Fry, 176
  Debra's Vegetable-Shrimp Stir-Fry, 93
  Garden Vegetable Soup, 97
  Marlene's Chicken and Vegetable Stir-Fry, 135
  Mushroom Sauce, 140
  Orange-Almond Chicken, 136, **137**
  Salmon Teriyaki, 165
  Sesame Sauce, 141
  Teriyaki Turkey Salad, 266
  Tofu Burgers, 86
  Unfried Crunchy Chicken, 128, **128**
Spa at Doral, 160, 232
Spaghetti
  Mediterranean Pasta, 162, **163**
  Shrimp in Tomato Sauce over Pasta, 206, **207**
  Spicy Spaghetti Marinara, 158
Spices, 45. *See also specific spices*
Spinach
  Linguine Montecatini, 160
  Mediterranean Pasta, 162, **163**
  Spinach Lasagna, 212
  Spinach Squares, 105
  Sweet and Creamy Spinach Salad, 248

Splurge Meals, <u>84</u>, <u>90</u>, <u>135</u>, <u>145</u>, <u>150</u>, <u>152</u>, <u>158</u>, <u>164</u>, <u>165</u>, <u>177</u>, <u>179</u>, <u>200</u>, <u>213</u>, <u>215</u>, <u>216</u>
Spoon bread
   Broccoli-Cheese Spoon Bread, 240, **241**
Spreads. *See also* Dips; Sandwich spreads
   Herbed Cheese Spread, 115
   Roasted Garlic Spread, 114
Sprouts
   Green Salad Roll-Up, 82, **83**
Squash. *See* Winter squash; Yellow squash; Zucchini
Stews, <u>42</u>
   Black-Eyed Pea Stew, 220
   Lentil-Sausage Stew, 200
   Pollo Loco, 188, **188**
   Slow-Cooked Pork Stew, 152, **153**
   Spicy Pork and Beans Stew, 198, **199**
   Tomatoes and Zucchini with Meatballs, 146, **147**
   Veggie Cassoulet, 218, **219**
   White Chicken Chili, 186, **187**
Stir-fries
   Brown Rice Vegetable Stir-Fry, 176
   Debra's Vegetable-Shrimp Stir-Fry, 93
   Marlene's Chicken and Vegetable Stir-Fry, 135
Stock, homemade, 45
Strawberries
   Buttermilk Fruit Smoothie, 120
   Corn Crepes with Strawberry Sauce, <u>301</u>
   Guiltless Banana Split, 307
   Purple Power Shake, 123
Stuffing
   Chicken Stuffing Casserole, 242
Substitutions, food, <u>42–43</u>, <u>46–47</u>
Sun-dried tomatoes
   Chicken Stuffing Casserole, 242
   Greek Island Chicken, 130, **131**
   Mediterranean Pasta, 162, **163**
   Mediterranean Stuffed Eggplant, 224, **225**
   Roasted Vegetable Wraps, 80, **81**
   Veggie Cassoulet, 218, **219**

Sunflower seeds
   Broccoli Slaw Waldorf Salad, 251
   Chopra Granola, <u>73</u>
   Tofu Burgers, <u>86</u>
Supermarket strategies, 31–32, 34, 36, 38
Suppers. *See* Main dishes
Sweet potatoes
   Orange Sweet Potatoes, 230, **231**
   Sweet Potato and Leek Soup, 101
   Sweet Potato Mash, <u>232</u>
Swiss cheese
   Almond-Mushroom Rice Casserole, <u>239</u>
   Twice-Baked Potatoes, <u>229</u>

T

Tahini
   Tahini Dressing, <u>254</u>
Tamari sauce
   Braised Tofu, 221
   Garden Vegetable Soup, 97
   Tofu Burgers, <u>86</u>
Tapioca
   Tapioca Pudding, 298
Tarts
   The Duchess's Chocolate Mousse Tartlets, 289
Tea, in salad dressings, 50
Tiramisu
   Tiramisu, 313
Tofu
   Braised Tofu, 221
   Mushroom and Tofu Fettuccine, 161
   Purple Power Shake, 123
   Tofu Burgers, <u>86</u>
Tomatillos
   Confetti Enchiladas, 144
Tomatoes. *See also* Sun-dried tomatoes
   Angel Hair Pasta with Clam Pesto, 164, **164**
   Baked Black Beans with Orzo, 87
   Black Bean and Corn Salad, 270, **271**
   Black-Eyed Pea Stew, 220
   Canyon Ranch Burgers, <u>100</u>

Chicken Fajitas, 142, **143**

Chicken Fettuccine, 182, **183**

Confetti Enchiladas, 144

Easy Rigatoni, 159

Ensalada Mexicana Vegetariana, 179, **179**

Fettuccine with Pot-Lickin' Chicken Sauce, 156,
    156

Go-Go Gazpacho, <u>63</u>

Joan's Jewel of the Nile Chicken Kabobs, 191

Lentil-Sausage Stew, 200

Linguine Montecatini, <u>160</u>

Mango Chicken, 132

Mark's Potatoes and Tomatoes Vinaigrette, 235

Mediterranean Zucchini, 228

Meximix, 213

Persian Cucumber Salad, <u>250</u>

Pollo Loco, 188, **188**

Quick Chicken Pasta Salad, 90

Red Chile Steak Burritos, 150, **151**

Salsa Mexicana, <u>119</u>

Santa Fe Sauce, <u>141</u>

Shrimp Creole, 174, **175**

Shrimp in Tomato Sauce over Pasta,
    206, **207**

Skillet Chicken with Tomatoes, 138

Spicy Pork and Beans Stew, 198, **199**

Spicy Spaghetti Marinara, 158

Spinach Lasagna, 212

Tabbouleh Salad, 275

Tomato-Crab Bake, 110, **111**

Tomatoes and Zucchini with Meatballs, 146,
    147

Tuscan Bean Soup with Sausage, 154, **155**

Unstuffed Cabbage, 223

Vegetable Lasagna, 210, **211**

Very Vegetable Soup, 209

Tomato sauce

    Broccoli-Stuffed Shells, 216, **217**

    Chicken and Rice Italiano, 126

    Chicken Fettuccine, 182, **183**

    Eggplant Parmesan, <u>222</u>

Jodie's Pineapple Pizza, 215

Pita Pizza, 109

Pollo Loco, 188, **188**

Portobellos and Goat Cheese, 106, **107**

Spinach Lasagna, 212

Vegetable Lasagna, 210, **211**

Tortilla chips

    El Dorado Casserole, 194, **195**

    Ensalada Mexicana Vegetariana, 179, **179**

    White Chicken Chili, 186, **187**

Tortillas

    Asian Veggie Wraps, 208

    Black Bean and Corn Burritos, 178

    Chicken Fajitas, 142, **143**

    Confetti Enchiladas, 144

    Easy Huevos Rancheros, 54, **55**

    Green Salad Roll-Up, 82, **83**

    Meximix, 213

    Quick Black Bean Enchiladas, 177

    Red Chile Steak Burritos, 150, **151**

    Roasted Fruit Wraps with Dipping Sauce,
        308, **309**

    Roasted Vegetable Wraps, 80, **81**

    Spicy Dipper Rolls, 104

    Vegetable Quesadillas, 84, **85**

Treats

    calorie-saving swaps, <u>46–47</u>

    serving sizes for, 20

Trifle

    Potluck Trifle, 314, **315**

Tuna

    Tuscan Tuna Salad, 261

    Wonderful Tuna Salad, 258, **259**

Turkey

    Confetti Meat Loaf, 192, **193**

    El Dorado Casserole, 194, **195**

    Taco Bake, 148, **149**

    Teriyaki Turkey Salad, 266

    Tomatoes and Zucchini with Meatballs,
        146, **147**

    Waffle Sandwich, <u>63</u>

Turkey sausages
    Garbanzo-Sausage Soup, 197
    Lentil-Sausage Stew, 200
    Tuscan Bean Soup with Sausage, 154, **155**
Turnips
    Salmon Chowder, 98, **99**

U

Umeboshi plum vinegar, <u>254</u>

V

Vegetable recipes. *See also specific vegetables*
    Brown Rice Vegetable Stir-Fry, 176
    Debra's Vegetable-Shrimp Stir-Fry, 93
    Marlene's Chicken and Vegetable Stir-Fry, 135
    Pita Pizza, 109
    Slow-Cooker Lemon Chicken, 139
Vegetables
    calorie-saving swaps, <u>46</u>
    eating more, 30, <u>243</u>
    fresh, cooking, 40
    fresh, storing, 44–45
    roasting, 189
    selecting, 36
    serving sizes for, 16
Vinegars, 45

W

Waffles
    Waffle Sandwich, <u>63</u>
Waist size, 7
Waldorf salad
    Broccoli Slaw Waldorf Salad, 251
Walnuts
    Black Cherry Baked Apples, 302, **303**
    Broccoli Slaw Waldorf Salad, 251
    Pumpkin Cake, 285
    Romaine Salad with Sherry Vinaigrette,
        256, **257**
    Tofu Burgers, <u>86</u>
Water, daily intake of, 30

Weight, ranges for, 7, <u>10</u>
Weight loss
    behavior changes for, 3, 6
    and body image, 23
    and exercise, 25–26, 28
    and food cravings, 23
    formal programs for, 23
    goals for, 3, 11
    motivation for, 6–7
    obstacles to, <u>35</u>
    personality quiz for, <u>12–15</u>
    personal strategy for, 7, 10–11
    rapid, effect of, 10–11
    strategies for, 20–21, 23, 28, 30
    and yo-yo dieting, 3
Weight-loss plan menus, 316–30
Weight-loss profiles, <u>2</u>, <u>24</u>, <u>29</u>, <u>37</u>, <u>41</u>, <u>49</u>, <u>92</u>, <u>108</u>,
        <u>112–13</u>, <u>134</u>, <u>168–69</u>, <u>190</u>, <u>214</u>, <u>234–35</u>,
        <u>288–89</u>
Wheat berries
    Multigrain Bread, **95**, 245
White beans
    Meximix, 213
    Quick Chicken Pasta Salad, 90
    Tuscan Bean Soup with Sausage,
        154, **155**
    Tuscan Tuna Salad, 261
    Veggie Cassoulet, 218, **219**
    White Chicken Chili, 186, **187**
Wine
    Big-Flavor Chicken, 129
    Broccoli-Stuffed Shells, 216, **217**
    Chicken Fettuccine, 182, **183**
    Greek Island Chicken, 130, **131**
    Potluck Trifle, 314, **315**
    Sherried Squash Bake, 233
    Shrimp in Tomato Sauce over Pasta,
        206, **207**
    Shrimp Risotto, 205
    Spicy Spaghetti Marinara, 158
    White Chicken Chili, 186, **187**

Winter squash
    Pumpkin Cake, 285
    Pumpkin-Ginger Rice Pudding, 300
    Sherried Squash Bake, 233
Wonton wrappers
    Wonton Fruit Cups, 306, **306**
Wraps
    Asian Veggie Wraps, 208
    Roasted Vegetable Wraps, 80, **81**

Yellow squash
    Joan's Jewel of the Nile Chicken Kabobs, 191
    Roasted Vegetable Wraps, 80, **81**
    Tomatoes and Zucchini with Meatballs, 146,
        147
    Vegetable Quesadillas, 84, **85**
    Very Vegetable Soup, 209
Yogurt
    Baked Catfish with Dill Sauce, 170
    Chocolate-Raspberry Avalanche Cake, 280, **281**
    Crab Salad, 260
    Go-gurt, 63
    Peanut Butter and Banana Shake, 122

Pistachio-Pineapple Yogurt Pie, 310, **311**
Rancho la Puerta Basil Yogurt
        Dressing, 254
Roasted Fruit Wraps with Dipping Sauce,
        308, **309**
Roasted Vegetable Wraps, 80, **81**
Salmon Chowder, 98, **99**
Smooth Sailing, 63
Wonderful Tuna Salad, 258, **259**
Wonton Fruit Cups, 306, **306**
Yogurt cheese, 50

Zucchini
    Asian Veggie Wraps, 208
    Grilled Summer Salad, 253
    Mediterranean Zucchini, 228
    Roasted Vegetable Wraps, 80, **81**
    Tofu Burgers, 86
    Tomatoes and Zucchini with Meatballs,
        146, **147**
    Vegetable Lasagna, 210, **211**
    Vegetable Quesadillas, 84, **85**
    Very Vegetable Soup, 209

Conversion Chart

These equivalents have been slightly rounded to make measuring easier.

Volume Measurements

U.S.	Imperial	Metric
¼ tsp	–	1.25 ml
½ tsp	–	2.5 ml
1 tsp	–	5 ml
1 Tbsp	–	15 ml
2 Tbsp (1 oz)	1 fl oz	30 ml
¼ cup (2 oz)	2 fl oz	60 ml
⅓ cup (3 oz)	3 fl oz	80 ml
½ cup (4 oz)	4 fl oz	120 ml
⅔ cup (5 oz)	5 fl oz	160 ml
¾ cup (6 oz)	6 fl oz	180 ml
1 cup (8 oz)	8 fl oz	240 ml

Weight Measurements

U.S.	Metric
1 oz	30 g
2 oz	60 g
4 oz (¼ lb)	115 g
5 oz (⅓ lb)	145 g
6 oz	170 g
7 oz	200 g
8 oz (½ lb)	230 g
10 oz	285 g
12 oz (¾ lb)	340 g
14 oz	400 g
16 oz (1 lb)	455 g
2.2 lb	1 kg

Length Measurements

U.S.	Metric
¼"	0.6 cm
½"	1.25 cm
1"	2.5 cm
2"	5 cm
4"	11 cm
6"	15 cm
8"	20 cm
10"	25 cm
12" (1')	30 cm

Pan Sizes

U.S.	Metric
8" cake pan	20 × 4-cm sandwich or cake tin
9" cake pan	23 × 3.5-cm sandwich or cake tin
11" × 7" baking pan	28 × 18-cm baking pan
13" × 9" baking pan	32.5 × 23-cm baking pan
2-qt rectangular baking dish	30 × 19-cm baking dish
15" × 10" baking pan	38 × 25.5-cm baking pan (Swiss roll tin)
9" pie plate	22 × 4 or 23 × 4-cm pie plate
7" or 8" springform pan	18 or 20-cm springform or loose-bottom cake tin
9" × 5" loaf pan	23 × 13-cm or 2-lb narrow loaf pan or pâté tin
1½-qt casserole	1.5-l casserole
2-qt casserole	2-l casserole

Temperatures

Fahrenheit	Centigrade	Gas
140°	60°	–
160°	70°	–
180°	80°	–
225°	110°	–
250°	120°	½
300°	150°	2
325°	160°	3
350°	180°	4
375°	190°	5
400°	200°	6
450°	230°	8
500°	260°	–